£ 9.09

Balzac

Balzac

V. S. PRITCHETT

The Hogarth Press
LONDON

Published in 1992 by
The Hogarth Press
20 Vauxhall Bridge Road
London SW1V 2SA

First published in hardback by
Chatto & Windus Ltd 1973

A CIP catalogue record for this book is
available from the British Library.

ISBN 0 7012 0987 9

Printed in Great Britain by
Mackays of Chatham plc Chatham, Kent

Cover design and illustration by Jeff Fisher

Contents

TO DOROTHY

The Complete Works

Many of Balzac's titles underwent changes and their chronology is sometimes uncertain. They are listed here in their final form; the dates are those
accepted by most authorities.

Cromwell (1819: not produced or published during the author's lifetime).

Pseudonymous works: by 'Lord R'Hoone', in collaboration – *L'Héritière
de Birague* (1822); *Jean-Louis* (1822); by 'Horace de Saint-Aubin' – *Clot-
ilde de Lusignan* (1822); *Le Centenaire* (1822); *Le Vicaire des Ardennes*
(1822); *La Dernière Fée* (1823); *Annette et le Criminal* (*Argon le Pirate*)
(1824); *Wann-Chlore* (1826).

Works published anonymously: *Du Droit d'Ainesse* (1824); *Histoire
Impartiale des Jésuites* (1824); *Code des Gens Honnêtes* (1826).

La Comédie Humaine

Titles of the constituent novels and tales are in the order in which they
appear in the Bibliothèque de la Pléiade series of 1935–7. This edition was
based on Balzac's 1845 catalogue and his subsequent modifications of it.

1. Etudes de Meurs: SCÈNES DE LA VIE PRIVÉE: *La Maison du Chat qui
pelote* (1830); *Le Bal de Sceaux* (1830); *Mémoires de deux Jeunes Mariées*
(1841–2); *La Bourse* (1832); *Modeste Mignon* (1844); *Un Début dans la
Vie* (1842); *Albert Savarus* (1842); *La Vendetta* (1830); *Une Double Famille* (1830); *La Paix du Ménage* (1830); *Madame Firmiani* (1832); *Etude
de Femme* (1830); *La Fausse Maîtresse* (1841); *Une Fille d'Eve* (1838–9);
Le Message (1832); *La Grenadière* (1832); *La Femme Abandonnée* (1832);
Honorine (1843); *Béatrix* (1839); *Gobseck* (1830); *La Femme de Trente
Ans* (1831–4); *Le Père Goriot* (1834–5); *Le Colonel Chabert* (1832); *La
Messe de l'Athée* (1836); *L'Interdiction* (1836); *Le Contrat de Mariage*
(1835); *Autre Etude de Femme* (1842).

SCÈNES DE LA VIE DE PROVINCE: *Ursule Mirouet* (1841); *Eugénie Grandet*
(1833); *Les Célibataires* – (i) *Pierrette*, (ii) *Le Curé de Tours*, (iii) *La
Rabouilleuse* (1840, 1832, 1841–2); *Les Parisiens en Province* – (i) *L'Illus-
tre Gaudissart*, (ii) *La Muse du Département* (1833, 1843); *Les Rivalités*
– (i) *La Vieille Fille*, (ii) *Le Cabinet des Antiques* (1836, 1836–8, 1839);
Illusions Perdues – (i) *Les Deux Poètes*, (ii) *Un Grand Homme de Province
à Paris*, (iii) *Les Souffrances de l'Inventeur* (1837, 1839, 1843).

SCÈNES DE LA VIE PARISIENNE: *Histoire des Treize – (i) Ferragus, (ii) La Duchesse de Langeais, (iii) La Fille aux Yeux d'Or* (1833, 1833–4, 1834–5); *Histoire de la Grandeur et de la Décadence de César Birotteau* (1837); *La Maison Nucingen* (1838); *Splendeurs et Misères des Courtisanes – (i) Comment aiment les Filles, (ii) A Combien l'Amour revient aux Vieillards, (iii) Où mènent les mauvais Chemins, (iv) La Dernière Incarnation de Vautrin* (1838–47); *Les Secrets de la Princesse de Cadignan* (1839); *Facino Cane* (1836); *Sarrasine* (1830); *Pierre Grassou* (1840); *Les Parents Pauvres – (i) La Cousine Bette, (ii) Le Cousin Pons* (1846, 1847); *Un Homme d'Affaires* (1845); *Un Prince de la Bohème* (1840); *Gaudissart II* (1844); *Les Employés* (1837); *Les Comédiens sans le savoir* (1846); *Les Petits Bourgeois* (posth.); *L'Envers de l'Histoire Contemporaine – (i) Madame de la Chanterie, (ii) L'Initié* (1842, 1848).

SCÈNES DE LA VIE POLITIQUE: *Un Episode sous la Terreur* (1830); *Une Ténébreuse Affaire* (1841); *Le Député d'Arcis* (1847, finished in 1854 by Charles Rabou); *Z. Marcas* (1840).

SCÈNES DE LA VIE MILITAIRE: *Les Chouans* (1829); *Une Passion dans le Désert* (1830).

SCÈNES DE LA VIE DE CAMPAGNE: *Les Paysans* (1844); *Le Médecin de Campagne* (1833); *Le Curé de Village* (1839); *Le Lys dans la Vallée* (1835).

2. Etudes Philosophiques *La Peau de Chagrin* (1830–1); *Jésus-Christ en Flandre* (1831); *Melmoth Réconcilié* (1835); *Massimilla Doni* (1839); *Le Chef-d' Œuvre Inconnu* (1831); *Gambara* (1837); *La Recherche de l'Absolu* (1834); *L'Enfant Maudit* (1831–6); *Adieu* (1830); *Les Marana* (1832–3); *Le Réquisitionnaire* (1831); *El Verdugo* (1830); *Un Drame au Bord de la Mer* (1835); *Maître Cornélius* (1831); *L'Auberge Rouge* (1831); *Sur Catherine de Médicis* (1830–46); *L'Elixir de Longue Vie* (1830); *Les Proscrits* (1831); *Louis Lambert* (1832); *Séraphita* (1834–5).

3. Etudes Analytiques *Physiologie du Mariage* (1829); *Petites Misères de la Vie Conjugale* (1830, 1840, 1845).

Les Contes Drolatiques (published in three sets of ten tales, 1832, 1833, 1837).

Plays: *L'Ecole des Ménages* (1839); *Vautrin* (1839); *Les Ressources de Quinola* (1842); *Pamela Figaud* (1842); *La Marâtre* (1848).

Acknowledgements

The writer owes a considerable debt to the important biographers of Balzac – André Billy, Stefan Zweig, and André Maurois – and to the graceful scholarship of Marcel Bouteron and Félicien Marceau. The excellent *Correspondance* and the *Lettres à Madame Hanska*, both edited by Roger Pierrot; *Balzac: Letters to his Family, 1809–1850*, edited by Walter Scott Hastings; and J. Lewis May's translation of the correspondence with Madame Zulma Carraud have been indispensable. I have also frequently consulted Herbert J. Hunt's exhaustive *Balzac's Comédie Humaine*. In addition to my own translations of biographical material I have drawn gratefully on the versions of Norman Denny and William and Dorothy Rose. In Balzac's works, though I have mainly relied on the translators of George Saintsbury's monumental edition published by Macmillan, New York, in 1901, I have also used the contemporary versions of *Les Illusions Perdues* by Kathleen Raine and the recent Penguin Classic edition of *The Chouans* by Marion Ayton Crawford.

The publishers are indebted to the following for permission to quote from their publications: W. H. Allen & Co. Ltd and Grossman Publishers, Inc. (Marceau, *Balzac and his World*); The Bodley Head Ltd (*The Unpublished Correspondence of Honoré de Balzac and Madame Zulma Carraud*); Cassell & Co. Ltd (Zweig, *Balzac*); Macdonald & Co. Ltd (*Les Illusions Perdues*. Published as *Lost Illusions* by Alfred A. Knopf, Inc. in the U.S.A. and Canada); and Penguin Books Ltd (*The Chouans*). The quotation from *My Past and Thoughts* (Herzen) is from the edition revised by H. Higgens, published by Chatto & Windus Ltd and Alfred A. Knopf, Inc., 1968. Maurois, *Prometheus: The Life of Balzac*, is © 1965 in the translation by The Bodley Head Ltd, reprinted by Harper & Row, Publishers, Inc.

The Wrongs of Childhood

In 1799, six years after the Terror, a son was born to the pretty young wife of Bernard-François Balzac, a husband thirty-two years older than herself, head of the hospital administration and Deputy Mayor of the pleasant town of Tours. The Balzacs were strangers to the place. Bernard-François had arrived there by shrewdly using the new opportunities which Napoleon's rise to absolute power had made available to people of his background. Napoleon was First Consul. He had returned with enormous plunder from the Italian campaign; he had made his attempt to break England's seaborne trade by the expedition to Egypt and had at least defeated the Turks at Aboukir. A load of Oriental antiquities was brought back to France – a matter that was in time to become very stimulating to the imagination of the little Balzac just born – and, in addition, a giraffe which was to have its effect on Paris fashions.

France was recovering from anarchy and the time had come for rising young men to rise further in her armies and in civil life, and for men like Bernard-François who had survived the Revolution by cunning to consolidate their gains. The moment for rewards had arrived. In Tours, far away from dangerous frontiers and serious strife, a General de Pommereul had been appointed Prefect – a reward, it is said, for giving Napoleon good marks in his military examinations – and in turn he found a job for Bernard-François. The man had long been 'in military supplies' in Valenciennes and Brittany. Tours was the headquarters in such matters for the campaign against the rebels in Brittany and was a succulent place for a man of fifty who felt he had earned a right to a peaceful life. And

1

so, he and his pretty Parisian wife had a substantial house in the main street of Tours, once called the rue Royale and then rue de la Grande Armée. The son born to them was Honoré de Balzac who would become the author of *La Comédie Humaine*, a work Napoleonic in the grandeur of its design. Indeed thirty years later he was to say, 'What Napoleon achieved by the sword I shall achieve by the pen.'

That anything Napoleonic could come out of a Tourangeau, a native of Touraine, was unlikely. The soft airs and indulgent life of that happy part of France may even account, in some measure, for the slow development of the young Balzac's talents. He was to diagnose the case with sceptical good humour in his portrait of 'the illustrious Gaudissart', the travelling salesman. He says:

The softness of the air, the gentleness of the climate, a certain ease of living and geniality in manners, very soon stifle any bent for the arts, dissolve the power of feeling and weaken even the strongest wills . . . If he leaves Touraine the native does well; if he stays he becomes like a Turk on his divan and spends his time making fun of his neighbours, congratulating himself and ends his life in perfect happiness. Touraine is in fact the Abbaye de Thélème, made famous by Gargantua . . . The man who settles for it becomes idle, happy and if by any chance he happens to be as ambitious as Napoleon or as poetic as Byron, some mysterious force will force him to keep his poetic impulses to himself and to turn his ambitions into daydreams.

But if the Balzacs were strangers and interlopers in the affairs of this happy country and did not conceal that they thought themselves exceptional, this gave them a valuable point of observation. In one sense, especially in his salty, sensual good humour and common sense, their son became half-Tourangeau. If he was brought up as a child among people who lived for the golden mean, the juicy greeds and the horseplay of country life in the meadows and vineyards and canny little towns of their river valleys, he saw that there was an opportunist and shady side to their lives: they were buying up the sequestered property of the great families who had been ruined by the Revolution. He listened as a child to perpetual talk of money, property and ambition in his home and was being grounded in themes that were to make the novelist at once a dreamer and a devastating observer of human obsessions and appetites.

People as strange and uprooted as the Balzacs were as likely to be monomaniacs, people who, if they ever come to earth, are astounded by themselves. When he was thirty Honoré cried out in his spluttering, boastful way: 'I am inexplicable. No one will fully understand me.'

He might have been describing his extraordinary father. A self-taught son of a poor Gascon peasant from the Tarn, one of eleven children who had slept on straw in their little house and had worked from childhood in the fields, Bernard-François rose in the world because of his unusual sagacity and effort. Brighter and more energetic than his brothers, he was taken up by the village priest and nibbled his way into the one promising opening for a rising man: petty jobs in the offices of country lawyers. The decisive moment for Bernard-François – and Honoré was to describe it in his novel *César Birotteau* – was when he set off, perhaps on foot, for Paris. The distance from the South was enormous. The father must often have told his children how he had only a louis in his pocket and how his only possessions were a pair of breeches, a pair of blue stockings, a sprigged waistcoat, a jacket, and three strong linen shirts or smocks. He was wearing iron-shod boots and carried a walking-stick. (Walking-sticks were to play a spectacular part in the fantasy life of his son.) This would be about 1760. Louis XVI was on the throne. Bernard-François had become a reading man and though, despite the priest, he had read his Voltaire and swore by Rousseau, he had no revolutionary intention in his head. Far from it. The original name of the Balzacs was Balssa. (By the time the Balzacs were in Tours it was a family religion with them to dream that they were kin of the noble family of the Marquis d'Entragues. They rolled the transcendent 'de' privately on their tongues.) Imaginary aristocrat and open Royalist, the peasant Bernard-François put on a certain courtly air, dropped the dialect of the Tarn, and saw that to make a career when he got to Paris he must make himself indispensable to 'key men'. How he managed this is mysterious; in his anecdotage his utterances are grandiloquent statements of his honesty and ability, for he was given to awarding himself large moral prizes. He does seem to have become in time secretary to secretaries of the Naval Committee in Paris and even claimed to have had some employment in the Conseil d'Etat. Quickly, when the Revolution came, he stepped astutely aside into local government, the Hôtel de Ville. His weakness was an impetuous Gascon tongue and a boldness which betrayed his Royalist sympathies. A friend saved him during the Revolution by recommending his escape to Valenciennes on the border north of Lille.

What does a poor but enterprising man do when caught up in social revolution and war? Mask himself and turn his coat of course. It was a mark of talent on his part that he got into those safe grazing grounds for men without capital: the organization of military supplies. It is typical of him that he at once found his key man here in a financier called Doumerc who held all the strings in this promising occupation, where accounts had to be laundered and transactions made presentable. The financier was grateful. When Napoleon at last imposed order on the Revolution, Doumerc found a comfortably-off wife for his good friend and also got him posted to that lucrative and unassailable job in Tours. There was more than ambition to Bernard-François. He was short and burly, the plebeian not concealed by the grandeur of his blue, silver-embroidered uniform with the high collar rising to his ears above a deep cravat. A man of abrupt, pithy remarks, yet obliging, he strutted in the street. The black hair was combed forward boyishly, the nose was bold, the whole face strong, the dark eyes quizzical. At the same time there was a look of alarm in them; something odd was going on in his head. Autodidacts are likely to be cranks and originals. The self-taught peasant and inveterate reader was sanguine, but intemperate only in his novel views on everything. He saw himself as an intellectual and *philosophe* of the Voltairean kind. He was a construct of what he had read. His favourite authors were Rabelais and Sterne and he took pains to model himself upon the character of Uncle Toby. He was well known for his preposterous 'observations'. One particularly struck his son: 'I refuse to argue with people who disagree with me.' The strange look in his eyes betrayed one who had more than a touch of the madness of the purely rational man.

The marriage of Bernard-François was one of his aberrations. He was, as has been said, thirty-two years older than his wife. She was the daughter of well-off drapers and embroiderers in the Marais quarter of Paris and brought a good dowry and hopes of inheritance: 260,000 francs, a decent sum for those days. (One can only guess at what this was worth, but since the exchange value of the franc and the pound was fairly stable in the nineteenth century until 1918 and if one allows for the great change in values since, it might be estimated that she brought up to £40,000 capital. It was reckoned that a middle-class man could live in comfort on 10,000 francs, say

£400 a year. A government clerk would have to struggle along on 2500 francs.) Bernard-François had no capital but he had his salary. He announced he was as strong as an oak, as polished as marble, and as unshakeable as the Pyramids. His young wife was an exquisite girl of nineteen and one can understand why the ladies of Tours found her unbearably dressy and far too flirtatious. There is a picture of her. She wears a hat coquettishly aslant on her curls; her blue eyes are long and icy. She looks neat, vain, and wilful, with a mind of her own. She was certainly drily aware that she had been given to an old husband as a reward for his professional services to a friend of her family and that the capital was on her side. She was not in love with her husband.

If one thing united the awkward couple it was a shared obsession, but one in which wife and husband took opposite yet complementary views. For tiny busy Mme Balzac, money meant minute accountancy and unresting thrift; for Bernard-François money was a dream. For him, a true eighteenth-century man, money was Fortune. And Fortune was a gamble, but not an ordinary gamble. It was one made certain by the rational approach. Nothing illustrates this better than Bernard-François's action in putting his savings into a tontine, a crude form of endowment insurance, invented before capitalism became sophisticated. Tontines had been abolished by the idealists of the Revolution but Napoleon had brought them back. One of the safest was the Tontine Laforge. The members paid a capital sum into it and shared the interest in their lifetime, but left the capital to their survivors.

As a freemason and rationalist, Bernard-François saw that Fortune, i.e. collecting the jackpot, must be sought in a scientific spirit. He was proud of his independence and physical vigour and he saw that longevity was the key to success. He at once took steps to see that he outlived the other shareholders. He turned health faddist. Exercise, going to bed early, diet, were the answers. He intended to live until he was 100, even to 150. Sardonically he referred to the tontine shareholders who died as 'deserters'. And so he drank milk and the sap of trees – even chewed slips of bark – and went to bed early after a frugal meal. He drank very little wine. He was one of those who go to extremes in order to achieve moderation; and this trait Honoré inherited. The thing to do was to arrive at the perfect state of physical health by preserving the proper balance of one's vital forces, and to be invulnerable in one's opinions. Honoré's sister,

Laure, tells of their father reading in the paper about a man who had lived to be a hundred. 'There you've got a man who knows the secret of how to live. He has conserved his vitality.' But it turned out that the man was a drunk and ate heavy meals at night. Information like this did not defeat the adaptable Bernard-François. 'All right', he said. 'That man has simply shortened his life.'

Young Mme Balzac lived a gay life in Tours and caused a satisfying amount of annoyance among the important ladies of the town. (In one of his late novels, *La Muse du Département*, Balzac notes how provincial ladies lose interest in their clothes.)

But the gay life of Mme Balzac came temporarily to an end. She was pregnant and there must have been many an 'I-told-you-so' in Tours when her first baby died twenty-three days after birth. She had been unable to feed it. In 1799 when Honoré was born he was sent off at once to a wet-nurse, the wife of a gendarme in the village of Saint-Cyr across the Loire. Two years later the sister called Laure was born and joined Honoré. For four years the children were without their mother. This rankled with Honoré to the end of his life. His many love-affairs always started with the declaration: 'I never had a mother. I never knew a mother's love.' This statement is not a self-pitying lamentation; rather it is an enlarging of himself. In it he asserts he is an exceptional, perhaps even a metaphysical being. Already the sunny little boy who played by the Loire and watched the sailing-boats find their way among the sandbanks and little islands of the river was becoming a double person who lived in his imagination. But despite her air of coldness and folly, Mme Balzac was a practical and devoted mother. Old Bernard-François was getting lazy and indulgent. He had read his Rousseau and believed in letting children grow in their own way. He ignored his family and went to his room to read his Sterne, his Rabelais, his history of China or the Pyramids. If Honoré was on bad terms with his mother very early and was very frightened of her severe and pretty eyes, it was because she had become the disciplinarian of the family. She too could dramatize: as she punished, so she too sent up the cry that the children were 'breaking her heart' and causing her dreadful suffering. In such situations Honoré stared sullenly and told lies. They were an effective defence and also, he discovered, an extraordinary pleasure. They ensured his liberty. A second sister was born, Laurence, a romantic child.

In the following years Honoré experienced two more of those

wrongs of childhood which are so stimulating to genius. Mysteriously, as far as he was concerned, he was abruptly sent off once more, this time to the Oratorian fathers at their college in Vendôme. Why? Mme Balzac, who had been forced into marriage, had fallen in love with a young man of her own age, Jean de Margonne, a young country gentleman and officer in the militia who lived in a small château at Saché and who rode into Tours to amuse himself. Mme Balzac was about to give birth to his child. To stop gossip she got the father to be the child's godfather. (An acacia tree was planted in the Balzacs' garden to celebrate the birth. Or so it was said.) The new brother was called Henri and – the other children sourly noticed – was the favourite who was soon out of control and could do no wrong. When they grew older and became aware of the situation, the legitimate Balzacs drily and openly described themselves as 'the children of conjugal duty'. Henceforth they became experts in irony. They referred, with double meaning, to 'our celestial family', an allusion to the Chinese studies of their father, the less than celestial state of their home, and their feeling that they were the most remarkable children in the town.

What did Bernard-François say? He was in his sixties and the old freemason merely read Rabelais aloud because he knew this shocked his wife. When the children grew up Mme Balzac said: 'Because of his age your father had the tact to say nothing.' After all, under the French marriage system, a woman found her liberty in marriage and often did as she pleased; and, in the disorderly times, love-children were taken into the family. Honoré was to have a sound precedent when he in his turn fathered three children on women already married.

Having sinned in the Margonne affair, Mme Balzac put on orthodox religious airs in order to quieten her conscience and stop the gossip of her neighbours. She had grown up when the Revolution had broken the influence of the Church. She had dabbled in Swedenborgian beliefs which had become fashionable. Like her mother before her, she was prone to believe in mysticism, magic, fortune-tellers, and Mesmer. But now she displayed public orthodoxy. She firmly took Honoré to the superb cathedral in Tours on Sundays. The boy was intoxicated by the mysterious sensations he experienced: they were feeding the powerful dream-life into which he had retreated at home where he sat either making jokes or in half-annoyed stupor, evading his mother's eyes; or stood, scraping in a slapdash way on his violin.

To Bernard-François, the attraction of Oratorian teaching was that it was free of the military discipline of the Jesuits and was a mixture of the spartan and the liberal. It also taught respect for the Emperor. More valuable to the novelist than his jealousy of Henri was his dispatch to this college. It was a rule of the Oratorians that parents must not visit their children more than once a year. Balzac – as I shall now call him – swore that his parents did not visit him once during the time he was there from his eighth birthday until he was fifteen, yet the college was only forty miles away. His sister Laure says this is a fantasy, but agrees that the mother rarely came and, in her stern way, kept him short of money. It was a school for rich boys. Though he went there as a healthy young animal, and came back later a famished and sleep-walking ghost, the isolation awakened his mind.

Like Dickens – whom he sometimes resembles – Balzac returned again and again to his childhood in his writings. The picture is always dark. Transposed in other characters – a gifted orphan or a sensitive young aristocrat – the boy appears in *La Peau de Chagrin* and *Le Lys dans la Vallée*. The most detailed account of his imprisonment (as he called it) is in *Louis Lambert*, where he splits himself in two and becomes the observer of a boy of immense precocity and visionary genius.

Whatever may be granted to hindsight, the account in this book reveals the growth of lasting obsessions. No easy-going father pretending to be Uncle Toby now; no mother, but vigilant priests. Pride forces the schoolboy into a solitary life among rich boys who mock him for his lack of money and because he does not get presents from home. The eighty boys lived a regimented life. The human stink of the place, Balzac said, damaged the organs of thought. In the lockers there was the secreted, decaying food, there were the rotting bodies of pigeons the boys were allowed to shoot. The jakes were foul. In the mornings the boys lined up to wash in two troughs before the masters and then moved to a table where the women servants combed out their dirty hair. (All his life Balzac was fastidiously clean in body even though, as people complained, his hair had a greasy look.) He had a special care for his small hands and feet; his skin was delicate. In the winter at Vendôme the boys were tortured by chilblains and sores. He complains angrily in *Louis Lambert* of the filthy and broken state of the shoes they all wore. It was an agony when the mud-encased laces broke. He was angry that he had either no gloves at all or that those he had were caked with dirt and unwearable. (One sees the beginning of his lifelong obsession with gloves and perhaps the reason for the large quantities he ordered when he grew up.) The lessons bored him. He was lazy or backward in class. The chief complaint against him was that he was a day-dreamer. The boys learned parrot fashion and Balzac was often caught out, at a loss to know what to say when the master barked out: 'Next?' Most of his leisure was cut down by impositions or beatings with a leather stock. The boys were called out before the class and were obliged to kneel on a table to receive the punishment.

But he learned a valuable trick very early: to be sent to the 'alcove', the punishment cell in the tower of the school or the punishment cubicle in the dormitories where one could be alone. One of the priests was cataloguing the library which contained a large and indiscriminate collection of books looted from the châteaux of Touraine during the Revolution. Eagerly Balzac helped the priest and was able to carry off books to the cell. Like his father before him the dreamer had found literature: extraordinary memoirs, even the writings of Chateaubriand, religion and history, everything. He compared his day-dreaming to that of a young girl dreaming about an imaginary lover – and the comparison is one of the many indications of the feminine strain in Balzac's virile nature. In the next six years Balzac read at random everything he could lay hands on. One of the striking things is a wide reading in English literature from Shakespeare, Milton to Defoe and all the English eighteenth century. He read through the Oratorian library. He sought nothing short of total knowledge. In *Louis Lambert*, of course, he is describing ostensibly the life of another self at the school, the projection of his belief in his prophetic genius, but there is no doubt that this double Balzac is real. In their eccentric way the Balzacs were a literary family. He wrote of Louis Lambert, the boy genius; 'From that time reading was a sort of appetite which nothing could satisfy.' (Notice the word 'appetite' – the boy was to grow into the novelist who, more than any other, saw men and women in terms of their appetites.)

He devoured books of every kind, feeding indiscriminately on religious works, history and literature, philosophy and physics. He had told me that he found indescribable delight in reading dictionaries for lack of other books . . . His eye took in six or seven lines at once . . .

And he remembered everything he read. He could remember even the position of a sentence on the page. And the images prompted by the words gave him 'a sort of second sight by which he could command all nature':

When I read the story of the battle of Austerlitz I saw every incident. The roar of the cannon, the cries of the fighting men rang in my ears and made my inmost self quiver.

He lost all sense of his own physical existence and lived like one 'leaving Space behind him'.

It is perfectly plausible that he was deep in the speculations of Swedenborg on the nature of angels and the power of the will, though he passed as being a very conventional Catholic. He had heard of animal magnetism. Reprimanded for day-dreaming one day the boy fixed the master with a long, unflinching stare of concentrated scorn – an early exercise in that magnetism of the 'brown eyes flecked with gold' everyone noticed when he grew up. He got the whip, the ultimate punishment, for repeating the stare a second time.

There were good and watchful masters at the school, but seven years is an eternity in childhood and in the end solitary reading left him stunned. He could hardly speak. His health broke under the strain which was imposed less by the school than by his own brain and will. He makes out that Louis Lambert wrote a spectacular Treatise on the Will, and if Balzac did not write such a treatise it is clear that his later stress on the power of the will was formed at this time. The imagination of Napoleon, that haunting victorious presence in the minds of the Vendôme boys, would have been nothing without Will.

The Oratorians were alarmed by the illness of their pupil. They asked his parents to take him away. He came home looking like a ghost. The doctor said he had brain-fever but Bernard-François, the immortal, was contemptuous of doctors. An open-air life would cure the fifteen-year-old boy. They sent him to Jean de Margonne's at Saché, despite the existence of Henri, for in Touraine the errors of love were taken amiably. For the rest of his life Jean de Margonne, who was bored by the country, welcomed Balzac eagerly and seems to have preferred him to Henri, his natural child.

The boy walked or rode from one friendly house in Touraine to another:

For the first time in my life [he makes Félix de Vandenesse say in *Le Lys dans la Vallée*] I could rest under a tree, walk fast or slowly as I list, without being called to account by anyone . . . the first taste of freedom, though exerted in trifles, brought unspeakable expansion to my soul.

At the moment when I walked down the valley of the Indre, the mill and its falls gave voice to the murmuring vale; the poplars laughed as they swayed; there wasn't a cloud in the sky, the birds sang, the grasshoppers chirped, everything had melody. I love Touraine!

But there was a distinction:

Never ask me again why I love Touraine! I do not love it as we love our childhood home or as we love an oasis in the desert, I love it as an artist loves art . . . but for Touraine I should not now be alive.

Whatever is lyrical in Balzac's writing, whatever is flushed with sensual laughter, has its source in that country.

It was now 1814 and Bernard-François was having difficulties in Tours. His key man and protector, the Prefect-General Pommereul, lost his job. There was trouble between the Church party and the Bonapartists as Napoleon's luck turned. The old admirer of Sterne sought to raise his prestige by literary exercises. He wrote several pamphlets. One on law reform and how to prevent robberies and murders. Criminals must be made to do work useful to society. Another pamphlet dealt with young girls who had been betrayed and left destitute: all charitable institutions should keep special posts for unmarried mothers. This was a subject the old man knew rather a lot about. Another pamphlet has a note of desperation in it. He proposed that his favourite object, a pyramid, should be built in the Tuileries or the Champ-de-Mars in honour of the Napoleonic régime. But the Allies had won. Napoleon was sent to Elba, the monarchy was restored; the Duc d'Angoulême paused at Tours on his way from Bordeaux to Paris to join Louis XVIII. France was weary of the Napoleonic slaughter and Tours obligingly turned its coat. Flags were in every window. A great Royalist ball was given. Bernard-François dodged it discreetly, but sent his son who was fitted out in a new blue jacket, silk stockings, his father's waistcoat, and pumps that made his feet swell. Hastily Bernard-François altered the theme of the pamphlet. It was rewritten to propose a compromise: 'An equestrian statue which the French people desire to erect to perpetuate the memory of Henri IV.' This achieved nothing. In the meantime his speculations with his wife's property turned out badly. To the end of her life Mme Balzac kept a careful account of her financial history: her husband had lost 60,000 francs of her money on land purchases and the Bourse. The Balzacs had to sell their house. The time had come for the old opportunist to get away. He appealed to the son of his old friend, the financier M. Doumerc, to get him the job of Director of Victualling to the First Military Divisions in Paris. Dressed in his now out-of-date uniform, Bernard-François looked like a patchwork of historical mishap when he moved off to the Marais quarter of Paris in 1814, the quarter of Mme Balzac's prosperous relations in drapery and the law. Their son was put into a Royalist and Catholic pension and took his lessons at the Lycée Charlemagne; and once more, in the interests of discipline, his mother gave him no money. He wheedled it out of his grandmother. He was now as tall as he would ever be: only five feet two inches high, with a long body and comically short legs and, not for the last time in his life, he looked like 'a Savoyard's monkey'. But good came of his changed life. He received from the school the decoration of the Lily and was inscribed as Honoré *de* Balzac, a device of the new régime to win over the provincial bourgeoisie to the monarchy. Bernard-François had occasionally ventured to insinuate the romantic 'de'. The odd thing is that Jean de Margonne, his wife's lover who was entitled to the particle and occupied a genuine small château in the countryside of châteaux, usually dropped his.

The Lawyers of the
Marais District

Napoleon had left his mark upon Paris, but it was still the Paris of
Louis XIV when the Balzacs arrived in 1814. It was a compact city
of 700,000 people, but on the north it did not extend far beyond
the Grands Boulevards: Montmartre and its windmills were in the
country, so were Auteuil and Passy and the Champs-Elysées. The
avenue was a country road with ditches of sewage on either side
and you could buy a glass of milk from the farmers who grazed
their cows in the fields beside it. Cossacks were camped there in
1814. On the south side houses just touched the Invalides and
Montparnasse. The luxury quarter was at the Palais-Royal but the
streets near it were a warren of mean alleys and slums which lay
between the Palace of the Tuileries, the Louvre, and the quarter of
prostitution behind the rue de Richelieu. When Balzac wrote *La
Cousine Bette*, he placed the vengeful Alsatian spinster in this sinister
quarter, in the Impasse Doyenne where Théophile Gautier in due
course would annoy his landlord by his wild fancy-dress parties.
The Jardin des Plantes was the fashionable park, popular because it
contained the giraffe which had been sent from Egypt. It had travelled by sea and had been fed on the milk of five cows during the
voyage. The animal's neck was the rage – the giraffe look came in
for women: a long neck with close curls to make the head look
small. Balzac, one notices, was always attracted by women with
long curving necks and closely curled hair.

The Marais, where the Balzacs settled, was a good way to the
east, between the rue du Temple and the Place des Vosges, then called
the Place Royale, a district from which the nobility had migrated in

the seventeenth century because of the infiltration of commerce, the bad smells, and the noise. They had moved across the river to the Faubourg Saint-Germain, leaving their mansions to lawyers and to petty trade. The Marais was now a mixed middle-class and artisan neighbourhood. Rising lawyers, even Presidents of the Court lived there, and prosperous traders like Mme Balzac's relations; but poor craftsmen and labourers crowded there too, also criminals, fortune-tellers, and actors and actresses playing at the local theatres – the Gaieté, the Ambigu-Comique, and the Cirque Olympique. Filth flowed in the narrow streets, mud was everywhere. Planks were put down so that pedestrians could cross without getting spattered. One of the minor titillations of life was the sight of women lifting their long skirts and showing their white stockings as they picked their way along. In *Les Illusions Perdues*, Coralie the pretty actress says sharply to her protector Camusot, the silk merchant: 'When a man loves a woman he surely doesn't let her paddle in the mud and risk breaking her legs, going on foot! It's only these tape-measure knights who like to see skirts with mud on the hem.' Camusot is scared and says she shall have a carriage 'the day after tomorrow'.

A large number of *pensions de famille* had sprung up in those days. They had increased because the population of uprooted families had increased after the Revolution and the wars. These pensions were inhabited by people of grand family who had been ruined, by speculators who had seen their sudden fortunes collapse, by soldiers on half-pay, returned prisoners of war, widows of high officers of the Grande Armée and, in the Quartier Latin, students. In the Pension Vauquer, in *Le Père Goriot*, Balzac described exactly what pension life was like.

In this period the cafés of Paris had no *terrasses*. One went to the café to read the papers, but the nervous traders of the Marais quarter made a point of reading *all* the papers, so that no one should guess their political opinions in these troubled times. There was one cheerful place, the Café Turc – since the expedition to Egypt the Orient was the fashion: the young Balzac dreamed of a slave-like Oriental mistress – where one sat in a garden. It had a tree-sheltered alley for lovers, a kiosk, a Chinese bridge. One could buy ices or beer and watch the side-shows – a sign of the return to pleasure after the hard times and butchery of Napoleon's battles.

The pursuit of pleasure was not the first thought in the minds of the hard-working people of the Marais. They got up at five in the morning. They toiled in small, dark shops and offices where the smells of the streets hung in the air and where outbreaks of cholera often occurred. They were in bed by nine at night and, at that hour, it was said if anyone looked at Paris from the tower of Notre-Dame he would see a glow of light over the Palais-Royal, a glitter in the Faubourg Saint-Germain where the aristocracy turned night into day, but only a glimmer from the Quartier Latin, and in the Marais complete blackout. In all Paris lighting was by candle, though a few newfangled oil lamps were coming in, heating was by wood-burning stoves and only the wealthiest who happened to have private wells had water in the house.

The very rich lived in private 'hôtels', but the classes in the Marais were divided by the floors they lived on. The better-off lived on the lower floors. The house of a high government official would not be carpeted by Boulard, the famous *tapissier* of the Empire, but it would have Venetian mirrors in coloured glass, panelled walls decorated in the manner of Watteau or Boucher. Besides his cook and maids he would have a valet who would change his coat and run downstairs to become his coachman. On the first floor one found a financier, on the second a lawyer or important civil servant, on the third a shopkeeper, on the fourth a worker, and in the attic some miserable wretch. There were stables below in the courtyard. Carriages were rare here, but cabs went by tinkling their bells; on the passable roads the newly invented omnibus appeared, with names like Béarnaise for the Legitimists, Constantine to commemorate the conquests in Algeria, and a whole collection of Gazelles, Diligentes, and Hirondelles. But for the ordinary man the best way of making the difficult journey from one quarter to another in Paris was by horseback. Paris was described as 'the paradise of women, the purgatory of husbands and the hell of horses'.

The Balzacs were, at first, comfortably off and well connected among the lawyers and business people of the Marais. Mme Balzac was vigilant of her son's morals and his studies at the Lycée Charlemagne. Honoré did not distinguish himself there. He came thirty-second in Latin. A letter to him shows Mme Balzac's stern, emotional methods. Thirty-second! What a disgrace. How heart-breaking for a mother! 'You will understand that a thirty-second at the Lycée cannot possibly be taken to the fête de Charlemagne tomorrow.' Farewell, she said, building up one of her scenes which were becoming commoner, to the rare pleasure of having all her children round her. She had been going to collect him at eight in the morning, there would have been lunch, dinner, and instructive chats. But (she carried on), his slackness and other errors left her nothing to do, but to leave him to his punishment: 'Quelle vie pour mon ceur.'

She watched his spending. We read in *Le Lys dans la Vallée*:

M. Lepitre occupied a fine old house, the Hôtel Joyeuse where as in all ancient residences of the nobility, there was a lodge for the gate-porter. During the hour of recreation, before the usher took us in file to the Lycée Charlemagne, the wealthy boys got breakfast at the lodge, provided by the porter called Doisy. Breakfast with a cup of coffee and sugar was in the most aristocratic taste, in consequence of the exorbitant prices to which the Colonial products rose under Napoleon.

What benefit to his education (she asked) would come from the greed for coffee and sugar? Did he know the value of the money he cost his parents? What would be the next vice? The gambling-rooms of the Palais-Royal, the prostitutes of the wooden galleries? She saw to it that a professor took him back to Lepitre's in the evening. Balzac had to confess that he owed Doisy 100 francs. An important incident: it is Balzac's first debt. His mother had driven him to it. Balzac's later appetite for debt looks like the desire to avenge the stinginess of his mother's habits and to compensate for a lack of love. He went on to a three-year study of law, for his parents had useful connections there. He was moved to a notary's chambers and now there seemed to be a chance to slip out and go down to the Palais-Royal; but he was still shadowed. Prostitutes and easy-going girls went there in the evenings to the wooden galleries that adjoined the grand arcades of the palace of the Duc d'Orléans. They called the evening parade 'faire son Palais'. At last his mother went off on one of her restless visits to Tours that were usually concerned with some little property of hers and the chance for slipping out improved. The second time he tried it was in 1815 but when he opened the door, there stood his mother. Waterloo was lost. Napoleon was on the point of abdication and she had travelled back to take her son off to Tours in case there were riots. She had known what revolution was. So ended the first frightened attempt at adventure. He was left, he said, advancing his age in the character of Félix de Vandenesse in *Le Lys dans la Vallée*, 'standing between boyhood, prolonged study and a manhood late in showing its green shoots'.

The only woman he was at his ease with was his maternal grand-mother. Bernard-François's relations never appear in the son's life: if they were alive they were working in the fields in the Tarn. There is a tale that a brother of Bernard-François went to the guillotine for murder. The grandmother who had created the severity of her own daughter had softened with age and had become peculiar. She adored the curly-haired youth who sat up playing cards with her in the evenings. If the portrait he draws of the rich old lady with her jewels and lace and silver in *Le Lys dans la Vallée* has something of her she was as 'old as a cathedral and as painted as a miniature'. He talked incessantly of the lectures on science that he had taken to attending at the Sorbonne. She pretended to lose at whist so that he could collect some pocket money. If he started buying handsomely bound books at this time it was she who paid and laid the foundation of a lifelong mania.

Whenever Balzac speaks of women at this period of his life he stresses his timidity and his poverty. One does not know what to believe. His sister Laure, who liked to think of her brother as a gallant libertine, says he had many 'strange intrigues'. It is pretty certain that he preferred older women to young girls. His grand-mother must have teased the stumpy youth. He had a comic tip to the end of his nose, he had already lost some of his top teeth. According to Laure, his grandmother betted him 100 crowns that he wouldn't succeed with a certain pretty woman in the neighbour-hood and he did succeed. Nothing in his letters or writings suggests this is true.

But it is certain that he loved listening to old women. There was one family friend who had been the mistress of Beaumarchais who fascinated him with tales of the playwright's life. These must have influenced him for he told his sister he was going to become a playwright like Molière or Beaumarchais but that before he did so he would have to formulate a philosophy. This is the first hint that the family joker had a buried and secret intention. He had written a poem or two in the manner of Chénier, the fashionable poet, but no one took that seriously. At home they called him 'the poet' to annoy him; but when he told his sister that he had to work out a philosophy of life first, the statement was deeply serious. He had confided to her that he had 'genius' and knew that for this, a formed attitude to life was essential. There were no signs of the playwright or novelist, but there were many signs of the man who would be his own encyclopedia and who would put it to visionary uses. He was, for example, excited by a new book by the family friend, Dr Nacquart, which contained a theory of the structure of the brain and spoke of the 'interrelation of body and mind'; they were in physical, organic communication with each other through the mysterious processes of electricity and magnetism. He started arguing for a Chair of Occultism, Magic and Hypnotism at the Sorbonne and one gets a hint of the sense of mystery and vision which will eventually add an extra dimension to the most factual passages of his novels. As we read from sentence to sentence there will always be a sense of words moving into what is uncertain in the power of human feeling and action. One can see at this stage he was half agnostic, half middle-of-the-road Catholic, but three writers of the thinking kind had a lasting influence on him.

First of all, through his mother and the current fashion, Emanuel Swedenborg is permanent as a shadow at the back of his mind. Swedenborg had been a natural scientist, a mathematician, an engineer – he had even, in the mid-eighteenth century, attempted to invent a flying machine. He was a scientist of genius who sought for a scientific interpretation of the universe. In time he moved to astronomy and then to the relation of the soul to the body. He was fundamentally a physiologist who argued the supremacy of the spiritual and divine and in the crisis of middle age he began to have religious visions and came to believe that a spiritual sun preceded the real sun and that a Divine Mind creates continually the physical world. The spiritual acted on the membranes of the brain. The visions introduced him to angelic beings – or transformed souls. Speculations of this kind appealed to Balzac's dramatizing instincts: in his thirties in *Séraphita* he wrote a highly dramatic and very Swedenborgian romance.

The other writers who influenced him are the scientists he heard of or read when he went to lectures at the Sorbonne. There was Johann Kaspar Lavater, the Swiss poet and physiognomist who died in 1801. He was a mystic who divined the soul in the details of the human face and Balzac's novels are full of these divinations. More important was Georges Cuvier to whose lectures Balzac listened. He was a naturalist who worked on the classification of mammals. His natural history was the starting-point of Balzac's lasting conviction that human beings could be classified, as social animals, in the same way. He prepared the way for Balzac's natural history of society.

We must add to these influences his passionate reading of the *Arabian Nights*: in a circuitous passage through his imagination, science and even his merely convenient religion were turned into dramatic magic.

But as an observer of society the young Balzac's enormous and fevered reading was less useful to him as a novelist than what he hated: the law. His studies obliged him to stick to the lawyer's chambers. In disputes about wills and property he saw human nature in all its shamelessness. In years to come, in novel after novel, in *Un Début dans la Vie* which describes the cynical larks by which the clerks relieved the boredom of toiling from five in the morning onwards over legal documents; in *La Rabouilleuse* which describes a woman's struggle to get an inheritance; in *César Birotteau* which analyses the legal processes of bankruptcy, Balzac would draw upon his young knowledge of the law.

His parents supposed that they had set him on a safe career. They knew nothing of his literary ambitions. All he had to do was to work in chambers, marry a girl with whose money he could buy a partnership in ten years and he would be made. And this was urgent. Bernard-François was now obliged to retire on a very small pension, the tontine had not yet become the cornucopia and Mme Balzac's speculations were not good. There was a family crisis. They would have to leave Paris for a cheap house outside at Villeparisis on the coach road to Meaux and Metz. They looked to the son as the hope of their old age. He had to come out into the open. He announced he was going to be a playwright. He refused to be

. . . a clerk, a machine, a riding-school hack, eating and drinking and sleeping at fixed hours. I shall be like everyone else. And that's what they call living, that life at the grindstone, doing the same thing over and over again . . . I am hungry and nothing is offered to appease my appetite. What do I want . . . I want Ortolans: for I have only two passions, love and fame and nothing has happened to satisfy either and never will . . .

He intended to be a writer.

There was a storm at home. What was he going to write? His reply was what any young man of the time gave. The way to begin was with a tragedy in verse. The public clamoured for historical tragedies in verse and Byron had shown the way: the great century of the European novel had not begun in France. The only novels read outside of *La Nouvelle Héloïse* came from England: Richardson and Sir Walter Scott and the Gothic stories of terror. The subject, Balzac announced, would be Cromwell.

This Bernard-François had to admit was topical. It would give Honoré, as a student brought up in the Napoleonic Wars, the opportunity for some rhetorical lines expressing his hatred of England:

> Exécrable Albion, je puis donc te haïr! . . .
> Puisse de mon pays s'élever un vengeur
> Qui, de l'orgueil anglais rabaissant la hauteur
> De vingt siècles de haine accepte l'héritage,
> Et sous une autre Rome engloutisse Carthage.

For the Napoleonic Balzac, Paris was ancient Rome reborn. He was to dislike English wealth and the English character – except in one woman – all his life. More important, because of the Revolution and the execution of Louis XVI the popular interest in the regicides was acute among Royalists and Republicans alike. In a few years' time Victor Hugo was to have enormous success with the subject. And the Balzacs reflected that there was certainly money in the theatre.

A lament went up from Mme Balzac: the easy-going Bernard-François was worried about his small pension. But the Balzacs were a literary family. Bernard-François regarded himself as a writer. He began to fancy the idea of being the father of another Sterne. And, in his wars with his wife and as a follower of Rousseau, he had always argued that the children should follow their own natures. In the end Mme Balzac, the educator, was overruled. She accepted the situation. It was laid down that they would support their son for two years in a garret while he wrote plays and the family, forced to economize, went off to Villeparisis. However, there was a condition: friends and neighbours in the respectable Marais were to be told that Honoré had gone off to relations in Albi. It was necessary for family pride's sake that the Balzacs should not be thought to be stupid enough to support a son in the idle pursuit of literature and fame. The drapers and lawyers of the Marais *worked* for their fortune. The governing clause in what was a very generous arrangement was that he should be kept poor. He was twenty.

A Passion for a Pretty Woman . . .
Her Name is Fame

The garret was on the fifth floor under the tiles of a poor house in the rue Lesdiguières, a working-class street on the far side of the once-aristocratic Place Royale and a short uphill walk to the cemetery of Père Lachaise. It was the first 'garden cemetery' of Europe, laid out only sixteen years before and the pride of France. From it there was an arousing view of the whole of Paris. There, in two novels, *La Peau de Chagrin* and *Les Illusions Perdues* – books ten and fifteen years away in Balzac's thirties – Lucien de Rubempré and Eugène de Rastignac would have dreams of conquering the city. The dream was Balzac's. In the garret, genius; in Paris, love, fame, and wealth; in Père Lachaise, the apex of the triangle, death. In 1819, at twenty, Balzac was committed to fame. He was intoxicated by his freedom; as for love, he wrote to his sister Laure, his confidante:

Fire has broken out in this neighbourhood, at 9 rue Lesdiguières in the head of a young man. The fire brigade have been working on it for a month now; impossible to put it out. He has got a passion for a pretty woman he has never met. Her name is Fame.

The attic was cold in the autumn and winter; the sky gleamed through gaps in the tiles. Already a furnisher, he had made himself a paper screen to keep out the draughts and wore a hood on his head. His mother had given him a mirror and was very offended when he exchanged it for a better one. He lived on very little: rent 3 sous a day, 2 sous for laundry, 2 for coal, 2 left over for emergencies.

We get our first glimpse of the gaiety of the young man. To Laure he wrote:

'I have taken a servant.'
  'A servant, my dear brother, how could you dream of such a thing?'
  'Dr Nacquart's servant is called Tranquille. Mine is called Myself. When I wake in the morning I ring for Myself and he makes my bed.'
  'Myself.'
  'Sir?'
  'I was bitten in the night. Look and see if there are any bugs.'
  'There are no bugs, sir.'
  'Good.'
He starts sweeping, but is no good at it. He raises the dust. He brushes my clothes, looks after my linen, cleans my shoes, waxes the furniture and all the time he sweeps he sings, laughs when he talks and talks while laughing. I take my breakfast and then, in case he is asleep, I tick him off, he is rude and I throw him out of the door and lock it.

He had made a start with *Cromwell*, but fatally and characteristically the idea of writing a light opera in the manner of Byron's *Corsair* began to distract him.

Oh sister, torment is the other side of the coin of Fame. Long live grocers, all day at their counter, and going to some hell-fire melodrama for relaxation. Happy people, all the same they do have to spend their lives between the cheese and the soap. So death to grocers. Long live men of letters. They are poor in pocket but people of note. So good night. Life and death to everyone.

Another day:

I don't go out much except to cheer myself up at Père Lachaise. Great news: I've eaten two melons. Send me some ideas for *Cromwell*.

He was trying to get the scene between the King and Queen right. It ought to be tender, melancholy, pure, fresh, but it escaped him. Hadn't Laure some colourful notions picked up from Ossian? Shouldn't he creep out to Villeparisis and meet her secretly at the Canal one evening? He signed himself 'Your brother the werewolf'. He was working at night. Suppose his attempts to be a writer failed? Times were troubled and countries look to their writers in political crises.

So, if I am strong enough – after all we don't know yet – I might choose something other than literary glory, I could be a famous man, a great citizen. I want to do good and make everyone happy. Nothing but love and fame can fill the vast place in my heart in which you nestle.

He wants to be rich so as to see the whole family settled. And if she sees any genius for sale in Villeparisis, please buy some for him. He needs it.

Apart from his parents and his sisters, the only person who was in the secret of his whereabouts was Dablin, an ironmonger of the rue Vieille du Temple, a decent little bibliophile and connoisseur in his spare time, who had a doubting but affectionate view of the young man's intelligence.

In his story *Facino Cane* Balzac later looked back on these days and described his life. His single passion, he said, was observing people and for that he felt that he had a mysterious faculty, far more valuable than all his reading of Malebranche's *La Recherche de la Vérité* and the new scientists. He wandered about the streets in the evening before settling down to work at night by his candle; the working at night indicates already his greed for life during the day.

As shabbily dressed as the workers and as easy-going, he had no difficulty in mixing with them and listening to their arguments when their work was over. His observation, he said, 'penetrated the soul'. He said he simply 'became them'. One night he followed a worker and his wife coming home from the Ambigu-Comique. They talked of the show, then about their personal affairs, the mother dragging a child along, not listening to it. They talked of their pay due the following day and how they would spend it; the price of potatoes, the long winter, what they owed the baker.

I could feel their rags on my shoulders, I walked in their worn out shoes. I was with them against the managers of their factory and with them when they were tricked out of their pay. I left myself to become them. Was it second sight?

Anyway I found this power in myself. I saw the value of this district with its heroes, inventors, practical sages, pressed down with misery and necessity, drowned in wine and spirits. How many dramas in this city of pain?

He went to the wedding of his charlady's sister — she earned only 40 sous a month from him. A touch of novelizing here: this woman was in fact Mme Comin, the Balzacs' family housekeeper. Her husband was a cabinet-maker. The party took place on the first floor of a wine shop in a room lit by oil lamps with tin reflectors: eighty people all dressed up with bouquets and ribbons, red in the face with drink and heat, dancing fiercely. 'A brutal happiness.' Three blind men played the violin, clarinet, and flageolet.

In *La Peau de Chagrin*, written ten years later in 1830–1, his youth becomes a visionary novelized poem. It is a poetry of what might be called the relation of human beings to things. Material objects partake of life, can almost throb with the mysterious electric fluid that, he thought, connected spirit and matter. The current passed through the roofs and chimneys he saw from his attic window. The book is a rhapsody in which desire and appetite spend themselves until they are annulled by death. It was in the rue Lesdiguières that Balzac set the passionate allegory which he was to live out, in all its detail. For every desire uttered and fulfilled the wild ass's skin contracts. The life of the imagination is killed when its desires are realized. Eros destroys as it fulfils. Here is the remembered attic.

Often I remember soaking my bread in milk, as I sat by the window to take the fresh air, while my eyes wandered over a view of the roofs – brown grey or red, slated or tiled, and covered with yellow or green mosses. At first the prospect may have seemed monotonous, but I very soon found peculiar beauties in it. Sometimes at night streams of light through half-closed shutters would light up and colour the dark abyss of this strange landscape. Sometimes the feeble lights of the street lamps sent up yellow gleams through the fog, and in each street dimly outlined the undulations of a crowd of roofs like billows of the sea. Very occasionally too, a face appeared in the gloomy waste, above the flowers on some skyed garden, I caught glimpses of an old woman's crooked, angular profile, as she watered her nasturtiums; or in a crazy attic window, a young girl, fancying herself quite alone as she dressed herself – a view of nothing more than a fair forehead and long tresses held above her by a pretty white arm . . . I liked to see the short-lived plant life in the gutters – poor weeds that a storm soon washed away . . . My curious world became familiar to me. I came to love this prison of my own choosing. The level of Parisian prairie of roofs beneath which lay gulfs packed with people penetrated my soul and were in harmony with my thoughts.

The two years were up. *Cromwell* was finished. Balzac went home to Villeparisis. He stood up to give a formal reading of the play to the family and Dablin who was called in to judge. Boisterously confident the young man read on until presently he saw boredom on everyone's face. Dablin bluntly said the thing was a disaster.

Even Laure was bored. Her future husband, a young canal engineer called Surville, tactfully proposed that a professor from the Ecole Polytechnique should be called in to arbitrate. He did so. His verdict was terrible: the boy could take up any profession he liked – but certainly not literature. Balzac was angry but not crushed. 'All right', he said. 'All it does is to show I am not good at writing tragedies.'

He was so thin after his life in the attic that his mother made him stay at home. His freedom had gone.

Although *Cromwell* was a failure, it was not the failure of a facile pen. It emerged from his usual deep reading. He consulted the Latin classics, he returned to Corneille and Racine. He corrected and recorrected. He was to begin with a masterpiece and because his mind was excited he worked on two novels besides. One was called *Stenie ou les Erreurs Philosophiques*. The family were impressed by the ambition and hard work contained in the failure and took him more than half-seriously. Like his father he was resilient. Having failed to start at the top of the tree he looked about him, as so many writers have done, for chances at the bottom: he knew he had to earn his living. And as a writer!

A new and lasting side appeared in his 'inexplicable' character: fame had failed, love had not appeared; money only remained as the goal. The high-minded poet and philosopher of the garret turned into the energetic popular scribbler who was prepared to write any saleable rubbish that came into a head that was giddy with ideas. He discovered a powerful mental vitality, all the stronger because of the forced repression of the sensual man. He discovered he had an endless store of self-dramatizing fantasy, an engine-like power of continual work, and the conscienceless cynicism of the born sales-man. It did not matter what he wrote or how he wrote, so long as he put himself to it and made what he was short of – cash. In short, he had an exuberance that could not be restrained. The famous decision to wait until he had 'formulated his philosophy' was not forgotten but it was pushed aside. He had got to win independence of his family. Whatever his sister may have said about his adventures as a lover, he knew he neither had the time, the money, nor the attraction for the easy or romantic girls who distract young men. He could stand apart, he could observe – but work must come before anything else, even sordid work. He must learn his trade, like any other apprentice in the Marais. One can see the opportunism

of his father and the self-discipline of his mother coming out in him
– the characteristics of his background, half peasant, half bourgeois.

The spirit of the times connived at his purpose. In order to appease
the public, still divided in its loyalties, the new monarch, the elderly
Louis XVIII, had lifted the severe censorship imposed by Napoleon.
Newspapers and magazines burst out and excited the reader by their
reckless contents. The day of the savage caricaturist, the clever
columnist and scandalous gossip had begun. If Napoleon had filled
the heads of his people with the idea of Glory, the vacuum he left
was now filled by the equally ruthless idea of money-making and
speculation. The ruthless soldier was supplanted by his sons, the
ruthless financiers. The idea of sudden Fortune and self-preservation
had replaced the glamour of victory and slaughter. Lucien de Rubempré and Eugène de Rastignac were the rising and cynical young men.
And there was another aspect to this, closer to Balzac's talents. With
the collapse of religious faith and the orthodoxy of the eighteenth
century, a new kind of writing was gobbled up by a public that
sought its entertainment in cheap novelettes of terror and cruelty,
sexual licence, improbable mystery and melodramatic fantasy. Now
murder, adultery, sexual aberration, violence, and supernatural ter-
rors were the exotic subjects. They were imported from the Gothic
novelists in England, for with the fall of Napoleon English fashions
ruled. A historical setting gave licence to tales of unheard crimes,
once an abbey or castle was postulated. Melodrama and a sort of
pornography were tastes of disturbed minds and pulp literature was
its medium.

In his visits to the bookshop-publishers who had their shacks in
the wooden galleries that crowded like a flea-market round the
Palais-Royal, in cheap restaurants like Flicoteau's near the Sorbonne,
Balzac had met solemn young men like himself trying to sell a
volume of verse or a play and had seen them turn to this money-
making trade of writing thrillers. He had to know a group of these
sparks who had hit upon a scheme of group-writing: two or three
would collaborate on a story, writing perhaps alternate chapters.
They stole their ideas from English writers like Walpole, 'Monk'
Lewis, Mrs Radcliffe, and then published the result over a pseudonym. The stuff sold. Balzac was invited to try his hand. He was well
placed for the task. He had always been deep in English literature
which he read in translation. He had read and reread the most
striking of the Gothic novels, *Melmoth the Wanderer* by the Irish-

man, Charles Maturin. The stories proposed to him exactly met the taste of his clever sister Laure who had just married her engineer and who, as yet without children, was living in the country and eager to help her brother if only to pass the time. She kept him supplied with new scenes of terror. She worshipped him. Her husband, a nice dull fellow and very jealous of Balzac, nevertheless joined the game. Balzac chose the name Lord R'Hoone, an anagram of Honoré, for his pseudonym. Early in 1822 he wrote to her: 'I am working like the horse of Henri IV before it was turned into bronze, and this year hope to earn 20,000 francs and found my fortune.' (He made nowhere near such a sum: it would be nearer 8000.)

I have to turn out the *Vicaire des Ardennes*, the *Savant Odette de Champdivers*, a historical romance of the R'Hoone family. Very soon Lord R'Hoone will be the fashion, the most prolific of all authors, and women will give their eyes for him and then little Honoré will ride, head high, crop full, in his carriage.

He was, we repeat, absurdly little. He sold one novelette, *L'Héritière de Birague* for 1200 francs.

What he had discovered was something of great importance to his future as a writer: he could write as fast as he talked and this was very fast indeed. He wrote a novelette in two or three weeks, working in long timeless stretches; he boasted that he could wear out ten crow-feather pens in three days, in his rapid hand that dashed like black rain across the uncorrected pages. He could hardly keep up with his fantastic invention and he did not care much how it all read. It was all offal, he said, but it poured out. Bernard-François was amazed but his mother was horrified. She had been brought up with a regard for syntax and prose style and his careless clichés shocked her. They got worse as he succeeded. It was true that he wrote under a pseudonym and that none of their friends would believe that a son of hers had written such stuff, but the bother was that the boy could not keep his mouth shut. He boasted. Or fell into despair. He either thought he was God or nothing – he was as unstable as herself.

What was to be made of a book like *Le Vicaire des Ardennes* in which a woman finds herself in love with a young man who turns out to be a son she has had in an *affaire* with a bishop? This book was seized by the police. Or *Le Centenaire* – a fantasy, a form to which he leaned now he had read Maturin's *Melmoth the Wanderer*

– which treated Bernard-François's obsession with longevity and became a vampire legend? The story is an early sign of Balzac's interest in sexual aberration: a villain extends his life again and again by murdering young girls and injecting their blood into his veins. Yet it was noticeable in these books that Balzac's observation of places and ordinary people was good. But he wrote to Laure when he was twenty-four: 'Now that I begin to know what I can do, I hate having to waste my time on this nonsense.'

Laure says he wrote forty novelettes in the trashy manner. As a matter of pride he insisted on paying his parents 1200 francs a year for his keep. He could rarely scrape the money together. He was confined to his cold room in the house at Villeparisis, made cold by the draught that came under Bernard-François's door: the old man, in his seventies, believed in fresh air. The son chafed at his lack of freedom. He could hardly ever get to Paris. He longed for a luxurious mistress, but what woman would look at a poor man! And the financial anxiety had increased at home. Laure was married, but now there was the dowry for Laurence, the second daughter, to be paid. Laure's husband was hardly a catch. For Laurence a noble attachment was sought. The elder Balzacs pushed and pushed until they found a very fine match indeed in a youngish aristocrat, Amand-Desiré de Saint-Pierre de Montzaigle. Mme Balzac had her old weakness for brainless young bloods. Bernard-François was enchanted by the 'de', but Honoré, who had strong views about love in marriage, could see nothing in the man but a good shot and an eternal billiard player whose real interests in life were gambling and – according to police reports – loose women. He was getting hold of a large share of the Balzac money in order to pay his debts. The wedding was a crude bourgeois comedy in the Balzac tradition. Two kinds of invitation were sent out. To their low friends the invitation came from M. and Mme Balzac. To the bridegroom's family they were M. and Mme *de* Balzac. The 'de' had been achieved at last. The cost in wretchedness and tragedy – though with some alteration – was eventually set out in one of the best of Balzac's early serious stories, *La Maison du Chat qui pelote*. In a year or two Montzaigle's behaviour became open and shameless. His creditors came to the house. He crawled home in the small hours. His young wife was ill and her beauty gone. Mme Balzac was not inclined to blame the noble Montzaigle, but she nagged Honoré for not being in a steady job and he had to spend his time dodging or placating her.

One sinister incident occurred before the wedding. The coachman's whip caught the father's eye. The old man, so proud of his appearance, his dignity and health, had not reckoned with accident. The shock did not kill him, but from then on he weakened.

The Balzac parents had reached the chronic stage of their restlessness. They changed houses. Mme Balzac was up and down to rooms she had kept in the rue du Temple. The once-pretty coquette had become fretful and anxious. Balzac reported sardonically on the family situation and the local gossip to Laure. Mother, he says, is like Nature as usual: in a terrible mood for five hours a day and then she recovers. Her health is up and down, so are her journeys to Paris. The smallest things upset her: 'Today I forgot to thank her. She came in and sulked, made a scene and would not say what it was all about.' Laurence enlightened him: he had forgotten to thank her for making him a black jacket. ('At my age!') The troubadour, as he calls himself, gets up in the morning knowing the day will never be long enough. He is always bent on rushing through a novelette in a week or two and is driven mad if he has to stop for lunch or dinner. His mother makes a scene if he goes off to work in his bedroom. Most of the time he has to work in the salon, listening to her say 'Oh, my head! Bring me some water.' Or 'Close the shutters.' She rails at her husband, telling everyone that he may have a good stomach, but he has a cold heart. He replies that she is a malicious woman and compulsive actress. Take any notice of her, Bernard-François tells his son 'and she will destroy you'. As for his son's novels, he says scornfully, everyone knows that novels are to the French what opium is to the Chinese! After that, looking very white these days, Bernard-François walks out of the house as often as possible. He even takes a room in Versailles, away from home. About this time the old man takes up his earlier habit of chasing after young girls and causes a scandal by getting a local girl 'into trouble'.

There are other scandals, Balzac reports. At the Maupertuys, he tells Laure, a miller's daughter has given birth to a bastard, a little Champi. We suddenly get a glimpse of the sort of thing the novelist will put into the *Contes Drolatiques*:

'Holy mother of God, I warned Maupertuys that I'd never let his daughter marry my son.'

'That's right', father says to M. Champi, 'and damn that, you can't stop the young man amusing himself.'

'That's true. We did the same ourselves and my son is a young beggar who knows how to f, g, h, i, j, k, l well.'

'It's human nature', father interrupts.

'Anyway the girl is back, she's put the baby out with her "aunt" as they say for her "uncle" to take care of. That's settled it and the gossip has stopped.'

'Bugger it. Life goes on', father says to M. Champi smiling slyly. And he knows more than he lets on.

Without knowing it Balzac is on the edge of a great change in his life. There is a certain M. de Berny living at the other end of the village, rather well-off, a short-sighted old man with a bad temper. He has gone completely blind now and his wife has had to take charge of their estate. She has taken on the management of the farm and is selling the hay and crops herself. She is a friend of Mme Balzac. Mme de Berny has either a secretary or tenant (supposed by the neighbours to be her lover) who really rules the household and now M. de Berny has stopped propagating – his wife by this time had nine children – this gentleman has firmly sent two off to college: 'The children of poor Mme de Berny are the only ones in the world', Balzac writes to his sister, 'who know how to laugh, dance, eat and sleep and talk in a civilized way and their mother is still very charming and devoted.'

Civilized talk! He was starved of it. Out of kindness Mme de Berny took him on as a tutor for her children.

La Dilecta:
Mother-Sister-Mistress

The young Balzac who thought Paris was ancient Rome reborn could not resist the sight of wealth in the richer parts of the city, in the Tuileries or the Palais-Royal. But he was soon humiliated by the difference between himself and the cool dandies who dressed in the English fashion and cultivated the special kind of bad manners that were the ritual of the English upper class, and who were outrageously familiar with the exquisite women he coveted. His clothes were outlandish. His waistcoat was too short, his coat was the wrong shade of blue and the tails overlapped at the back. He wore awful nankeen trousers. His gloves were only fit for a policeman, he said, and his boots were clumsy. He had no watch, no beautifully jewelled cane. Genius unrevealed might be fermenting in him but he looked like some anxious little clerk from the Marais. He walked with downcast eyes. To dine at Very's was beyond him; he resorted to Flicoteau's in the Quartier Latin with the rest of the students to eat mutton cutlets or plain beef and to fill up with bread and potatoes at 20 sous a time. It was the 'temple sacred to hunger', with salvation lying in the words *pain à discrétion*.

But the lines written from Villeparisis in 1824 about the Berny family contain the hint of an awakening. The first and the most rewarding love affair of his life was about to transform him. He was twenty-three when he went as tutor to the Berny children. M. and Mme Balzac might think that they had close claims to friendship with the grander Bernys at the other end of the village because M. de Berny, too, had idled years before in the blessed pastures of military provisioning; but if the two families saw a lot of each other in Villeparisis and if Mme de Berny, a year or two older than Mme Balzac, was kind enough to give her a lift to Paris in her carriage from time to time and to listen patiently to her jokes, there was a distinct line drawn between them.

M. de Berny came of an old noble family and was well-off. His wife, the mother of nine children including an able son and pretty daughters, had had a startling and romantic career. As a girl she had been brought up in an exalted circle at the summit of Balzac's dreams of history: the court of Louis XVI at Versailles. The King and Marie-Antoinette had been her god-parents. She was the daughter of the German court harpist and a Lady of the Bedchamber. In the Terror she had been hurriedly married to M. de Berny who was many years older than herself; the couple had been imprisoned and it was only the fall of Robespierre that saved them from the guillo-tine. Marie-Antoinette had sent Mme de Berny a lock of her hair and a pair of ear-rings from the scaffold itself. The novels of Sir Walter Scott, the most important and most widely read of all novel-ists in Europe, had given Balzac a passion for the romantic dramas of history: here in Villeparisis was living history, just along the busy street where the long-distance diligences of the road to Metz had their posting houses. Mme Balzac was glad to see her son on terms with the Berny children, for Mme de Berny had a very eligible, well-dowered daughter. A good marriage would establish him. She encouraged her son's visits to the house.

Mme de Berny was a busy, plumpish, agreeable woman in her forties, whose eyes were sad. One gets a glimpse of her husband, perhaps, in the portrait of the quarrelsome and moody card-player of *Le Lys dans la Vallée* who makes his wife's life a martyrdom. Young Balzac liked playing cards and may very well have soothed the irritable old man with a game or two and relieved the tension between the couple. At any rate he became tutor to the children and Mme de Berny treated him as if he were one more son. He gazed at her and she teased him. Her favourite son who had died would have been exactly Balzac's age. He ignored the pretty daughter and fell in love with the mother, a woman twenty-two years older than himself. He saw in her the mother he felt he had never had. In *Le Lys dans la Vallée*, written many years later when Mme de Berny was dying, he wrote:

In the first woman we love we love everything about her; her children are ours, her house is ours, her interests are our interests, her unhappiness is our great unhappiness. We love her dress, her furniture. We are more distressed to hear her crops are damaged than we are when we are losing our own money . . . in other women, later, we look for them to enrich our worn out feelings with the feelings of youth.

There was another attraction in Mme de Berny. Like himself, she had 'philosophical principles'. Soon after her forced marriage, and to escape what Rousseau would have called its taint of prostitution, she had gone off with 'an abominable Corsican' who had left her after five years with a child. She returned to her husband. M. de Berny was tolerant enough to allow the child to visit her from time to time at Villeparisis and the story was well known in the village. The melancholy smile that put an interesting shadow on the sensual grace, gaiety, and wit of busy Mme de Berny was the smile of a woman who had once (and perhaps more than once) loved passionately. Dark-haired, with a bold Greekish nose, expressive lips, and an ironical voice that now and then gave an engaging foreign sound to some of her words, she had an easy self-command and the manners of court life. Balzac was the talkative and sanguine young man who was able to make one laugh at his fantasies. The children liked him. His manners might be uncouth; he might be vain and, like many short young men, he was apt to tip up on his toes and boast of what he was going to do. He was a shade common, but he could hardly contain his peasant energy. When he talked to Mme de Berny about his trashy novels, she recognized the agony and appeal in his voice and agreed that with his imagination he was capable of something better. On his side she was what he instinctively sought, something mature women found themselves telling him, with an intimacy that might surprise them afterwards: a life story. In telling it to this apparently naïve and serious young man, she became pensive. His curling black hair was brushed up from a fine forehead, the large eyes burned and conveyed an unspoiled and penetrating sincerity. His father, who was vain of being as strong as an oak and as polished as marble, had handed down a marble smoothness to the superb forehead and column-like neck of his son. The greedy moving mouth invited; he seemed to contain a store of sensuality innocent until now. One gets short glimpses of Mme de Berny, some of them direct, in his later work. In *Madame Firmiani*, for example:

Her mocking caresses, her criticism, do not wound, she does not nag in discussion, but brings it neatly to an end, her rush of feeling is not slavish. She is affable and laughing; she never bores and leaves you happy with yourself and with her grace in everything she touches. She is natural. No straining, no asserting, her feelings are simply expressed because they are true. Though frank, she never offends. She accepts a man as God made him, forgives his faults or absurdities. Tender and gay, she compels before she consoles. If you see a fault in her you defend it. She commands respect, but there is always in her voice the eagerness for an unknown future which a young girl has.

He could only gaze at her. He saw that she despised her husband.

In this, his first love affair, he was timid. He ventured into significant gesture, laborious strategies, but no utterance. His mind was bemused by the amount he had read. He searched for a manner, exalted and literary, suited to a woman who had lived in a royal court. They talked about Rousseau. There lay a key: he saw himself as a new Rousseau addressing a new Mme de Warens. The parallel was striking: she was twenty-two years older than himself. There was also something appropriately tragic in this difference. So, unable to speak, he wrote and rewrote and polished a long declaration of love – and kept a copy. He had been told in Paris that women love boldness and surprise. In his letter he said he knew she would laugh at him but he shrewdly directed his aim at her melancholy:

You are unhappy, I know, but you have riches in your soul that you do not know, and which can bring you back to life. When I first saw you, I saw you had the grace that surrounds all those beings whose misfortunes come from the heart. I love in advance those who suffer. So for me your melancholy had a charm, your unhappiness attracted . . .

Think, Madame, that far from you exists . . . a being to whom you are more than a friend, more than a sister, almost a mother but still more than all this: a kind of visible divinity to whom his every action is referred. If I dream of greatness and fame, it is so that I may use them as stepping stones to bring me nearer to you; if I attempt great things it is in your name.

All his life he was a prolific letter writer and especially of love letters. They are cast in the grandiloquent convention of the period and since (as he often said) a studious man lives in the imagination, love letters are essays in creating feeling and convincing oneself that it exists. Also, he said, they improved one's prose style. In fact, in all those early carefully drafted and copied letters (or what has survived of them), Balzac is writing a novel and will wake up to find it is truer and more binding than he knew or perhaps intended.

Mme de Berny was astonished. She *did* laugh. But politely and kindly. She told him that he was a young man who did not know what he was talking about and that she was old enough to be his mother. Once started, he did not stop. Letters came tumbling in every day, arguing, pompous, ecstatic, and impudent:

If I were a woman of forty-five and I was still good-looking – how differently from you I would behave . . . If I were a woman of spirit who knows the world I would not refuse to pick the apple that tempted our first parents.

But he was simply an adolescent without graces:

I am like those young girls who are gauche, stupid, timid and soft and hide their fire.

He became solemn and took a heavy philosophical tone. He discoursed weightily on love in terms he imagined would suit a cultivated woman who had grown up in a royal court. He was anxious to show his mind was loftier than the Balzac family mind. He turned to literature and pretty well copied a page from Maturin's *Melmoth* and held forth on the nature of love. Mme de Berny found herself being lectured.

To love is the exaltation of our being, the inspiration of the poet . . . it is to swim in the universe, see nature other than she is, to rebel against all received ideas . . . This coming together of all the forces in us happens only once. At the age of twenty we live only once, as one dies only once.

Mme de Berny saw to it that her children were always with her when he was about; she became fussed when the children saw that something was going on in the mind of their demented tutor. He accused her of being insincere as 'a follower of Rousseau'. 'Our lives', he pronounced, 'should be guided only by this axiom, "Take all the pleasure you can."'

In the terrible youth of her generation, the sense that life was short had been implanted; but Mme de Berny resisted. He went too far. She told him he must never come to the house again.

But even if she was experienced enough to recognize Balzac's declarations as the importunities of a young man out for his first conquest, she could not be but flattered. There was a certain thrill in turning him down and in behaving with a propriety which had not always governed her life as a woman. She became thoughtful. He had brought to life her knowledge that she was married to a man she despised and in love had been cheated. She took back her prohibition and became protective. If the difference in age was fatal, she recognized his cleverness and vitality. She could, at any rate, form him. On that understanding with herself she met him in the garden of her house and argued with him. Her sexual feelings were awakened. She allowed him to kiss her. Every evening after that he sat on the seat in her garden waiting for her to slip out to him. 'I love you to madness', he said. In the end, she gave in and both were stunned by their new situation. In a fluster Mme de Berny told him to be discreet: Balzac was at first reckless, then – to her disappointment – suddenly prudent. But Villeparisis was a watchful village. Soon Mme Balzac saw that Balzac had stopped working half the night on his novels and then heard the appalling rumour that her son was sleeping with a woman older than herself. 'She is trying to get her claws into him' – the old cliché came at once to the reformed sinner's lips. She sent the young man off to Bayeux to stay with his sister and finish his book. The parting was agonizing for the lovers, but Mme Balzac thought she saw relief at the rescue in Honoré's eyes. The only thing that annoyed Mme Balzac was that Mme de Berny would insist on walking down the street with her, as if nothing had happened, 'for the entertainment of the whole village'. All Mme de Berny would say was that Honoré's manners were improving.

Letters went back and forth between Bayeux and Villeparisis, but in October he returned. He had finished a novel, *Wann-Chlore*, an improvement on his earlier work, and he sounded cured. But he was not. Neither was Mme de Berny. Literature and its exalted phrases had vanished from their heads. Her fears and doubts had gone. She told him she had got her freedom – whether from her husband, from some other attachment, or the remorse that had dragged on for years and had been caused by her flight with the Corsican, one cannot tell. She had rediscovered sexual love and, on her side, it would grow uncontrollably as she aged. Balzac wrote of their new meeting:

Every day I find new beauties in you . . . Laure, the consecration of the garden seat, that festival of love that we thought dying, has reinspired it, and from being a tomb, the enchanted spot now seems to me an altar . . . I place my destiny in your hands, my whole being, my whole soul, swearing that it has gained only by yours.

To her, the boy of twenty-three is 'my adored master'. And so he will remain until she dies twenty years later. The affair will never be over, despite his infidelities, for either of them. Mme Balzac took the break bitterly. Her one consolation during this time was a curious investment. She had taken a dying nephew into her house and nursed him. He died and left her 90,000 gold francs. The Balzacs moved back to Paris. Balzac got a room of his own in Paris and Mme de Berny visited him there.

The Dreams of a Printer

For Balzac, Mme de Berny became – and was all her life – the Dilecta: the first, most purely and terribly loved (he said), who contained all the elements of woman the artist needs – mother-mistress-sister. The word 'wife' is missing: until the last six months of his life he would not know what a wife was. His feeling for the Dilecta was profound, grateful, and lasting, though inevitably because of the difference in age and differences of temperament, she would not be the only woman in his life. In his unguarded way he began his love affairs with other women by telling them about her and he was naïvely astonished at what La Rochefoucauld called 'the greatest evil that besets us': their jealousy. He wrote to the most jealous of all, Mme Hanska, the Polish lady whom he married just before he died:

It would be unjust if I did not tell you that between 1823 and 1833, an angel sustained me in my horrible struggles. Mme de Berny, although married, was like God to me. She was mother, mistress, family, friend and admirer; she made me a writer and consoled me as a young man, she formed my taste, she wept and laughed like a sister, she came to me every day to soothe away my pains like a sleep . . . More, although she was under the thumb of her husband, she found a way of lending me 45,000 francs and I paid off the last 6000 (with five per cent interest, of course) in 1836. But she rarely raised the question of the debt. Without her I would simply have died. She guessed when I had not eaten for days; she foresaw my needs with angelic goodness; she fostered the self-respect that saves a man from what is base, a pride which stupid people imagine nowadays to be

38

self-complacency, the pride that Boulanger has perhaps over-stressed in his portrait of me.

When she was fifty and he twenty-eight, Mme de Berny wrote to him in one of her jealous fits:

Goodbye, Didi, I love you all the same, with your rages, your lack of tact, your thousand moods, indeed all your faults which I even love for their sake. Happy to forgive you so that you too will forgive. I love you though you are off the leash, and I adore you for everything that makes your sweet heart beat and for your tender soul.

And later, with all the naturalness of one whose passion is blindly absorbing, she is grateful for having been made to feel so intensely by the young man. Does the sentiment come from half-German heritage? It does not, all the same, cloy, nor is she desperately acting a part.

I love you not merely from day to day but from minute to minute and each minute gives me the joy which is a whole life in itself. It absorbs everything, past, present, future . . . Oh heavenly darling stay in your ecstasy, live in my memories. It is only so that I tell you how happy you have made me. You will never know what you are to me . . . Last night was worth ten centuries to me . . . Step forward, strong in your own con-science as far as I am concerned, you owe me nothing, you will never owe me anything, I shall always be at peace. My memories will always be more beautiful and rich than earthly reality. Source of my love, oh gracious angel . . .

The unformed, almost unknown, young man (she repeats) is her 'master'. Very early she had called him, with a dig at Mme Balzac, an eagle hatched by a goose. She had discerned the master – but one who was so far master of nothing. The word 'master' was important to ambitious young men of his generation: those brought up on the stories of Napoleon's victories. If older Frenchmen had been shaken by the Napoleonic slaughter and the panic of Wagram, the young still thought of Austerlitz and the romantic campaign in Egypt. They were stunned and confused by Waterloo and the Abdication.

In his *Confessions d'un Enfant du Siècle*, Alfred de Musset said the children of the Revolution and the Napoleonic Wars

. . . well knew that they were destined for sacrificial slaughter; but they thought that Murat was invulnerable. The Emperor had been seen to cross a bridge with so many bullets whistling round him that no one could believe he was mortal. And even if one had to die, what did it matter? Death was beautiful in those days, so great, so splendid in its crimson cloak. It looked so much like hope . . . the very stuff of youth.

But the genius of Napoleon had indeed consumed the *peau de chagrin*, the wild ass's skin, and had left a vacuum in which the Napoleonic reality was translated into a dream. It was not surprising that the young Balzac should boast that he would achieve by the pen what Napoleon had achieved by the sword and he was not the only one of his generation to think of mastery. But what was there to master?

The answer lay in the new wealth that now seemed possible, in the new advances in industry, the appetite for goods and pleasure, in speculation and colonial power: these sprouted after thirty years of *gloire* built on sacrificing and suffering. As Félicien Marceau has written in *Balzac and his World*, the young brothers of Napoleon's thirty-year-old colonels felt the only mastery left to them was the mastery of society. For this the adventurous and scheming young men needed the help of influential women. Napoleon had taught these young men that the world owed them a debt and a race of fops and dandies copied English fashions and set out, not armed with pistols, but with intelligence. The new generation, Félicien Marceau points out, 'were like soldiers, reckless, cowardly, impatient for pleasure, contemptuous of danger. They were shameless and indifferent.' They were out for power and fortune and – 'up to their eyes in debt, they didn't give a damn'.

Balzac was far from being a tiger or dandy but he was a climber: he had found a woman who, if not socially influential, was cultivated. The mastery, Mme de Berny discerned, was there. If he felt he was an eagle he was still no more than a promising young hack who was selling a dangerous facility as a cynical writer of Gothic shockers, not very well written. He was far from fortune, for all he received was the pay of a hack and not one of the most successful ones. The germs of mastery lay in his growing power of becoming a self-made encyclopedia. He was turning himself, albeit journalistically, into a natural scientist whose subject is people and if journalism scatters the eager mind and tends to paint people from the outside in brusque explanatory outline with a coarse brush, there was wit and strength in Balzac's writing.

Mme de Berny heard from her young lover the day-to-day struggles of his early life among the poets, editors, critics, and hacks in Paris. He set it all out with vivid actuality and judgment in the middle section of *Les Illusions Perdues*. The revival in journalism in the Restoration had a very sordid and corrupting side and in presenting the scene, Balzac assumes a detachment by dividing his own volatile character between several personages. He never draws his own portrait. He is in part the ambitious but gradually tempted and weak Lucien de Rubempré, the young man of dubious aristocratic connection who writes his first article on a little round table in an actress's dressing room by the light of rose-coloured candles with her lover, a pharmacist, standing by. And in a serious if idealized way one sees something of him in D'Arthez. The cynical Lousteau says about the typical young man who rushes to Paris to be famous and 'take Fashion by storm':

Poor beggars, they pick up a living by writing biographical articles, Paris news items, odds and ends, or books commissioned by those astute dealers in blackened paper who would rather publish trash that sells ... Take myself, for example, I put my best ideas into a series of articles for a scoundrel who passed them off as his own, and who on the strength of these samples has been given a job as a sub-editor.

Balzac was agog as he watched the mechanics of the new journalism. Finot, the son of a hatter, is the first to employ Lucien on his paper that is run like a hat shop. Finot says:

You will be paid for all articles at the rate of five francs a column [less than a pound now]. You need only pay contributors three francs, so you will make a bonus of 15 francs a day and get the editorial contributions free. That brings it up to 450 francs a month. But I want to retain the power to attack or defend men and affairs in the newspaper as I wish – always allowing you to indulge in private likes and dislikes that don't interfere with my politics. I may be a Ministerialist or an Ultra, I haven't made up my mind; but I want to keep up my connection with the Liberals ... So do get Florine to work this little scheme and tell her to put the screw on her druggist because I have only 48 hours in which to conclude the deal.

D'Arthez and his young friends, on the other hand, have integrity. They eat at Flicoteau's and help each other out. In some words of D'Arthez one hears what was soon to become important to Balzac if he could only achieve independence. He wanted to become another Walter Scott.

You can adapt the Scottish novelist's form of dramatic dialogue to the history of France and still be original. There is no passion in Walter Scott; either he himself is without it, or it is forbidden by the hypocritical laws of his country. For him woman is duty incarnate. With one or two exceptions, his heroines are all exactly alike . . . But woman brings disorder into society, through passion. Therefore you must portray the passions – then you will have at your disposal immense resources that the great Scottish novelist had to forgo in order to provide family reading for the prudish English. In France you have the contrast between Catholicism, with its charming sins and brilliant manners, and the sombre figures of Calvinism, during the passionate years of our history.

Those 'passionate years' – in the best of Balzac – were to be his own time.

He had moved into a room in the rue Tournon in the Quartier Latin where his mother, frugal and severe as she was sometimes, secretly paid his rent, so competing with Mme de Berny who came to see him, secretly at first. She found a multiple young man: an atheist who turned out an orthodox *Histoire Impartiale des Jésuites*; he even essayed a treatise on Prayer. Very much in the manner of his father he was given to 'utterances' and ironical 'observations' which he turned into pamphlets. Having failed to write a tragedy he dashed into writing comedies. They were never staged. There was a vogue for 'Codes' done in a bright and sardonic style: Codes for Honest Men, Commercial Travellers, Gallantry. Balzac turned out one on the first theme.

None of this scribbling brought him much money. He thought of turning from journalism, which he half despised, to almost any other enterprise which would give him independence, particularly to business. He was quick to recognize profitable ideas in trade and although he was always to be a disaster as a businessman, his ideas often turned out well when put into hands more patient than his own.

In 1826 in this period of crisis, with Mme de Berny pushing him towards independence of his family and Mme Balzac pulling the other way, he had one of these excellent ideas. If one could not win independence by writing, there was great promise in a new and special kind of publishing. Families in the rising middle class had discovered that to have a collection of classics in the house gave them status and Balzac saw that there was a market for cheap pocket editions on thin paper. He proposed, as a beginning, to publish cheap volumes of Molière and La Fontaine, illustrated by engravings and introduced by himself: cost to the publishers 5 francs a volume; sale price 20 francs; or 13 francs to the bookshops. Mme Balzac and Mme de Berny were united for once. The older Balzacs, as eager as their son, found a hard-headed friend from whom they had bought a farm in Brie who would put up 9000 francs. Mme de Berny put up another 9000. The only Balzac to object was Laurence, the romantic daughter, who was disillusioned in her aristocratic marriage. She wrote to her brother:

How can you plunge into trade about which you know nothing? To make a fortune in business you must have only one idea in your head; if you start with nothing behind you, you must have only one thought from the moment you get up to the moment you go to bed . . . Your imagination will run away with you, you'll think you have an income of 30,000 a year and when one starts day-dreaming like that judgment and good sense fly out of the window . . .

She said she would rather see him a poor, serious artist in a garret doing serious writing than loaded with money and business.

Balzac wrote his introductions to the first two volumes. The venture failed. Only twenty copies sold. They were too dear. The hard-headed friend wanted his money back at once. Balzac was obliged to get rid of the unsold stock for 24,000 francs to a bookseller. It had cost 16,000 francs. A profit? No. Balzac did not understand the tricks of commerce. He was paid in bills on firms that were nearly bankrupt. The discounters paid scarcely 30 per cent and his chief debtor paid him, not in cash, but in an unsaleable stock of books. There was an unpleasant scene between Balzac and the publisher who called him a liar; he was provoked by the young man's bumptious manner. The failure was not entirely his fault. In France in the 1820s and 1830s there was not enough coin or paper money in circulation. The 200-franc note, say £30 or $70, was the smallest. The consequence was that one half of society was 'drawing' on the other in dream-like exchanges of promissory notes.

Nothing succeeds like success; but nothing so intoxicates as the first unjust and unbelievable failure of a resilient young man. Like his mother, Balzac was no sooner down than he was up again. There is something light-headed in the judgment of the quarrelling Balzacs in what followed. To them – the father, an old man with literary dreams and pamphlets in his head; the mother, with her shopkeeper's anxiety about the financial future – their eldest son was the only hope for the family. There was certainly none in Henri, the spoiled love-child who absorbed the emotional side of her nature. She had always been mistrustful of literature as a way of earning money, unless it could be somehow a sort of shop or manufactory, equipped, and in solid bricks and mortar. So when their hard-headed friend said that Balzac's publications were too dear because he had not printed them himself, the whole family, including Honoré, saw what must be done. He must turn good solid printer. He could even print his own works. The friend was expert at exacting terms for the protection of his own risk; he would put up money if others could be found. Mme Balzac went to rich Mme Delannoy, the daughter of old Doumerc who had put Bernard-François on the road to fortune in Tours, and she willingly put up 30,000 francs against the Balzacs' guarantee. Mme de Berny put up the rest. Not only that, she got her husband to write a recommendation to the Ministry of the Interior when Balzac applied for a licence. He was to have a charm for husbands in all his love affairs.

The idea was to buy up a small existing printing works and this was suspiciously easy. The rush for profits in a market that had too suddenly expanded had led many small men to disaster. There was a dubious side to the new affluence. Wages were low: workers earned only 18 sous a day because of price cutting which was the great evil of early nineteenth-century capitalism even in advanced industrial countries like England. The new machinery was expensive and bankruptcies were very common. Between 1826 and 1830 many banks closed down. It was not surprising that the Balzac partners soon found a bankrupt printing works to be had cheaply in one of the most famous little streets of the Quartier Latin, the rue Visconti. It was an ugly new building. Again, in *Les Illusions Perdues* there is Balzac's own description of it.

A dark ground floor consisted of one enormous room lighted by an old-fashioned window looking on to the street, and by a large sash window opening on a courtyard at the back ... There was also a back passage leading to the master's office ... Customers always preferred to come in by a glass door opening on to the street, although this meant going down three steps ... If they happened to be gazing at the sheets of paper hung on cradles made by cards suspended from the ceiling, they bumped into the rows of cases, or had their hats knocked off by the iron bars that held the presses in position.

He watched the compositor ('the monkey') pick the type out of the 250 compartments of his case, reading his copy. At the back of the workshop was his dark office and upstairs was a flat for himself where Mme de Berny (who had sold her house in Villeparisis) came to visit him. He had nailed blue muslin on the walls.

Trade was in Balzac's blood. Everything connected with work absorbed his encyclopedic curiosity. In novel after novel he gives us details of how people earn their livings and make or lose their money; and printing, so essential to his art, so fascinated Balzac all his life that he often wrote beside the printers in their workshops. But it is doubtful if a close study of the history and the materials of a trade is the best preparation for success in it; it is certainly fatal for this to be the sole interest. Deep and even meddlesome as his exhaustive curiosity was, it was fundamentally literary. He might set about learning the full history of paper-making, and be quickly expert in the technique of new processes, but the knowledge was for him, albeit unconsciously, an end in itself, a 'furnishing' – and how often one has to use that word when one thinks of him! – a furnishing of his imagination.

Still he began modestly enough. He hoped for a big sale of popular pamphlets. There were booklets on the Art of Tying a Cravat, on Managing Domestic Servants. There was an anecdotal dictionary on the street signs of Paris. He moved back to printing cheap editions of the classics; and in support of contemporary literature he printed the second edition of Alfred de Vigny's successful *Cinq-Mars*. The young Prosper Mérimée, four years younger than himself and with the advantage of coming from a cultivated family, offered his play, *La Famille de Carvajal* – very much in young Balzac's taste for melodrama. The book was based on the famous tale of Beatrice Cenci that had attracted many writers. But when the fastidious Mérimée called at the workshop in the rue Visconti he found his printer was a thin, dirty young man who did not stop talking. Like many who knew Balzac at this time he was put off by the missing upper teeth. Mérimée affected English dress and manners and reported that his printer was an enthusiastic muddler and very arrogant with it, too. He sat lording it in his office and when he was not talking his head off, he was reading. His fits of aggression arose, in part, from his own impatient sense of failure. Men like de Vigny and Mérimée were about his own age and had already won a high reputation. They belonged to the inner circle of the Romantics who were beginning to dominate the writing of their time. De Vigny was an aristocrat. Mérimée came of a family eminent in the arts. Balzac was no more than an unknown scribbler in the Paris Grub Street. There were sinister family traits in two of the pamphlets he had printed: one, intended for chemists, argued that it was possible to ensure a long life by taking pills – his father's obsession – and another was on how to satisfy one's creditors without paying a penny.

The strange thing is that the novelist who was to be unique among novelists in understanding the influence of money in human affairs and who never stopped talking about making his own fortune, was so unpractical. He enjoyed giving absurd discounts. He even enjoyed not being paid at all. He loved signing promises to pay: it was all dream-like. He had no notion of keeping his private expenses separate from those of his business. His life as a printer was like a reckless love affair with his trade.

Once more the customers did not come but, once more, the instinctive solution for him was to increase the stakes. He was quick to see the importance of new techniques and understand them. He heard of a new printing process called the Fontereotype: he saw it was revolutionary. It dispensed with the use of a crucible for casting the matrices and the need of reversing and correcting the cast pages. A type-foundry was for sale in the neighbourhood; it was going cheap, once more because it was bankrupt. He persuaded his partners to buy the foundry.

This experiment in empire-building was sound enough. You published and printed yourself and you got the custom of other printers. Full protection! There was also a good deal of the advertising man in Balzac: in this he was like his famous travelling salesman the 'illustrious Gaudissart' who sold subscriptions to newspapers and life insurance. Balzac produced a handsome illustrated album of the new types and designs he could supply – funereal, mythological, and astronomical. The irresistible album was sent out to the trade. Once more the customers resisted. Balzac knew all about business – as a matter of literary research – but never thought of going out to get it. The fact is that he had not ceased to think of himself as a serious novelist. The whole object of this gamble had been to give him a solid income and assure his independence as a writer.

In 1828 creditors appeared in the rue Visconti. The original partnership broke up and now, in a last effort to save everything, Mme de Berny came openly into the business – until then her presence had been private and discreet. A new agreement was made, to last twelve years. Old Bernard-François declared that now Honoré was going ahead like a flash of lightning. 'In five or six years Honoré will have a fortune', he said, 'he will owe it to his talent, his hard work and the 50,000 francs I have given him.' (It was his wife's 50,000.)

Mme de Berny's efforts to establish Balzac's freedom had failed and Mme Balzac had her own stern opinions on the disastrous outcome of the love affair. She saw she was the only person capable of getting her bewildered and incompetent son out of the mess, and who could prevent the word bankruptcy – so shameful in the Marais – from being uttered. She put in one of her cousins, a calico merchant, to liquidate the affair. In the liquidation she took over her son's share of the debt to the tune of 37,600 francs, and Mme de Berny's son and a partner took over the foundry. Mme de Berny had advanced 45,000 in two years. She asked only that he repay 15,000 francs as and when he could. Balzac himself, eight years later, said he had repaid 6000 francs. The matter remains in the twilight that always clouds the detail of Balzac's finances. In fact, freed of his mismanagement, the business thrived under Mme de Berny's son; but at the age of twenty-nine Balzac owed his family alone 50,000 francs. Instead of achieving independence he had to start life again with a total debt of 100,000 francs on his shoulders.

He was stunned and stupefied. He watched his mother push him out of the way while she took charge. And from this moment a new Balzac appeared. He had been jolted off centre into that position of bemused detachment so valuable to the artist, even though to the normal observer he might be thought irresponsible. For despite his lifelong groans about the burden of his obligation, the real lesson of his failure to him was the opposite of what would occur to the ordinary man who learns prudence in misfortune: he had lost his financial virginity and saw before him in the licentious territory of debt a Promised Land. He was liberated at last. There was nothing to do but to settle to serious writing about the realities of daily life that he knew so painfully well. There, in that Promised Land, increasing his debts year by year, he would gladly work himself to death in the delusion that he was paying them off. If there was one governing passion in his life, it was for work.

Amid his debts he had acquired his lasting capital. He understood the mechanics of society. He knew how trade was financed, how speculation worked, how banks and money-lenders operated, how deals were made; and he knew the passions that were roused by a society given to the worship of money. When he came to write *César Birotteau*, the tale of the perfumer who was ruined by speculation in land on the site of the new Madeleine, he described the processes of the law of bankruptcy with an accuracy that lawyers were unable to fault. But that book was still ten years away. In the meantime, just as Napoleon was undisturbed by the slaughter of his troops, so Balzac rose above his disaster.

Bankruptcy and Genius

To his amazement the very independent young Balzac was brusquely pushed by Mme Balzac into hiding from his trade creditors. He hid in the flat of a young critic called Henri de Latouche, a kind if touchy young dilettante who thought there was promise in Balzac's latest novel, *Wann-Chlore*. When the scare passed off this first experience of conspiracy and escape was so exciting that he lost all interest in the cause of it. He was irritated by the fact that he had to go and sign papers at the liquidators. The whole episode was an annoying interruption of his dreaming state.

When the coast was clear he left Latouche and appeared, as if nothing had happened, at a little house in the rue Cassini, near the Observatoire. In 1828 this quarter was on the outskirts of Paris almost in the country, a melancholy region of waste land, unmade roads and paths between market gardens and haunted by footpads. Creditors would have had difficulty in finding the house. A foundling hospital, a home for the deaf and dumb, a convent or two, were the only landmarks. The bells of the convents were dismal. Balzac's family had rallied to him. His mother had loaned him 200 francs, the house was taken in his brother-in-law's name: tenancies in the name of someone else or even of imaginary persons henceforth became a permanent feature of Balzac's life. Not only out of necessity; he loved mystery. For the next nine years – with intervals of flight to his sister Laure in the country, to Saché and Angoulême when Paris was too hot for him – the house in the rue Cassini was his home. He let the ground floor off to an industrious painter. He rescued what furniture he had from the printing works, including the blue muslin curtains. These he nailed up again in the new home. There was a back door, opening to stairs leading directly to his bedroom, by which Mme de Berny could discreetly slip in. She was very distressed by the disaster and had taken lodgings near by in a street appropriately called the rue d'Enfer. On the main door, in one of his fits of fantasy, he put the inscription 'L'Absolu, Marchand de Briques'. The joke was also one more disguise.

Here Balzac's revelation of the energizing poetry of debt took one of its lasting forms. If he was a born writer, he had already shown himself to be a compulsive furnisher, a man who believed in the magic of objects bought on credit. It was part of his *gourmandise*. He began buying clocks, a candelabra, statuettes, knick-knacks, and a great deal more besides. His austere friend Latouche thought his tastes effeminate and indeed the virile Balzac seemed to nest womanishly:

You haven't changed at all. You pick out the rue Cassini to live in and you are never there . . . Your heart clings to carpets, mahogany chests, sumptuously bound books, superfluous clothes and copper engravings. You chase through the whole of Paris in search of candelabra that will never shed their light on you, and yet you haven't even got a few sous in your pockets that would enable you to visit a sick friend. Selling yourself to a carpet-maker for two years! You deserve to be put in Charenton lunatic asylum.

The carpets were heavy, soft, and blue. In time the study was in mahogany, upholstered in red leather, and there was a fine glass mahogany bookcase filled with luxuriously bound books. They bore the coat of arms of his imaginary ancestors – the device of the d'Entragues. In time his own works would stand there in a handsome edition: and next to them would be an equally expensive volume containing a collection of the bills falling due – or, for him, never falling due. He chose a sunless room for his study – he worked at night. It contained a small statue of Napoleon, to egg him on. The knick-knacks were indeed odd: a little glove, like a child's; a little white satin shoe; a little rusty key which he called his talisman. The armchair was in brown silk with fringes. The work-table itself was surprisingly small and plain and was covered with green baize.

To mark the transit from reality to fiction and to invoke mystical powers, he put on a white robe when he sat down to write at night. He liked to think of himself as a monk. The robe was soon to be held by a belt of Venetian gold, and from it hung a paper knife, a

pair of scissors, and a golden penknife. On his feet he wore Moroccan slippers.

Three more items stand out in this inventory: a marble bathroom 'fit for a duchess', a glass case containing a piece of silk on which were embroidered a pierced heart and an inscription, 'Une Amie Inconnue'. He had a mistress already but there was always another, a dream-woman, in his head. The object that indicates the worker is mundane: an alarm clock. It wakes him up in the evening when he settles to work all night till six in the morning by the light of four candles in the candelabra. When he finishes he goes at once to the bath. He has a mania for cleanliness and for the perfect condition of his hands. He regards his small clean hands as a sign of his aristocratic inheritance. He boasts that no ink ever stains his robe. The clean monastic austerity is at variance with the grotesque untidiness of his clothes and the greasiness of his unkempt hair, when he puts on a very old hat and goes out. But he is not always shabby. He has started to run a lifetime's account with Buisson, the fashionable tailor. There is a bill for black trousers, a white waistcoat, a chamois waistcoat. Nothing can be done about his legs which are too short; but if he remembers to do his coat buttons up he looks passably, if always a little comically, well dressed.

When she heard of his mahogany bookcase and newly bound books, Mme Balzac sent up a scream. He got his sister to intervene for him. He had been lent 200 francs, he said, 115 of which was rent. How could he be living in luxury on the remaining 85 francs! The usual evasion.

This stupid young man (he wrote to his sister) is locked in his study. He has got to kill half a ream of paper, cover it with ink. He may seem reckless to others but he has a good heart; a hard word knocks him out. He needs, he says, large-hearted friends, people who know how to live to the full. Certainly he worked. He was doing articles, stories, sketching an historical novel – 'a volume a week'. His mother's angry letter, he says, has cost him 20 francs, the price of two nights' work.

But – the marble bathroom? Fit for a duchess? There *was* a duchess. We must go back to the drama of his venture as a publisher and printer. Whether Balzac was sexually innocent when he met Mme de Berny we do not know. Innocence is not uncommon among much-mothered, intellectual young men obsessed with their ambitions. Balzac would often say that sexual restraint was indispensable to the dedicated artist and even that 'once a year' for health's sake was enough. This may have been one of his fantastic sayings. What is certain is that his affair with Mme de Berny had its roots in his desire to belong to another, more cultivated family; but having won his liberation, and however elevated he may have been by her love, he was certain now, and emboldened, to move towards other women. Ambition and a new self-confidence and the Romantic stress on liberty in love would drive him and even if he had not been a Balzac he would be – like so many men of genius, conscious of rising in the world – a romantic snob. Three years after his success with Mme de Berny his head was turned, not by a young and pretty girl, but one more middle-aged woman, Laure Permon, Duchesse d'Abrantès. This affair was a stormy distraction in the life of a young man attempting to establish himself as a publisher and printer. She was the widow of General Junot, a fellow officer of Napoleon when he made his first leap towards notice at the siege of Toulon. Napoleon had made him a duke. Titles always went to the heads of the Balzacs and for Honoré – who was in the early stages of becoming 'the secretary of history' – the Duchess was an irresistible history lesson. She was the intimate history of Napoleon's court in person, for she had been brought up at the Tuileries as a girl. Mme de Berny had been at the court of Versailles. He had been entranced by her stories of the *ancien régime*: in the Duchess he had met his first grand figure of Napoleon's parvenu nobility. She had been famous for her wealth, her dinners, her salon. As a young woman she had been the mistress of Metternich who was to be a haunting presence in Balzac's life.

It is thought that he met the Duchess through his sister at Saint-Cyr, near Versailles, where his touchy brother-in-law was Director of Military Studies. There is also a tale that he met her coming out of a money-lender's in Versailles. If this is true it suggests the dilapidated state of the great lady's fortunes. Extravagant and now Bohemian, she lived in a small house at Versailles with her four children and a tribe of unpaid servants and when he went there Balzac must have noticed that the house was barely furnished. She had already sold most of her fine furniture, her jewellery, and her silver. A masterful and cunning woman, now in her late forties and getting stout, she saw in Balzac exactly the young man she needed: a clever ghost-writer, journalist, and publisher. There was now a huge public demand for historical memoirs of the immediate past and the Duchess wanted a publishing young man to collaborate in writing hers.

He saw a small stout woman, carelessly dressed in coffee-, and even opium-stained clothes and shabby shoes; but the uncorseted aristocratic slattern with dark hair all over the place was famous for her toilette and she wore the fashionable shawl like an empress. Her voice was hard, mocking, and precise. Her nose was a large and aggressive beak. She was said to be a good-natured liar but very charming with it. She was soaked in perfume. A scurrilous Versailles lawyer called Lambinet said that this was because she smelled like a polecat. But Balzac's imagination was carried away by her history and her distinction. Aristocratic women (he wrote) always beguiled by their remote smiles, their manners, the value they put upon themselves, and the distance they put between themselves and the world. They flattered all the vanities in one, he said, that were half-way to love. Two active vanities, two unlikely embodiments of professional self-interest, two people unscrupulous about money had met. The Duchess showed him her manuscripts. (She was to publish sixty volumes in the end, some by his hand.) She told him about Napoleon: the young novelist had a greed for vicarious lives and, once he had got over his awe of her, he knew now how to attract women of a certain age. Young girls bored him; they were sulky if not petted, he said, touchy, self-centred, and their company was unprofitable.

At first he and the Duchess were friends; but, hearing so much of the Napoleonic he determined to make her his mistress. He remembered the Napoleonic tactic of sudden assault. There was a good deal of the coxcomb in him. He began, as he had begun with Mme de Berny, with letters that are marvels of pomposity, hyperbole, and bombastic self-portraiture. She was amused and turned him down. He was annoyed but returned with a long essay comparing the characters of proud and unconquerable women with the sensitive. He dragged in Clarissa Harlowe whose sensibility is crushed by virtue, and the fighting heroine of Maturin's *Melmoth*. And then he drifted into one of his educational excursions into entomology: like insects men and women cautiously put out feelers towards one another and the antennae of 'certain souls' recognize each other instantly. In another letter he got on to the delicate subject of the gap in age.

Balzac had a sure instinct when he concentrated on the misfortunes of women for, to a woman, are not her misfortunes her romance? Balzac's success with women sprang from his compelling interest in their adventures. He went straight with bold and skilful sympathy to what was secret in their lives. The Duchess drily reminded him – and this was a mark of that jealousy which is so often the beginning of love – that she had heard he was already in 'silken fetters', a reference to Mme de Berny. Balzac knew his moment had come. It was the moment to expand and assert that he was a slave to no one. He was a man with a will of his own and not (he said) to be led by apron-strings and nurses. If he had one quality (he said), it was energy. Amid a life of misfortunes – and just as she had done in *her* misfortunes – he had known how to present 'a calm front'. As for himself, he has never told anyone about them. This was quite untrue. He had told not only Mme de Berny but everyone else. Domination was intolerable, he said. He would not be made a lackey: 'I cannot be led or governed.' And then came the exuberant outburst of the Gascon bombshell. Moralists could judge him as they wished, but they could never grasp the exceptional man:

I have the most extraordinary character and I study it with the detachment I apply to the characters of others. In my five feet three inches I contain every possible inconsistency and contrast, and those who find me vain, extravagant, obstinate, frivolous, illogical, fatuous, negligent, idle, unpurposeful, unreflective, inconstant, talkative, tactless, crude, unpolished, difficult and of uneven temper are no less right than those who would say I am economical, modest, courageous, tenacious, energetic, hard working, constant, reserved, full of finesse, polite and always cheerful . . . In short, learned or unlearned, talented or inept, I am astonished by nothing more than myself. I conclude that I am simply an instrument played upon by circumstances . . .

The Duchess was amused. He added more gravely:

Does this kaleidoscopic state arise out of what Chance has installed in the souls of those whose aim is to depict every condition of the human heart, to paint all feelings so that by the power of imagination they may themselves experience the feelings they paint? And is the gift of observation simply a kind of memory designed to assist the strivings of the imagination?

Exceptional herself, down on her luck, the Duchess might be hard-headed but she liked the risk of the exceptional. And, at all costs, she needed Balzac's help for her memoirs.

Balzac was soon telling her what he had years before said to Mme de Berny, now in her fifties, that life for a woman of her age was not over and the sun would rise again in her life. The Duchess reflected that the sun might just as well rise; on condition that he got down to work with her. She allowed her head to be turned once more. Soon he was calling her his beloved angel. The word 'angel' was part of his vocabulary of love; it was a fashionable word with Swedenborgian overtones. It was awkward that, like Mme de Berny, the Duchess was called Laure – it was also the name of his mother and sister – so, adroitly, he called her Marie.

Looking back on this period of his life and at a love affair that to others seemed grotesque, he wrote:

The sudden revelation of the poetry of the senses is the powerful link which attaches young men to women older than themselves; but it is like the prisoner's chains, it leaves an ineffaceable imprint on the soul, implants a distaste for a fresh and innocent love.

Mme de Berny knew that at some time she would be replaced but she supposed it would be by a young woman of his own age. She could not have expected that he would pursue a woman little younger than herself. On her side, the maternal tenderness had turned into a sexual passion, all the stronger because of her maturity. He was her god, her master – to this word she clung.

It is thought that Mme Balzac told Mme de Berny of the affair. There was of course anger, there were jealous scenes and misery. Balzac had behaved shamefully and ungratefully. He had 'soiled a pure love'. The Duchess had brought out the worst in his character. Balzac's defence was the defence of the artist:

The man accustomed to make his soul a mirror reflecting the whole world must necessarily lack that particular kind of logic and obstinacy which we call 'character'. He has a touch of the strumpet . . . He longs like a child for everything that takes his fancy. He will love to idolatry and then abandon his mistress for no apparent reason . . . Men and women may without dishonour indulge in many loves – it is natural to go in pursuit of happiness. But in every life there is only one true love.

Mme de Berny ordered him to break with the Duchess for two years. He loved Mme de Berny, but he was indignant and embarrassed. He had sworn to the Duchess that he was not dominated. But the wretchedness of Mme de Berny moved him; he knew what he owed to her. He blustered, he lied, he evaded, but at last he gave in. The silken fetters were indeed stronger than the anecdotal embraces of the Napoleonic Duchess who sent him a contemptuous letter:

... If you are so weak as to do as you are told, poor man, your state is more to be pitied than I supposed ... Have the kindness to send me back the books which the librarian at Versailles has already asked me for ten times and were only lent to you in my name ... I can't help laughing to see, after a few days, that my reason has completely returned to me ... One month, no six weeks! God, it is enough to make one die laughing.

He had discovered it was inconvenient for a publisher to be harassed by three mothers but a pattern had been established.

At last the two years were up. In the rue Cassini Mme de Berny would slip in unseen by the neighbours. Sometimes the door was locked. Often she was shut out. Was the Duchess there? Was there some other woman? Had he gone off to amuse himself in Paris? She worked on his proofs, ran messages to editors.

If you had been kind [she wrote], you would have told me yesterday when you sent me the Review that you wouldn't be there at three o'clock. I really don't like being told by all your servants that you are not at home – so would you tell me, sun or rain, whether I may venture to the rue Cassini at three?

She would speak to him fearlessly, she could read him clearly; but she valued the love he had made her feel and was large enough and tender enough to control her possessiveness. She knew his pride, she wrote, his outbursts of temper, his crudity, his lack of tact. She understood his lies came from timidity, pride in his independence, and fear of hurting. He was unbearably younger – that was what she had to suffer. She could tell him quietly that he had genius: but she begged him not to shout his genius from the housetops. She thought about him, longed for him, for his company, desired him every hour. And she knew and was grateful that he came to her at once when he was in trouble and that with her he worked best. The affair with the Duchess did not last long; but as with so many of his mistresses, there was never a complete break. He helped her, on and off, as a fellow writer for years. His friends, both men and women (Théophile Gautier said), were obliged to recognize that Balzac was one of those unreliable creatures who are known for their disappearances and absences. He returned as eagerly as he left.

In this first year at the rue Cassini he was emerging from his dazed state. He must stop ghosting and collaborating under an assumed name. He must write something worthy of the secret 'de' in his imagination, a book to be signed for the first time Honoré de Balzac. The early Romantics of the eighteenth century had been philosophers; they were being followed in the 1820s and 1830s by Romantics who saw their subject, as he did, in history. Scott and James Fenimore Cooper were very present in his mind. His contemporaries, like Vigny and Victor Hugo – who was writing *Notre-Dame de Paris* – had chosen the past and they had succeeded because the public who had lived through so much bloody history wanted to read about the passions – but at a picturesque remove. Balzac was groping his way to the realization that history was not far off. It was probably now; it was certainly within living memory. He had only to look back to Tours where as a youth he had heard so much about the Royalist rising in Brittany – the *Chouannerie*. A year or two before he had started a novel called *Le Gars* on the subject. It was to be the story of a beautiful dancer, the illegitimate daughter of a nobleman, who is sent by the government to get the confidence of the leader of the Royalist rebels and to lure him into betraying his troops. Balzac had made a false start, but he always kept his false starts. He had a store of them. He would begin two or three things with excitement and then tiring of them put them aside. Now creditors had discovered the rue Cassini. With Scott in mind he decided on something more ambitious than *Le Gars*. He would go to the real scene. People who had been caught up in that civil war were still alive.

Balzac was an industrious exploiter of family friends. When he was a printer he had tried to raise a loan from the son of his father's old protector in Tours, General de Pommereul. The loan was refused. But now, using his wits once more, he begged the son who lived in Fougères, in the heart of the *Chouan* country, to allow him to stay for a few weeks. The son was now a general. 'The financial events', Balzac wrote, that had 'shaken the Paris business world' had brought him 'to a halt'. Honour had been saved, but at the cost of his fortune: 'I am going to start writing again and the agile pen of the crow or the goose must help me gain a living and repay my mother . . . I won't take up much room.'

The Pommereuls were delighted. They were bored in their château and knew he would entertain them. The General's young wife was a gay woman and she wrote describing his arrival:

He was a tiny little fellow with a big head and a wide body made absurd by ill-cut clothes. His old hat was too small for his head; but once he took the hat off one forgot everything else. I could not stop looking at his head. If you haven't seen his forehead and his eyes, you won't understand the effect of them – a wide forehead that seemed to be lit by a lamp, brown eyes flecked with gold, which seemed to speak. In his gestures, his way of speaking and holding himself, he was so bursting with confidence, good nature, simplicity and frankness that it was impossible to know him without liking him at once – his humour was exuberant and contagious. In spite of his misfortunes he was not in the house more than a quarter of an hour and we hadn't even shown him his room, before he had the general and me laughing till tears came into our eyes.

Of all the accounts of Balzac's talk, hers gets exactly his manner and method. He had engaged to pay for his keep by telling the Pommereuls stories. All the people he spoke about, he said, were alive *now*. 'They love, suffer, whirl in my head, but I shall soon have them organized, classed, labelled in books – famous books.'

He had an extremely convincing way of telling them. One was certain that what he told 'had actually happened'. He would begin something like this. 'General, you must have known the X family in Lille, not the X's of Roubaix, but the ones who are connected with the Z's of Béthune? Well, something occurred in that family as dramatic as anything in the Boulevard du Crime.' Off he went and we were spellbound by his words and his imagination. When he finished one came back to earth with a start. 'But is that true?' we'd say. Balzac fixed one with his subtly dancing eyes and then with a laugh that shook the windows, as usual: 'Not a word of truth in it', he'd say. 'It's pure Balzac.'

The Pommereuls bought him a new hat in Fougères and then took him to see the farms and the châteaux, the fields and lanes where the savage peasant war had taken place. The rebel peasants were called *Chouans* because of the weird owl-like cries by which they signalled to one another at night. His hosts noticed the extraordinary powers of absorption and self-projection which he had claimed when he was following and listening to people in the rue Lesdiguières.

Les Chouans is a powerful study of the cruelties and deceptions of a civil war between fanatic peasants and trained soldiers, but the hand of the new Balzac is seen in the domestic detail. We have this glimpse of the scene in the home of Galope-chopine, the guerrilla:

At nightfall a dreadful uneasiness crept into Galope-chopine's cottage, where life until then had been so artlessly carefree. Barbette, carrying her heavy load of thorn-broom on her back, and her little boy with a supply of grass for the cattle, returned at the family's supper-hour. As they came in, mother and son looked vainly to see Galope-chopine, and never had this wretched room seemed so large to them, its emptiness was so pervasive. The fireless hearth, the gloom, the silence, all spoke to them of impending misfortune.

When it was quite dark, Barbette bestirred herself to light a bright fire and two *oribus*, which is the name given to resin candles inland from the coastal belt to the Upper Loire, and on the northern side of Amboise in the country round Vendôme. She moved about her preparations with the slowness of a person overwhelmed by deep feeling. She was listening for the slightest sound; and often, misled by the gusts of wind that whistled about the house, went to the door of her wretched dwelling and returned sadly again. She washed two *pichés*, filled them with cider and placed them on the long walnut table. Several times she looked at her son who was watching the cooking buckwheat cakes, but was unable to speak to him. At one point the little boy's eyes rested on the two nails that served as support for his father's fowling-piece, and Barbette shivered as she noted like him that the place was empty. The silence was broken only by the lowing of the cows or by drops of cider falling periodically from the bunghole of the cider-cask. The poor woman sighed as she prepared and filled three earthenware bowls with a kind of soup made of milk, broken pieces of buckwheat cake and boiled chestnuts.

'They were fighting in the field belonging to the Beraudière farm', the little boy volunteered.

'Run and look', said his mother.

The boy ran to the field, and saw the heap of corpses in the moonlight, but no sign of his father, and returned joyously whistling; he had picked up a few hundred-sou pieces that the triumphant Counter-Chouans had trampled underfoot and left forgotten in the mud. He found his mother sitting on a stool by the fireside spinning hemp, and shook his head.

Balzac wrote much of the novel at the Pommereuls in eight weeks, and the General's wife, seeing he was thin, said he needed fattening. She was a good Catholic and a good cook.

Mme de Berny missed him: 'My precious one, it will soon be ten, take your Minette on your knee and let her put her arms round your neck . . . But you are not to fall asleep and to make sure you don't I give you one of those kisses we know so well.' But she knew, she said, that he didn't want her there. Still, she said, she was lucky in one thing: the Duchess wasn't with him.

She asked if the Pommereuls were happy. She hoped so. It would be nice to know they were as happy as he and she. 'There is so much misery in the world . . . '

When the novel appeared in 1829 it was signed Honoré de Balzac and was his *succès d'estime*. The critics praised it but said it was 'after Sir Walter Scott'. Of course. And they fell upon the careless writing. It sold only 450 copies and it brought him little money, for his way of writing was disastrously expensive and would remain so. His habit was to write as carelessly as he talked and Balzac's brilliant, sceptical discursive talking voice gave a spell to all his writings; but once he got the proofs he slaughtered them. Incidents, chapters were moved about and every passage was covered with corrections that spread like a swarm of obliterating flies over the text. He rewrote the whole book. New proofs were sent for, and the same happened, again and again, as new ideas came to him. Passages were cut out and stored often to become the sources of other stories, or even articles. Printers were tormented by the crow-pen scribble dashed off by the excited writer by candlelight. Publishers threatened because of the expense of the corrections. A notable part of Balzac's earnings was always lost in having these costs deducted. The corrections were a tribute to his exuberance and invention, but they were ruinous. He rushed on from a bit of one book to a bit of the next. He made a habit of declaring a book was finished when he had merely written down a few ideas, or a few pages, and was throwing it over for a time in favour of some other work he was late in delivering.

One unlucky but eventually profitable annoyance occurred after the publication of *Les Chouans*. A few years before the publisher of *Codes* had moved on to a new idea: *Physiologies*. He had given Balzac money in advance for a Physiology of Marriage and he had not bothered to write the book. The publisher now insisted on it.

The Wild Ass's Skin

Like Dickens, Balzac contained his age and again like Dickens he had an immediate sense of his public. When later on he was criticized for pot-boiling he said hotly that an artist who has no private means and who is not supported by some sinecure in the government has to pay attention to popular taste and the demands of editors. Whatever may be said of *La Physiologie du Mariage* – the book was signed 'By A Bachelor' – it was wittily addressed to the public taste of the moment and drew out something central to his own nature. Its publication in 1829 made him notorious if not famous, and established him in the minds of a large number of women readers. They might be angry, they might be admiring, they wrote hundreds of arguing, confessional, or ecstatic letters to the writer who was so much on their side and who had the gift of intimacy. For the rest of his life women were his chief corrsepondents. The man with three mothers was an expert on his subject.

For if there was one thing the 'celestial' Balzac family knew all about it was domestic love. Not the cold campaign of seduction in *Les Liaisons Dangereuses* of Laclos; not the analysis of the varieties of the passion which Stendhal had examined in *De l'Amour* only a few years before, for Balzac lacked that psychological fineness; but love in the married state, love in the household. Indeed he might have quoted Sterne:

Love, you see, is not so much a Sentiment as a Situation, into which a man enters, as my brother Toby would do, in a *corps* – no matter whether he loves the service or no – being once in it, he acts as if he did . . .

He had listened to his father's 'utterances' drawn from *Tristram Shandy* and Rabelais, as the father sat at home with a restless wife who had presented him with another man's child. He had seen his sister Laurence die early in a marriage that had become wretched. He had listened to the unhappy life stories of the tender Mme de Berny and the vicissitudes of the career of the Duchesse d'Abrantès, a woman of the world. One can hear these voices mixed with his in the book. Balzac had the journalist's talent for having it all ways. Blatantly imitating Stendhal, he spiced his confection with anecdotes and aphorisms, and with satirical gambols like his praise of the female headache:

O migraine, protectrice des amours, impôt conjugale, bouclier sur lequel viennent expirer tous les désirs maritaux . . . Honte au médecin que te trouverait un presérvatif.

That might have come from Molière. The book is genial, frank in its sexuality, and has a streak of the vulgar. Its conclusion is very moral: a plea for sincere love. The fact is that the roving bachelor liked even his loose women to be settled among their household goods. The hope for the married woman lies in the art of becoming the mistress-wife. The book owed its success to Balzac's adroit perception of a change in women's attitudes since the eighteenth century. In its defence of married women in their virtues, sufferings, or in their delinquencies it caught a tide that was running for female emancipation and had become powerful.

The Napoleonic Wars had made love sudden and short, and marriages unstable, desperate; but now two impulses appeared in the minds of the 'new' middle-class woman. In one she was tempted by a longing to revive the illicit intrigues of the aristocracy of the *ancien régime*; but, with inborn respectability, she required a moral veil to be cast over what went on under the system of the arranged marriage and the dowry. She required an appropriate hypocrisy: vice was eager to pay its tribute to virtue. (In *La Cousine Bette* Balzac notes the change when Mme Marneffe, the new courtesan, puts on sentimental, religious, and moral airs and always speaks of her 'fall' as she skilfully bleeds her lovers.) The second impulse was more elevated. It was directed to a mystical emancipation. It was concentrated in the Saint-Simonist movement and particularly in the figure of Barthélemy Enfantin who held that 'the definite moral law can only be revealed by Man *And* Woman, and that its application must be the result of their harmonious association'. Another cult directed to the emancipation of women was called 'Evadaïsme' –

the word combines the name of Adam and Eve. The status of women was raised, according to this doctrine, by putting Eve's name first. The leader of this cult, Ganneau, called himself Le Mapah. He wrote innumerable pamphlets, one of which contains the verse quoted by Enid Starkie in her book on Petrus Borel.

> Mary is no longer the Mother. She is the wife,
> Jesus Christ is no longer the son. He is the husband.
> The old world (confession) is coming to an end.
> The new world (expansion) is about to begin.

The noisy man-woman who wore trousers, smoked cigars, and was popularly known as the *lionne* appeared in the imitations of George Sand and was a by-product of this new theology. If Balzac's common sense leaves such speculations aside in the *Physiologie* he had his own quasi-scientific interest in androgynous beings.

In the meantime Balzac had found a public. He turned to writing *feuilletons* for the new reviews like *La Revue de Paris, Le Charivari*, which published Daumier's drawings, and the gossipy *Caricature*. And in one series of *La Femme de Trente Ans* he strengthened his hold on his readers. He had shrewdly noted one more change in social wishes. The conventional notion was that after her marriage by the time she was twenty a woman ceased to be interesting; yet at thirty she was still young. Women who had been forced into marriage, who were isolated, betrayed, took lovers and were abandoned, were forced to come to terms with circumstance: it is Mme de Berny's story. The joke that went round Paris was that a clever new writer of light novelettes had extended the age of love for women by ten years.

The Balzac we know begins to appear. His hand as a writer of 'black' romance is seen in the terrible drama of *El Verdugo* in which a Spanish father tells his son to execute the whole family to save it from the dishonour of being executed by the French invaders. But after this Balzac abandons fashionable romance for the daily life he knows best. In the collections of stories he eventually assembled under the title of *Scènes de la Vie Privée* there are stories of the sentiments: the wife deceived by her husband, the woman abandoned by her lover, the old age of a woman whom marriage has deceived and whose lover is in conflict with her daughter. And, more important and coherent, there is the portrait of Gobseck, the money-lender; the delightful study of a rebellious girl – said to be drawn from the young Laure – in the *Bal de Sceaux; Le Curé de Tours* with its portrait of the innocent old Abbé who is destroyed by making an enemy of his landlady; and *Colonel Chabert*. The last two are very fine short stories and although Balzac came to despise the form in time, he showed an absolute mastery in it. He moved with discursive ease among stories that depended on exact observation of circumstance, moved on to the changes of feeling and behaviour of men and women brought up under different dispensations: the old survivors of the *ancien régime* in their châteaux in Touraine; the people who had known the Revolution and the wars; and the people of the restored monarchy. Again and again we hear his explaining voice, with his sudden eager phrase 'voici pourquoi – that is why' such and such an event emerged from the circumstances he has set out. 'That is why' is at the heart of his stories. His characters are items of social history, but warm and alive. He had, up till now, spent his time listening to everyone – above all listening to women, lawyers, returned soldiers. He had met many veterans at the house of his brother-in-law at Saint-Cyr and there were thousands in Paris anyway. The story of Colonel Chabert comes from one of those encounters and its content is worth examining for it already shows Balzac as more than a raconteur or conventional realist. The story opens with a minute but vivacious description of a lawyer's office and its bumptious, slangy clerks – 'puddle jumpers' – who are shooting pellets of bread at an old man dressed in a coachman's coat passing in the street below. Balzac is a master of office slang.

The old man comes into the office and stands, monosyllabic before the mocking clerks who treat him as an idiot. His skin is transparent, he is a motionless, shabby living corpse with the air of a tragic idiot.

> 'I am Colonel Chabert', he says.
> 'Which Colonel Chabert?' the clerk says.
> 'The one who was killed at Eylau', he replies.

We are at once in the middle of a terrifying story of how the Colonel has groped back to life from under the bodies of a mass grave on the battlefield and has managed after a year or two to crawl back to France. He is a man who is officially 'dead' and therefore has no identity. He has come to the lawyers to establish that he is living and to trace his wife who has married again and, of course, has inherited his money. The struggle to recover an inheritance is a theme to which Balzac continually returned. Where Balzac shows his mastery is in setting the central part of the story in a lawyer's office, for this establishes that the dead man's return to life is really a return to a world dominated by greed; and it enables Balzac to make two reflections that bear not only on the surface of the tale, but on its moral theme. Of the lawyer's dirty office, with its clerks who jeer at the poor wretches who come to get justice or revenge there, he writes:

... after the second-hand clothes shop, a lawyer's office is the most horrifying of street markets our society has to offer. It is on a par with the gambling house, the courts, the lottery office and the brothel. What is the explanation? Because perhaps they place dramas of the human soul in a scene which is utterly indifferent to their hopes.

In how many scenes in Balzac are we struck by the indifference of the environment which has been realistically recorded. But in his comments on the Colonel's decision to return to beggary because of his contempt for the vulgar meanness of his wife, the honest lawyer seems to be speaking for Balzac's pessimism. In our society, the lawyer says, the priest, the doctor, and the lawyer are the people who stand apart because they are bound to lose all respect for the world as it is.

I have seen a father die penniless in a garret abandoned by his daughters to whom he gave 40,000 francs a year. I have seen wills put on the fire; mothers robbing their children, wives reducing their husbands to madness, so that they can live in peace with their lovers. I have seen women corrupting the tastes of their legitimate children so that they destroy themselves, in order that ... she can give everything to a love-child.

Such tales are pure Balzac – one notices for example the plot of *Le Père Goriot* in that list – and one begins to see that he himself is the observant lawyer of the passions before he is their psychologist. But upon his definitions he always imposed something else: the quality of dramatic vision. This visionary insight turns Colonel Chabert into something more than a wronged soldier. Coming back from the dead, he *looks* dead to this world, a ghost, a creature to be mocked and disbelieved. His false death becomes a resource – a fierce decision to remain a ghost rather than accept life as it is now lived by those around him.

In all Balzac's characters there is not only the physical man or woman shown exactly in feature and in the clothes they wear, but there is also some gleam of a vision, sordid or strange, by which they live. Like the characters of Dickens, they live by a self-imagination. Balzac was an exhaustive user of his life. He will tell a story; in the next story he will reverse the situation, playing variations on his themes. When he was telling these tales of circumstance he turned from time to time to the visionary or allegorical stories and these open up the way into his inner life as a man: the *Contes Philosophiques*.

What is inside this shrewd, warm, meaty, well-organized, and distinctly opportunist novelist in his early thirties? Fundamentally, underlying the common sense, there is the outstanding characteristic of the whole Balzac family – monomania, a power that drives them all to the single consuming passion. It makes its appearance in the first long work he published and which lifted him out of promise into achievement: *La Peau de Chagrin* of 1830–1.

He had written a good deal of the topical book on marriage when he was being taken about by the Duchesse d'Abrantès and the worldly voice in many pages of that book must have come, as I have said, from her. Now he went back obediently, embarrassed by his ties, to appease Mme de Berny. He was dodging his debts and choked with the journalism by which he had to live. He had agreed to write a Monograph on Virtue and, being a good trencherman, a Physiologie Gastronomique. Mme de Berny sadly appealed to him to take her on a holiday in Touraine and – we can surmise – though she admired his appetite for life, she may have warned him. He began to write his first memorable philosophical tale.

They travelled over the bad roads by diligence and arrived at a pretty little cottage outside Tours on the banks of the Loire, called La Grenadière, on the water's edge. With her, and back in the country of his boyhood, he always recovered the lost and buried life that reawakened his imagination. There is a touching account of the young man in his thirties rowing the woman in her fifties on the river: she is wearing a pretty grey dress and a cape with blue ribbons in it. She takes off her gloves and trails her hand in the water. They take a steam-boat all the way to Nantes and another to Saint-Nazaire. The sea air blows the staleness of Paris out of him.

If you only knew what Touraine is like! One forgets everything there. I don't mind that the people there are stupid; they are happy. Happy people generally are stupid. Glory, politics, the future, literature are just pellets for killing lost dogs. Virtue, happiness, life – its 600 francs a year on the banks of the Loire. Put your foot in La Grenadière, my house at Saint-Cyr . . . [He was thinking of his childhood and the house where his nurse, the gendarme's wife, had lived] beside a marvellous river, the banks covered with honeysuckle . . . Touraine has the effect of *foie gras* on me and one is in it up to the chin: the wine is delicious. It does not make one drunk: it beatifies. I have gone down to the sea by river at three or four sous a league. I have felt my mind widen as the river widens. I have swum in the sea, breathed pure air and sunshine. How I understand pirates and adventures and rebels! My dear friend, literature at the moment is nothing but a trade for prostitutes who sell themselves for 100 sous; it leads nowhere . . . My idea is to drift, discover, risk my life – sink an English ship!

The artist is reawakened. As usual more than one book came into his head: once he had started work on *La Peau de Chagrin*, the idea of writing a series of bawdy tales in a pastiche of medieval French came to him. He began on those as well. Behindhand with his journalism, he sent Mme de Berny up to Paris to deliver a third of an article he had written. She ran into the Revolution of 1830, the three violent days which put Louis-Philippe on the throne. Balzac was indifferent to that. He ended a letter to a friend: 'When at night one sees the beautiful skies here, one just wants to unbutton one's flies and piss on the heads of all the royal houses.'

Later in the year he went to Mme de Berny again. She was now living with her children at La Bouleaunière, a house she had taken on the Fontainebleau road near Nemours. There he finished *La Peau de Chagrin*. It is one of Balzac's torrential pieces of writing. Appropriately for a fable written in the nineteenth century, it is a book about the nature of power: it defines his life and is prophetic of his own fate. Like the work of all novelists, Balzac's novels are diffused autobiography; but in certain books Balzac draws on his youth directly again and again. In long portions of *Louis Lambert*, in *Le Lys dans la Vallée*, in *Les Illusions Perdues* he presents revised, transposed versions of the same experience. He is obsessed by the past, by projecting the sources of his inner life, by self-explanation. In *La Peau de Chagrin* there is not only his literal experience as the poor young man of the rue Lesdiguières, but there is the impelling fantasy that will shape, sustain, and in the end destroy him.

The story might come out of the fantastic tales of Hoffmann or the *Arabian Nights*; also it has an amusing connection with Balzac's early follies as a reckless buyer of bric-à-brac. We see in Raphaël, the poor student, the young Balzac dreaming of love and wealth, buying the magic skin in the notorious wooden galleries of the Palais-Royal, torn between a humble love and the adolescent dream of a luxurious mistress, moving towards the scene where he will grasp the magic skin and have his first wild desire granted. He has been warned that desire burns us up and that the will to enact it destroys us. The plot is too well known to need further description, but we see that the fantasy is a diagnosis. It is Balzac's first exposure of the cynical and ruthless individualism which is corrupting and will go on corrupting a materialist society that worships money and power. The nasty little crimes of the lawyer's office are now transposed into a romantic key: in glorifying the lust for gold society is being denatured. Raphaël's personal adventure shows the spiritual consequence of conforming to the spirit of the times. He desires the female idol of the city, Foedora, the woman who allures and maddens by the coldness of her heart and never satisfies. She plays with the intellect of the young man, for she knows that to listen to the fevered young intellectual is to enslave him. He hides in her bedroom to watch her going to bed and he hears her groan 'Oh God!' in apparent weariness with the sterile life she is leading. He is quite wrong: 'Yes, I remember', says Foedora, 'I was thinking of my broker when I said it. I had forgotten to ask him to convert my fives into threes, and during the day the threes have gone down in price.' The moral is that Raphaël's intellect has made him a dreamer, the dream realized enslaves him, and is never satisfied. He now desires great wealth, the skin shrinks; he shuts himself away but disaster follows. His hiding place is discovered by Pauline, the humble girl who loves him, and he dies in one last bout of sexual excess.

The allegory has its moments of melodrama: Balzac will always be prone to that, but it is on the whole absorbed by eloquence and invention. The tradition of Molière is powerful enough to allay the absurdities of the Hoffmann-like romance and the construction has the skill of dance and counter-dance. It is a brilliant coup of Balzac's irony – for he never quite surrenders to extreme ideas – that, in his bitter withdrawal from temptation, Raphaël infects the cautious old antique-seller from whom he bought the skin with a desire for the debauches he has so prudently avoided and brings him to destruction.

Critics complained that the eloquence was commonplace. As

Gautier, the aesthete, and other friends agreed, Balzac 'appeared not to know his own language'; but it flowed, it had the spell of the voice of a talker who is carried away and who depends on the presence of his personality. Balzac is always felt as a sanguine presence in his writing, breathless with knowledge, fantasy, and things seen. He likes a strong outline. He admired Monnier, the cartoonist; and the coarse line of caricature is often used to carry him across the large, argued panorama he is drawing. But Gautier, who believed in Balzac's greatness, also said that no great writer was so humble about his prose and struggled more to improve it. Naïvely he asked advice; his revisions and rewritings show the trouble he took with his awkward sentences.

With all its defects, even the confusion about the content of the parable, *La Peau de Chagrin* made him a famous and important figure in Paris. He was no longer an apprentice. Women tried to find out if he had ever known the icy and luxurious Foedora. About Raphaël's love for her he wrote what was true of all his love affairs, even his love for Mme de Berny when he made his declaration to her: that, at the beginning, love was an idea in his head before it was in his heart or even his senses; that he was moved by the will to dominate and make himself loved; and then suddenly he lost control of himself and found that what had begun in the head turned into a love that enslaved.

As for Foedora, he said in a letter, 'The total of the women who have had the impertinence to recognize themselves as Foedora now stands, to my knowledge, at seventy-two.' She is obviously a *belle dame sans merci*, an adolescent's dream. There is a rumour, all the same, that once Balzac hid in the bedroom of Olympe Pélissier, a courtesan of the time who was the mistress of Eugène Sue, the dandy and enormously successful writer whom Balzac envied. Olympe could have made that remark about her investments, for she had been left a small fortune by an American lover and on it had risen from poverty to prudent wealth. But she was noted for warmheartedness. Balzac, when accused by his Polish mistress at the end of his life of having been Olympe Pélissier's lover, gave a denial that is so elaborate as to be unbelievable. He claimed that he had been no more than her confidante during one of her quarrels with Sue; and it is a fact that Balzac and Sue were lifelong friends. But Mme de Berny was very jealous of her: 'I shall not be able to come and see you today', she wrote in a note, 'but I'm afraid you are not going to fulfil your promise to get rid of Olympe . . . All this chasing after other women has left too many stains on our love . . . '

In the next two or three years he turned many times from his realistic studies to other revealing *Etudes Philosophiques: L'Elixir de Longue Vie, Le Chef-d'Œuvre Inconnu*. But above all *La Recherche de l'Absolu* of 1834 contains the theme of a destiny that is the directing force in his imagination.

Our passions, vices, our inborn extremism, our pleasures and our pains are torrents of the mind flowing through us. When a man concentrates on violent ideas at any given point, he is destroyed by them as if he had been pierced by a dagger.

In this sense, all Balzac's characters have a core of monomania: that is to say from the Romantics he rejected he has retained the notion that the driving force in life is something disconnected from social circumstances. Balthazar Claes will willingly burn all the furniture in his house in order to keep his furnace going – the furnace that is required by his obsession with the discovery of the quintessential metal or substance out of which matter and spirit are made. In his own life Balzac was to burn himself out. He was about to pour out books like *Louis Lambert, Eugénie Grandet*, and *Le Père Goriot*, the stories of a secret society, *L'Histoire des Treize, Le Médecin de Campagne*, and *Le Lys dans la Vallée*, and very many other works. To say that he worked is inadequate: he seemed to have a ceaseless engine in his brain. At eight in the evening he would go to bed and be awakened at midnight by Auguste, his valet, and what he called his monastic life began. He put on his monk's robe of white cashmere with its golden chain and sat down by the light of four candles at the small table. He said of this table: 'It has seen all my wretchedness, knows all my plans, has overheard my thoughts. My arm almost committed violent assault upon it as my pen raced along the sheets.' The paper was in small sheets with a bluish tint so as not to irritate his eyes. He wrote hour after hour and when he flagged and his head seemed to burst, he went to the coffee-pot and brewed the strongest black coffee he could find, made from the beans of Bourbon, Martinique and Mocha. He was resorting to a slow course of coffee poisoning and it has been estimated that in his life he drank 50,000 cups of it. When dawn came he stopped writing and, imitating Napoleon, lay for an hour in a hot bath. At nine messengers brought him proofs from the printers and he began the enormous task of altering almost everything he had written and in that hand-writing that drove printers mad: the completed novel might run only to two hundred pages, but in its successive stages the manuscript might run to two thousand. This was work for the morning. He broke off for a light lunch of an egg or a sandwich. Back to proofs and letters in the afternoon; at five he saw a few friends and after dinner, by eight o'clock, he was in bed once more.

In this period, under Louis-Philippe, the so-called Citizen King, the middle classes had found a protector: but if the wealth of Paris increased year by year, the city and indeed all France lived in a state of social irritation. The ideas of the Revolution still moved the underpaid working class. The King, who made a point of strolling down the Boulevards with his family like an ordinary citizen, was a talkative, intelligent, good-natured man ruled by the stern will of his sister. Queen Victoria said he was as clever and talkative as any Frenchman who 'in great and small things took a pleasure in being cleverer and more cunning than others, often when there was no advantage to be gained by it . . . ' In caricature he appeared as a comically pear-shaped figure, the soul of slack respectable domes-ticity but the traditional intransigence of the Bourbons underlay this dullness. He had been put on the throne by the rich middle class who alone had the vote in a corrupt parliament where all elections were rigged. His enemies were the Legitimists or ultra-conservatives on the one hand and the socialists and liberal heirs of the Republican tradition on the other. There were strikes and riots and eight attempts on the King's life. The ambitious politicians of Balzac's novels are nearly all manipulators in Louis-Philippe's parliament.

Life in Paris became hectic in its gaiety in the 1830s. Outbreaks of cholera seemed to drive the Parisians to wild bouts of pleasure in the Carnival of 1832. There was general bacchanalia. There was a craze for fancy-dress balls and banquets – Gautier, younger than Balzac, was turned out of his rooms in the Impasse Doyenne because of the rowdiness of his parties. There was a craze for new dances – the *valse éperdue* and the *galop infernal*. The *cancan* was brought in by soldiers returned from Algeria and soon became smart. Fantas-tic balls were given at the Opéra where people went mad. At one there were six thousand in the crush. Delphine de Girardin, the pretty wife of the owner of *La Presse* and a great friend of Balzac's wrote: 'Every quarter of Paris is in uproar. The Faubourg Saint-Honoré is jigging. "Il tourne, il roule, il se rue, il se précipite, il s'abîme, il tourbillonne, il fond comme une avalanche." It is hell let loose! It is Bedlam on the spree.' One understands, after this, the picture of orgy in *La Peau de Chagrin*.

Balzac was putting on weight. If, as he said, he lived like a monk he was a very different kind of monk in his free hours, and perhaps he had more of these than he ever admitted. He had the gross energy required by the double life.

He took an extra floor at his house in the rue Cassini. His mother complained that although he must be earning a comfortable 10,000 francs a year he had not paid off a penny of his debt to her. Far from it. He had added 15,000 to his total. Eager to be as dandified as Eugène Sue, he ran up heavy bills with Buisson the tailor. He spent enormous sums on gloves – eight pairs at a time. He bought new furniture, and Aubusson carpets were laid.

Werdet, a publisher's salesman who had set up in business for himself and got Balzac for his list, found him vainglorious and contemptuous. 'A man who publishes me will need a large capital', he said. There was a row: but Werdet went again and found Balzac directing the laying of more Aubusson. His mood had changed. 'I can't afford carpets in *my* house', said Werdet. 'I'll send you some', said Balzac. And did so. Balthazar Claes burned his furniture; Balzac burned up his money.

These were the years when the English tilbury was the fashion. Balzac bought one and two horses for it, also a violet carriage rug with a coronet on it. He took on a liveried groom. The livery itself cost a pretty price. He drove to the Opéra, the Champs-Elysées, or to the Café Tortoni where he provided a new sensation: a heavy cane with a jewelled knob. Indeed he had a collection of these canes; one had a lock of fair hair passed through a gold ring in the knob which also contained an emerald. The caricaturists fell upon the cane. There, in plaster model, stands the short fat man with the sly, bombastic, and toothless grin, carrying an instrument as massive as a drum major's staff. They mocked the coronet; they ridiculed the coat of arms engraved on his silver. The device was grotesque. A naked lady and a cockerel supported the fantasy and the scroll beneath was inscribed 'Night and Day'.

How far away we are from the young man who, in his frightened way, had written his pompous declaration to Mme de Berny.

His bills for champagne were enormous and Werdet swears he saw him at Very's eating a hundred oysters, twelve cutlets, a duck, a couple of partridges, a sole, and a dozen pears. When he served his guests an ordinary wine from the grocers he would swear it had come from some fabulous vintage. And of his rum he once said it had been kept in casks on the sea-bed for a thousand years.

Display he loved above all. When accused by his soberer friends he said that a writer will never hold his public unless he advertises himself by his eccentricities.

Mme Balzac continued to appeal to her son who at last agreed to pay her 500 francs a month, but he evaded paying or paid late:

My son, since you do not hesitate to live in the style of Sandeau and his friends [Sandeau had been George Sand's lover], collect mistresses, knobbed canes, rings, silver ware, furniture, may your mother not frankly ask you to keep your promises.

In the salon of Delphine de Girardin, the newspaper owner's wife, Balzac captivated his listeners by his talk. He talked with all his body. He would bend down as if to pick up something on the carpet, she said, and suddenly would stand on tiptoe as if about to follow his own sallies into the air. His cheeks were ruddy, his voice resounded. His eyes shone with kindness: 'Good nature radiates from him. To his friends he abandoned himself.' But Delacroix and Gavarni found him noisy: 'Wide-eyed at everything you said, boasting about things he knew nothing about, eating like a pig when he is at home.' It was true. When he was not following his monastic régime he guzzled sardines and *rillettes*. But his talk continued its fantasies. He proclaimed that his tea came from the special garden kept by mandarins only for the Emperor of China. It was picked by virgins at sunrise and they presented it to the Emperor on their knees. A little was sent by caravan to the Tsar of Russia and Balzac had been privileged to have a supply of it through the Ambassador. At Delphine de Girardin's house he boasted that he had given Jules Sandeau a white horse and kept everyone agape by the account of where he had found it. He even turned to Sandeau and asked him if he was satisfied with it. As if he had suddenly been borne out of the real world he would announce that he had secret powers which had told him exactly where Toussaint Louverture had hidden his treasure in the West Indies and was so carried away that he fell to sketching maps to prove it. When in 1836 he wrote the story about Facino Cane, the Venetian who could see gold through walls, he was evoking a faculty which he more than half-believed he possessed.

The idea of a 'coup' of sudden wealth haunted him: he constantly assured his mother that in 'a few months' all his debts would be cleared. In him the family obsession with money was not avaricious; he was far from being a miser and despised Victor Hugo for his frugality. The fact is that he was not highly paid for his work; though he had a large number of readers all over Europe they bought editions pirated in Belgium and he got nothing from them. His earnings from novels were small compared with what he got from articles in the press.

Although he was famous he was still not absolutely sure that literature was his vocation. The society he moved in was not High Society: it was a well-off Bohemia, cut off from the aristocracy of the Faubourg Saint-Germain who still hesitated to have anything to do with Louis-Philippe's Paris or indeed with his government. It rankled with Balzac that Lamartine was a marquis and Hugo a vicomte, and that both had government appointments. He had met the raffish Duc de Fitz-James who was trying to pull together a party of Legitimists and Balzac drifted towards them, partly out of romantic snobbery, but also by growing conservative conviction. Mme de Berny, whom he now saw rarely, though always in time of trouble, protested against a royalism which was to be more royal than Louis-Philippe's. The aristocrats were cynics, Mme de Berny said; she had been brought up at Versailles and knew them well: 'They are ungrateful and ruthless users of people for their own ends, and won't change anything just for you, my dear.'

Balzac turned from his novels to writing a series of political articles. They revealed him very much as a man for the middle of the road with only a limited faith in democracy. France, he says, must have a hereditary, constitutional monarchy, with a powerful upper chamber to protect the rights of property; privilege must be guaranteed in some way. The lower house must represent the middle class who stand between the highest class and the masses: complete liberty to 'the easy class' whose duty is to enlighten the masses and turn them away from revolt. There were riots among the ill-paid workers in the Lyons silk industry. The answer to that was: the State must enlarge the middling population . . . 'I am for fusion and consolidation', but Balzac felt the middling bourgeoisie were unfit to govern. The weakness of Louis-Philippe was that he had no plan. What he was asking for was another Bonaparte, a vigorous and not a lazy government.

The Artist and the Faubourg Saint-Germain

One night, evidently not one of his monastic nights, Balzac slipped on the steps of his tilbury as he went to climb in after the opera and fell heavily on his head. He was getting plump and was always in a hurry. The rumour went round Paris that the mountebank with the short black moustache and the jewelled cane had gone really mad. He used the accident as an excuse to get out of Paris, for he was badly shaken. Creditors and publishers were after him as usual, and he took the opportunity to go down to the austere, grey stone house at Saché outside Tours to stay with his old friends, the Margonnes. They gave him his room at the top of the house and there he sat down to work and slept in the narrow bed in the pretty alcove.

He was being pestered for the rest of *Louis Lambert*. This work, published in 1832, was an analysis of the growing mind of a youth of genius. Balzac considered it the most important of his philosophical novels, though its main interest today is that it describes his own youth at the Collège des Oratoriens at Vendôme. Mme de Berny did not like the book: she said he was 'crying his own genius from the housetops'. She really meant that it was a pretentious essay rather than a novel. At the same time he was working on an instalment of that very different intellectual exercise, the *Contes Drolatiques*, written in sets of ten and done in the manner of Rabelais. They are tales in the erotic tradition of the misbehaviour of nuns, abbés, and other picaresque characters of the small towns of Touraine, but written (in order to bring out the lewd succulence of the adventures) in a concocted medieval French. One can hear him grunting with pleasure in this saucy pastime: it was the kind of thing that sold, whereas he would get little out of an obscure book like *Louis Lambert*. The archaic pastiche gives a sportive flavour to the *gauloiserie* and even has overtones of *Finnegans Wake*. One gets a sight of how Balzac's normal consciousness streamed:

Ah! fit elle, tu es le plus parfaict moyne, les plus joli, petit moyne, moynant, moynillant, qui ajt jamais moyneaudé . . . El chut en mal d'amour, allant du prime sault à fund de ses mizeres, venque tout est feu entre la première convoitise et le darrenier dezir. Et ne savoyt pas, comme else appris lors, que, par les yeulx, pourvoyt se couler une essence subtile causants si fortes coursoions en toutes les veines du corps, replis au cueur, nerfs des membres, racines des cheveulx, transpirations de la substance, limbes de la cervelle, pertuys de l'eppiderme, sinuositez de la fresure, tuyaux des hypochundres et aultres, qui, chez elle, furent soundain dilatez, eschaulder, chatouillez, envenimez, graphinez, herissez et frigauans comme si mille pannerees d'esquilles se trouvoyent en elle. Ce feut une envie de pucelle . . .

Two – 'La Succube' and 'Péché Véniel' – are polished in their mannered way. Balzac was showing that he could swing from the highest metaphysical speculation to its earthy, wine-soaked opposite. His sensuality fermented. He did not include the tales in *La Comédie Humaine* which he called his Madeleine – the church was being built at this time. The erotic stories, he said, should be regarded as the arabesques of a laughing child, scrawled round the base of the edifice that was to celebrate 'les forces humaines'. M. de Margonne liked having Balzac to stay for his ribald conversation, which shocked many people, especially Mme de Margonne. It is a sign of Balzac's tiredness that he claims to be writing a novel about Wagram, *La Bataille*. He refers to this book year after year, but there is no sign that he did more than make notes for it. It belongs to the pile of random pages which he accumulated during his life and from which he drew a page or two to pad out other works. His references to it seem to be a trick of emotional evasion. When he is accused by his mother or his mistresses he says: 'I am working on *La Bataille*.' He is entering one of his untruthful phases.

From Saché he wrote frequently to his mother whom he had left in the rue Cassini to face the music, for his creditors and publishers were in frantic chorus. He appointed her, he said, mistress of his affairs: she still headed the list of women he enslaved. Make excuses to the publishers and editors, he says. Impatient at her groans, he tells her to sell the tilbury on which he owes 1000 francs and to sack the groom, and send him his summer trousers which Buisson must have finished by now. And send his proofs to Mme de Berny: 'I'm working hard. My coffee does me no harm – indeed it suits me. The only thing that plagues me is my chastity; it keeps me awake at night.' Can't she understand that all these business matters take his mind from his writing? He tells her of the scores of pages he has to turn out and adds, of course, that he is working on *La Bataille*. He wrote to his sister Laure that his 'heart bleeds' for his mother, and one glorious day of good luck he will reward her, but:

. . . she has an imagination just like mine; one moment she can see nothing but misery and trouble, the next nothing but triumph. I understand that. Tell her that I write this with tears in my eyes, tears of tenderness and despair for fear of what may happen to her and I crave that such a dear, devoted mother will be with me when at last we have come through.

'Triumph' was the word used. He knew he had imperilled the family fortune. The guilt rankled but new ideas or expense swept it out of his mind. His mother begged him to get married. In these months he had the desperate idea of marrying a rich widow, a baroness, and sent her a copy of *Scènes de la Vie Privée*. The matter, as he said, had to be approached with caution; it would take him six months before he was clear of debt. Nothing came of the half-hearted scheme. Marriage was one more passing idea. It was his spoiled brother, Henri, who had the triumph. They had packed him off to the West Indies where, as a last hope, he was expected to make a fortune as a slave owner; shortly after landing at Port Louis in the Île Maurice, he had married his landlady, a widow and – in the Balzac tradition – fifteen years older than himself. The fortune was to be a myth, but for the moment Mme Balzac and his sister were overjoyed that at last one of the males of the family was settled. Balzac ate humble pie and with the resentment which sometimes leaks out in the self-pity of his letters to his mother, he wrote:

M. de Margonne has heard nothing yet; he won't be back from Tours until this evening. I'll tell him. Dear little Henri: *you* were his first thought and I envy him his happiness on being the first of us to make you happy; it has made me cruelly regret the road I have taken, and to have not done rightly by you; but I can only hope the day will not be far off when I shall be able to give back to you at least a small part of what you have done for me.

The letter is dated 23 June 1833 and he adds:

You know where I keep the note of my bills – it is in the 2nd box of my shirt drawer labelled Bills Owing. Please see whether I have made a note for the end of June and the beginning of July, and remind me in every post to send you your money.

Balzac enjoyed his own *risqué* stories but tired of Margonne's. Mme de Margonne was a cold, plain, hunch-backed, house-proud woman who drove him mad by making him stop work in order to come down on time to meals. He said good-bye to the Margonnes and on a scorching hot day left the little streams and coppices of Saché and marched vigorously the twelve miles into Tours, encumbered by his weight and his chastity, to catch the diligence. He was bound for Angoulême to stay with the Carrauds, old friends who had been at Saint-Cyr where Major Carraud had directed the Military School. After the coup of 1830 which moved Louis-Philippe from the Palais-Royal to the Tuileries and the throne, the poor Major had been downgraded and was now in charge of the gunpowder factory at Angoulême – a wretched exile for his clever wife who was bored by provincial society. They had a pretty house and were always delighted to take Balzac in when, mysteriously, he was on the move. In the summer of 1832 the Duchesse de Berry had landed in France to stir up an insurrection in Brittany which was soon squashed and a number of Balzac's passing acquaintances among the Legitimists were arrested. They included the Duc de Fitz-James whom Balzac had met in the so-called *loge infernal* at the Italiens – a sort of hell-fire club mildly imitated from England.

But Balzac's ambitions were really directed to the Faubourg Saint-Germain rather than to politics. His mind, once more, was on a woman: the Marquise de Castries. She was one of his thousands of correspondents. She held a salon to which she invited writers and she had written him a letter of admiration for *La Peau de Chagrin*. She pursued with all the flattering skill of a hostess. He was often at her salon in the rue de Grenelle late in the evening, where the tilbury waited for him. A new dream of being loved was in his head but as usual he was too awed by her social position (and too full of brilliant talk also) to utter his feelings; so he had copied a love letter written by Louis Lambert in the novel of that name and had sent it to her. The love letters of his novels had more than once been put to double use. This one began in the well-known style: 'Ange aimé, quelle douce soirée que celle de hier! Que de richesses dans ton ceur, ton amour est donc inépuisable comme le mien.' Her love? Well she was going to Aix and had invited him to stay there. There was talk of going on to Italy with her. On the hot tramp from Saché he was trying to work out how to raise the money for the journey.

The Marquise de Castries was another 'woman of thirty' (probably more), pretty, with a mocking look. Her gay faintly reddish hair was a crest of curls. She had a neat mouth, a quick, charming, coquettish temperament. A matter which Balzac seems to have ignored was that she had been badly injured in a riding accident after her marriage and was so crippled that she had to walk with a stick. He saw this as an elegance. What impressed him was that she was the wife of a marquis who later became a duke, a real Legitimist from whom she had long been separated. Soon after her marriage she had loved the son of Metternich and had had a son by him. He had been given the title of Baron von Aldenburg. Then, tragically, her lover had died. She knew all about Balzac through her uncle, the Duc de Fitz-James whose Bohemian tastes brought him to the salon of Olympe Pélissier. Gazing at the Marquise, Balzac believed he saw the courtesan within the aristocratic corsage; and she was a marked step-up socially from Mme de Berny and the Duchesse d'Abrantès.

The Marquise appeared to promise everything in the course of their flirtation; but Balzac was unsure and he went to the Carrauds for refuge and counsel. He could well do so, for of all the women he knew Zulma Carraud was, in a sense almost as deeply as Mme de Berny, a friend. Mme de Berny was never jealous of her affection for Balzac. And how different Zulma Carraud was from the Marquise! She was a plain, sweet-faced woman whose eyes lit up with a spontaneous intelligence. She was proud of her humble origins. She had strong Republican views – she was as indignant about Louis-Philippe's suppression of the Lyons silk workers as she was about the Legitimists – and she was better than Mme de Berny as a sound literary critic. She too had written to Balzac in her time, but reproachfully; she had denounced *La Physiologie de Mariage* for its cynicism. He had argued back. Their correspondence lasted for years between meetings. Her husband, the Major, was a silent misanthropic man of strict probity who instead of rising to glory in the Napoleonic Wars had wasted away as a prisoner of the British. The experience had ruined his health and career; he fought his bitterness by turning to intellectual interests – he was a mathematician. He was, as was usual in the marriages of the period, much older than his wife who was devoted to his grumpy integrity. The couple were united perhaps by compassion. Bored by provincial life, the intelligent Zulma Carraud longed for the visits of her genius. When he came he often got her to answer many of the letters he received from women; she was an expert imitator of his manner. She was a tender but outspoken woman, without any desire to dominate or drive. She is one more of the half-mother, half-sister figures in Balzac's life. In her letters to him Zulma is affectionate but her conscience is true and stern; in his letters to her the conventional high-sounding romantic style, the standard diction of passion with its literary turns, is rarely used: he writes plainly, vigorously, to defend himself. He knew she was a woman of principle. He had been shaken, for example, by her dislike of the note of cynicism about marriage in the *Physiologie*. His reply was diplomatic:

The feeling of repulsion you have felt, madame, after reading the early pages of the book I gave you, does you honour, and is so delicately put that no author could possible be offended by it. It shows that you could not be at home in a false and treacherous society and that you are not one of those who belittle and sneer at everything and that you are able to stand with dignity in the solitude where mankind is always great and noble and pure.

If she will read on to the end of the book she will find, he says, that he believes deeply in the power of virtue in women.

As the friendship deepened she told Balzac that when he was battered by the absurd life he was leading, he must 'hold her in reserve'. Why did he waste his intelligence on a useless social life? She begged him particularly to give up his infatuation with politics – especially for climbing into the society of the reactionary aristocrats. High Society, she warned him, is treacherous and it prides itself on ingratitude. It regards gratitude as ill-bred. Aristocrats are worthless. They have always hated and oppressed the people and she is of the people.

But if she was severe about the *Physiologie*, she was not a prude. She enjoyed and admired the *Contes Drolatiques* and, in fact, the story, 'Les Bons Propos des Religieuses de Poissy' came from her. When she was a child, she said, a gentleman in Issoudon had sent a bundle of breeches to the nuns as a gift for the poor; and the dear innocent old nuns had never seen such garments in their lives. Some said the breeches must be jerseys and tried them on over their heads and put their arms in the legs, buttoning the things under their chins. Puzzled, they called in a young nun who cried out 'Sisters, you have soiled yourselves by contact with this odious garment; it is the seat of mortal sin.'

Zulma Carraud went on insisting that Balzac was too great an artist to take part in the sordid politics of the day, but knowing Balzac's snobbery she had guessed, even before he told her, that there was a woman behind the political articles he had been writing. Balzac fought back. He had been called to a high destiny by people of the highest distinction:

An irresistible something draws me to Glory and Power. It is not a happy existence. I have a taste for women's society and a longing to love and be loved, that has never been completely satisfied. Despairing of ever being really loved and understood by the woman of my dreams, never having encountered her but in one form, that of the dispenser of pure affection, I fling myself into the vortex of political passions and into the stormy atmosphere of literary ambition.

The whole thing was a gamble but, he said, in a phrase which contains the driving force of his character, he would sooner suffer in 'a high sphere' than in a low one. Better the thrusts of a dagger than to be pricked by pins. He added: 'In this desert, believe me, that a friendship like yours and the knowledge that I can find sanctuary in your loving heart are the gentlest consolations.' He was all for a quiet life in the country and marriage – Zulma often recommended that – but he could never, he said, stand being married *and* poor.

Had he looked at his *peau de chagrin*, she wrote back, since he spent all that money on refurnishing his house?

From Saché he had written to her about the Marquise. He is slaving away, he says – she can tell that by the coffee stain on the letter. But – it comes out frankly:

I have to go clambering up to Aix in the Savoie after someone who is, perhaps, making a fool of me; one of those aristocratic women you have a horror of, I am sure; a woman as beautiful as an angel whom one credits with a beautiful soul; a true duchess, disdainful yet very loving, dainty, witty, full of coquetry – like nothing I've ever seen: one of those elusive spirits who says she loves me and wants to keep me immured in a palace in Venice, (you see – I tell you all), and commands that I write for her alone; a woman to whom you have to go down on your knees and worship and whom one delights to conquer; a dream woman, jealous of everyone and everything. Far better to come to Angoulême and be godly and quiet, hear the mill wheels turn and fatten oneself on truffles, to hear from you how to send a billiard ball into the pocket, laughing and talking – instead of squandering one's time and one's life to no good end! I will try to come.

Mme Carraud wrote back at once:

Your room is ready, the tea is made, I have prepared the cream myself and I have brought in the brie myself. An affectionate heart offers you rest and quiet – a rest so needful in the artificial life to which you are condemned . . . For we do not love you just because you are famous; we enjoy it as if we were part of it; often we mistrust it. So you are in love. You are in love with one of those creations of yours which chance has brought within your reach. You are still asking yourself if she has a soul! Honoré, dear Honoré, ought you not to have more faith? . . . This woman, this sylph-like creature, so greedy of your fame that she wants to swallow it up for herself alone – she *must* have a soul to compensate you with, a soul where, when you have foregone everything including your friends, will be the haven you need. You who know so much about women – how can you be so misled by your delirious imagination . . . I'll love her if she can embellish a single hour of your life – and if she doesn't plunge your heart into the bitter waters of disappointment. If that should ever happen you know where you can come for consolation. Here you can work, the evening we can talk by the Charente and look at the moonlight sparkling on the waterfall; and if it helped the flow of your writing I'd sit with my embroidery, near your table, silent but ready to speak if you ask me anything. That would make me lose the fear you make me feel in spite of myself and which I blush to confess, because it is very nearly an insult.

He stayed a month. That July he was thirty-three. He corrected the proofs of a new edition of *Les Chouans*, worked on *Louis Lambert* from eight at night to four in the morning and finished it in ten days, and fiddled with *La Bataille*. In one night he dashed off a story called *La Grenadière*. He played billiards. He visited the university and a student dropped his books in excitement at the sight of him; at the barber's, women snatched up locks of his hair which had grown long. He told Zulma Carraud what he had told his mother when she reproached him for his dissipated life, that he had been chaste for a year. She went on warning him against the Marquise and pressed her theme that what he needed was a good docile wife at the rue Cassini. She did this too well. To her horror Balzac made advances to *her*! She was distressed. Perhaps she was tempted for she felt his power. She half-loved him but she knew his character. Ashamed and apologetic, he left at once, for Aix. She wrote angrily to him:

Why did I send you to Aix, Honoré? Because we have not one idea in common . . . You are at Aix because you are going to be bought by a Party . . . I, plain of feature, undersized and lame, will never win over a man for whom such seductive traps are laid. You are at Aix simply because you just wanted a *woman* and I am not that: because sexual deprivation has simply made you love the whole female sex and I am too proud to yield just to that. You reckoned to persuade me by holding out the hope of some 'unknown paradise' . . . You didn't guess I was too proud to be initiated. You don't understand the delights of voluntary chastity . . . What madness to think of approaching me!

But in a few months, after his disillusionment at Aix, she wrote, almost with regret:

I really believe a woman like myself, only more womanly, would have suited you. An artist needs a disinterested woman, who knows how to efface herself when her lover leaves the real world, and waits to receive him with a smile on her lips and joy in her heart, when he comes back to it; she must be able to put up with everything for the man who lives by dreams, is bound sometimes to stray, but her tolerance must not be obtruded, for tolerance is bitter when one is the object of it . . . I came years too late . . . In another skin I would have been born for you.

Her influence failed, but her letters are charming and his are revealing. He admitted that:

. . . the selfishness of a man who has to depend on his ideas for a livelihood is something appalling. To be a man apart from the rest one has to begin by really cutting oneself off from them. It is a martyrdom.

It was generally agreed by those who talked of genius since the time of Byron that genius was martyrdom. It was in the middle of the confession of his love of the Marquise that he made his clumsy advances to Zulma Carraud. It did not strike him, the distraught egotist, that this was odd, nor that his promises of a 'paradise' of sensations was importunate and vulgar.

How to get to Aix was the problem for him. He had no money for fare or hotels yet (he now wrote to his mother) this was the moment to strike. The strange thing about Mme Balzac was that she also could lose her head when the question of salvaging her fortunes and getting her son to pay his debts to her arose. She eagerly scraped together small sums of money – mainly from the family friend, the widowed daughter of Bernard-François's old benefactor – to send him on the road to fortune. Balzac always inspired affection. The incredible elderly Mme Delannoy agreed to pay off his immediate debts so that he would be free to go; not before gently reproaching him for the coarser pages of the *Contes Drolatiques* which had shocked her. She had also heard, she said, that he kept bad company in Paris. Resigned to his extravagance, she to begged him to try and keep his head just a little bit and remember that his real friends were not in the great world.

At the end of August, Balzac got into the diligence on the four-day journey to Aix, borrowing 150 francs from Major Carraud at the last moment. He was going to stay with a marquise and go on with her to Italy! Travel by diligence was expensive. There was the cost of meals and inns on the road, and there were the tips which particularly annoyed him; he hated small payments. In one of his rare bouts of prudence Balzac counted his money and travelled *Impérial*, the cheapest seat, on top among the luggage. At one of the posting houses at Lyons he was a trifle late for the start. The horses moved just as he rushed to put his foot on the step. Once more, as in the tilbury affair, his hurry and weight were against him. He fell and was dragged a yard or two and the iron of the step tore his trousers and gashed him to the shin-bone. The pursuer of the Marquise arrived limping in agony at Aix. Almost his first encounter was a comic reminder of the life he had left behind a few months before in Paris. He was confronted by something like a female Balzac: a Mlle Adeline Wilmen, the actress-mistress of a M. Sannegan to whom he owed 1000 francs for a horse. Her lover, she said, had just lost a lot of money gambling in the town. She asked for the money he owed. A blow! But Balzac knew his actresses and refused to pay before tracing Sannegan – 'because I didn't know if he was still with her'. He found him. Sannegan, not wishing to hand any money over to the girl, congratulated Balzac and said he'd have the money himself! So a letter went off to Mme Balzac telling her to send him 1200 francs – he'd pay Sannegan and keep the extra 200. And he enclosed a letter for Adeline – who must have gone back to Paris – in order to shut her mouth and stop her spreading tales at the Vaudeville. In fact, he paid over no more than 600 francs because Sannegan admitted he had swindled him 'a little' and said he'd make it up by giving him a horse when he got to Paris.

After this low comedy the stay at Aix was at first very promising.

It appeared to get more and more promising, but it ended in disaster. Foedora, the icy lady of *La Peau de Chagrin*, had come alive and although Balzac remained on reasonably friendly terms with the Marquise in years to come, he always spoke with a shudder of hatred of her for the rest of his life. It is curious that in her first letters to him she had reproached him for the portrait of Foedora. At first she seemed kind and passionately drawn to him, but one notes that she discreetly placed him in a pretty and cheap little pension by the lakeside while she stayed in an hotel at the spa a few streets away. But, of course, he had come not only to pursue but to work. Love never stopped his work.

Letters full of requests poured out to his mother. He was quick to tell her his room cost only 2 francs. He worked from the early morning till six at night and had his coffee, an egg, and a cup of milk sent in. At six he dined with the Marquise at her expense and stayed with her until eleven. He was writing that never-finished novel, *La Bataille*, another *Conte Drolatique*, and correcting the proofs of *La Femme Abandonnée* – a story that must have brought Mme de Berny to mind.

What went wrong during those encouraging têtes-à-têtes? Both Balzac and the Marquise were excitable talkers. They exchanged sorrows, hers being far more painful than any Balzac had; but this he would scarcely notice as he held to his familiar story that he was a solitary without friends, one who had never known love, who lived a monastic life, and was all shyness and timidity. On her side, she had the strong political interests of her class – the royalism of the *ancien régime* – and the remorse of one who had 'defied society' by leaving her husband and who believed in a strong conventional Catholicism which would keep the masses in order and perhaps allay her remorse as well. She was, like all women, impressed by the range of his mind and under his absurdly dressed-up appearance would be aware of that marble forehead, the strong smooth neck, and the burning eyes: if he was droll his male fervour was compelling and could even persuade that he was handsome. And there was something feminine in his maleness which matched her coquetries; it amused her, while still admiring his powers, to play with him, to attract him to the sofa and at once to slip away neatly to the nearest chair. Women, Balzac noted, are always indulgent to the folly they create in others. She petted him with a brief kiss. They went on expeditions. They climbed the mountains. They visited the Grande

Chartreuse, they went to Geneva. She enjoyed the joke of calling herself Mme de Balzac in an hotel register, but shared no room with him. He panted in pursuit, but she always eluded. But she was flattered to be in at the birth of a new novel, *Le Médecin de Campagne*, which the Chartreuse, their conversations, and the rise of his erotic temperature had infallibly brought to his mind. The book shows that he and the Marquise were at one about the need for a strong monarchy, a strong Church, a strong social authority. He puts his opinions in the mouth of Dr Benassis, a veteran of the Napoleonic Wars, who seeks to raise the peasants from misery by a skilful, paternal, piece-by-piece improvement of their economy. Once more Balzac shows his business-like eye for what needs to be done practically, and his intense penetrating observation of the customs and characters of the peasantry. While he courted the Marquise his mind was more than half on what he saw in the mountain cottages and the fields.

But the Marquise baffled him and his frequent letters to his mother comically convey the state he was in, exaggerating his hopes, prevaricating to his publishers, and even proposing that she consult his clairvoyant on the situation.

The letters are brisk, practical, and demanding. The tilbury seems to be back again: get it out, don't employ the old groom. Don't pay the bookbinder, make Gosselin, a new publisher, play fair and release one of the *Drolatique* tales, the one Zulma Carraud had told him. Is Mame, his other publisher, pressing for the revised manuscript of *Les Chouans*? He is working like a demon – he'll do this new novel, *Le Médecin de Campagne* in a few days! In the meantime the ill-dressed lover suspects his appearance is holding up his conquest, so send him (along with any galley proofs) half a dozen pairs of yellow gloves and two pairs of boots – the price is too high in fashionable Aix – and by now his new fantasy is that he is *correcting* the unwritten *Bataille*. It is a sign that he has lost touch with reality and is desperately concealing his doubts. But, boots, boots, please! And add a bottle of that Eau de Portugal, indispensable to aspiring lovers, also hair lotion. And go to the bookshop to get the works of Tabouret. Most important: he encloses two strips of flannel which he has worn on his stomach. Take this to the medium so that she can tell him the cause of the trouble – presumably the wound in his leg, perhaps the wound in his heart – but keep the flannel in its paper wrapping so that the bodily secretions on them are not weakened. And – rather touching – he asks his mother not to tell Mme de Berny that the wound on his leg has opened again. Again one remembers he has several mothers. And, by the way, sell one of the horses; Sannegan has promised him a new one. And, before he forgets it, tell the *Revue* to set up the story 'Les Orphelins' at once. Think! he says: in six months because of his demoniacal work, the whole family will be free of debt. A postscript tells her to address the result of her consultations with the medium to Mme de Castries – so perhaps he had persuaded the Marquise that her weakened back would improve by the flannel cure. At Aix, Balzac lived in the financial as well as the amorous future. No sooner was he back from his drive with the Marquise to the Chartreuse than he wrote to his publisher, Mame.

My mother will shortly receive – if she hasn't indeed already received, a complete ms. entitled *Le Médecin de Campagne*. Now pay close attention. For a long time I have been struck by the importance of popular success by publication of books that reach the masses – a little vol in 8° like *Atala, Paul et Virginie*, the *Vicar of Wakefield, Manon Lescaut* . . . books for the masses. The point is that this new book is one which common people can read.

He has taken the New Testament and the Catechism, he says, as models! Mame will be able to read it complete, at a sitting – a new experience for any of Balzac's publishers. But he can't put his name to it – because he is already committed to another publisher. He wants 1000 francs for the edition because he is going to Italy. He is not going to return to Paris until he has fulfilled all his obligations and is free of debt.

All of this was untrue. Nothing had been written. Yet once he had written chapter headings Balzac was convinced he had completed any book.

But at Aix there was no progress, nor at Geneva. The lady proposed to take him, in the company of the Duc de Fitz-James, to Italy. Perhaps she would lose the prudence she had shown in the watchful society of Aix. Until he went there Balzac believed that Italy was the country of instant passion, free of French formalities, flatteries, and schemings. More letters to his mother and a lot of day-dream estimates of his probable expenses in Rome and Naples; more prevarications to the publishers, and some talk of acting like a man of honour. The couple got to Geneva and there Balzac was convinced at last that the seductive glances of the Marquise were leading him to triumph. They went to visit the Villa Diodati where Byron and Shelley had lived and perhaps these literary influences and the portrait of Byron hanging above the lacquered furniture convinced him that now was the moment for bold action.

What happened between the Villa Diodati and the Hôtel de la Couronne at Geneva? We do not know. But Balzac, always too eloquent in his self-dramatizations, tacked a chapter on the end of *Le Médecin de Campagne* when he eventually wrote it. The Doctor describes how his self-effacement as a practical Christian among the peasants was caused by the cruelty of a woman:

The day before I was everything to her, the next day nothing. The day before her voice was all music and tenderness, her eyes full of enchantment, the next her voice was hard, her eyes cold, her behaviour brutally off hand. In one night the woman in her died – the woman I loved. For a few hours I wanted vengeance, to make her hateful to the world.

In the Villa Diodati the hostess who liked to take up great writers may have had the ravishing sensation that she was queening it in some ideal salon, and some of Byron's glory may have been reflected upon the unpromising figure of the novelist. She probably had the sensation of being in the inner temple of art; but there is a difference between the temple and the bedroom. Balzac, too, priding himself in his belief that the supreme moment had come, went into what we can only suppose was action. We do not know what action. Perhaps he was too sudden. All we know is that he was abruptly slapped down and that he was enraged and mortified. Remember that if she had a cold heart, she had a mysteriously injured body. We can believe that she was sincere when she eventually replied to one of his savage letters a year after that the tragic death of her lover, the son of Metternich, and her accident were God's punishment for her adultery. Her pretty eyebrows raised in astonishment at his brutal rage. At the crucial moment she felt that to become Balzac's mistress would be to deny the memory of the tragic love of her life. It seems likely that she was physically repelled. She had a cutting tongue. He had his revenge in the *Duchesse de Langeais* eighteen months later. It is the portrait of a woman without heart.

The artist was always more powerful than the successful or injured lover in Balzac. If the Marquise de Castries is one of the starting-points of the *Duchesse de Langeais*, the background of the portrait is deepened and elaborated. From the start the social historian 'places' the Faubourg Saint-Germain and the psychological and political characteristics of the aristocracy: the love affair is conducted through the clever conversations about political and religious values. And the whole, when finished, became part of *L'Histoire des Treize*, in which a group of free-lance conspirators by calculated acts revive the notion of Napoleonic daring. Acts of revenge play a considerable part in Balzac's stories. The final violent scene in the novel in which the rejected lover *almost* enacts a sadistic vengeance by carrying off the Duchess by force and prepares to brand her on the forehead with a heated iron, is one of Balzac's melodramas from his early 'black' period. In the novel the cold Duchess has been frightened and softened, even awakened as a woman, by finding she can no longer govern the man she has tortured. Balzac even appears to grant that she is naturally chaste. The branding does not occur but it is, characteristically, one of his occult symbols. It is not quite beyond belief that a man like Montriveau, the explorer, who had until now never known a woman, should feel impulses of savagery and sadism when his passions had been so studiously played with. He would become a force and all the important characters of Balzac, even when observed with minute everyday realism, are driven by forces outside their self-knowledge. In this they have their share of Balzac's belief in the mysterious, organic mingling of the material and spiritual worlds. The branding-iron and the talisman, even the absurd piece of flannel, show this force manifesting itself in magic, magic itself being the vehicle of the unconscious. But that the Duchess should crave for an act of cruelty and need it in order to love passionately reads like crude psychological theory. If he had known how to wound, Balzac would have used ridicule.

In time Balzac and the Marquise became friends again for he could not entirely resist her fashionable salon with its eighteenth-century décor. He expected women to be useful and he feared to make a powerful social enemy. On her side, as a pursuer of men of talent and, above all, as a hostess, she could not bear to be dropped and indeed played one masterly trick on him. She got her old Irish servant to write love letters to him signed Lady Nevil, letters warming to a proposal of a rendezvous at the Opéra. She knew Balzac's vanity would not resist that. She invited him to dinner that night and watched with amusement his anxiety to get away to the rendezvous with the mysterious lady. 'Don't worry', said the Marquise,

'I'll take you there.' And did so. It is maddening that we do not know what happened: Balzac himself denied the whole story. He also denied his denial by saying that the maid had warned him beforehand. But his rage had died; other women took the place of the Marquise and hatred on both sides declined to a guarded friend-ship of regret, and on her side perhaps even desire. She was certainly piqued by the rumours of his love affairs, but about these he took up his customary stance – that he was alone, living the life of a chaste monk, working eighteen hours a day, and not seeing a soul. Men and women had very little existence for him when they were out of his sight: they were turned by his imagination into other beings.

He left Geneva humiliated and went to weep about it all to Mme de Berny at La Bouleaunière – the devoted consoler. Did he tell her – as he privately told his sister – that he was about to become a father? The girl was another Marie – Marie de Fresnaye, young and married – who asked for nothing but to be loved for a year and to have a child by him. He regarded this as a wonder and it was: for once he was not plagued by jealousy. It is thought that he drew her physical portrait the following year in *Eugénie Grandet* and dedi-cated the novel to her. She is said to have been a tall, placid, clumsy young woman. Nothing more is known of her. The affair occurred when he was telling Zulma Carraud, his mother, and his sister that he had been chaste for a year. That much-reported burden of chastity was one more invention. He was about to tell another lady who had been writing to him, at first anonymously, from Poland, that alone, afflicted, in his monastic cell, toiling all night, he had been chaste for three! The genius, gourmand, and talker, alive in all his senses, was an exalted child and with all the cunning, the instant greed and fears of a child.

Madame Hanska

The one woman to whom Balzac always revealed himself completely was his sister. They were alike in temperament, they had been allies in childhood, they could tell their secrets without fear of moral censure. She enjoyed his passing fantasies. He was an artist and therefore something of a pirate or raider. She understood that and he did not have to pretend or placate. She knew that to have genius is to conspire and she laughed *with* him at his deviousness and understood the springs of his nature. He confided in her alone when he had a secret of great importance and he knew she would read it all the more exactly if it were put in a mystifying way. In October 1833 he wrote a letter to her that jumps without explanation straight into the tale of a deeply private imbroglio. A year had passed since his humiliation in Switzerland; now, almost in the very same spot, he has turned the tables:

I am happy, very happy in mind, completely, honourably happy. Alas, a damn husband has not left us alone a single second for five days. He hangs on to his wife's skirt and to my waistcoat. Neuchâtel is a little town where a woman, a distinguished foreigner, can't walk a yard without being watched. I have been living in a furnace. Self-control doesn't suit me. The important point is that 'we' are only twenty-seven, 'our' beauty dazzles. 'We' have the most lovely black hair in the world, a smooth skin, a pet of a small head, a heart only twenty-seven years old, naïve, a real Mme de Lignolle, wild enough to throw her arms round your neck in front of everyone. A gliding eye that becomes voluptuous when it is still . . . I am drunk with love.

But he has to take his precautions. The letter becomes shadily allusive:

I don't know who to tell about it, above all not to Her, the grande Madame, the terrible Marquise who certainly suspected something when I said I was going again to Switzerland . . . nor even to that other She, the poor simple and delicious bourgeoise who is in fact very much a Blanche d'Azay.

This sounds like a mixture of one of the models for the heroine of *Eugénie Grandet* and the naked Moorish dancer in the tale 'Péché Véniel' in the *Contes Drolatiques*, and his sister would understand that, in love, his imagination turned first to the ideal images of literature.

He went on in an aside which he knew would not shock her in the least:

And I have fathered a child, that's another secret for you, the sweetest and most naïve of beings who fell at my feet like a flower from heaven, who came to me secretly, refused to let me write to her, and asks for nothing from me except 'Love me for a year. I will love you all my life.'

We hear of other 'Shes', one:

. . . who is still more possessive of me than a mother is of the milk she gives to her child.

and another without capitals:

. . . who demands her daily ration of love and who although as voluptuous as a thousand cats, cannot be called *gracieuse* nor indeed a real woman . . . so I confide my joy to *you*, dear sister . . . Only a real Balzac will understand.

There was no need to tell Laure that he had been chaste for a year. Indeed, she would have been very disappointed at such depressing news. And we come to what he and Laure enjoyed: the intrigue. Laure must on no account tell Mme de Berny.

More had been going on in Balzac's life than we shall ever know but in this letter we have had our first glimpse of Mme Hanska, the Polish Countess who Balzac was to pursue for the next seventeen years in a stormy and often broken love affair, until in the end, in 1850, she agreed to marry him out of pity a few months before he died. Until now his known mistresses had nearly all been well enough off, but not exorbitantly rich. Mme Hanska was not simply an aristocrat; she was almost an empress and enormously wealthy. The man who dreamed of adding wealth and love to his rising fame saw them embodied in Mme Hanska. Even Balzac's ambition in love, fed on the *Arabian Nights*, had not conceived wealth and power on such a scale. One more of his 'women of thirty' – she liked to pass for twenty-seven. She was really thirty-two – married to a sick husband twenty-two years older than herself, bored in the isolation of his huge estates in the Ukraine, the Countess nourished a lonely mind on Rousseau, Schiller, Goethe, and the latest French novels. She had read Balzac's *La Peau de Chagrin, La Physiologie du Mariage*, and the *Scènes de la Via Privée*, instantly recognizing his great qualities. She had written him a fan letter in 1832. It was glowing but tentative; as so many fan letters are it was really a literary exercise in self-love. It was signed simply 'L'Etrangère' and she added 'I shall remain so all my life.' She asked him to put an advertisement in *La Quotidienne* if he was willing to receive further letters. Balzac was used to fan letters from women, but he could not resist a mystery. He put a brief advertisement in the paper. A second letter had come to him when he was with the Carrauds at Angoulême. She wrote again at great length:

Your soul embraces centuries, Monsieur; its philosophical concepts appear to be the fruits of long study matured by time . . . I know you through my spiritual instinct; I picture you in my own way and feel that if I were to set eyes on you I should exclaim 'That is he'. Your outward semblance probably does not reveal your brilliant imagination; you have to be moved, the sacred fire of genius has to be lit, if you are to show yourself as you really are, and you are what I feel you to be – a man superior in knowledge of the human heart.

My heart has leapt as I read your works. You elevate woman to her true dignity; love in her is a celestial virtue, a divine emanation; and I admire in you the admirable sensibility of soul that has enabled you to perceive this.

Only three or four of her letters have survived – and by Balzacian accident. They were stolen from him by his black-mailing housekeeper, many years later, before Mme Hanska obliged him to burn the rest. They contained phrases of sexual intimacy and she was frightened for her reputation with her family. One can tell from his letters, which are all preserved, what she was writing. She took a high and authoritative tone; she was religious and hoped to see Balzac rise above the scepticism and the taint of libertinism which she found in *La Physiologie* and *La Peau de Chagrin*. She required more of the 'divine' in his genius. Almost at once the lofty soul revealed a morbid weakness: she was suspicious and, one must add, without humour. The handwriting of one of his early replies was different from the hand he first used. She was right: he got Zulma Carraud to reply to many of his unknown admirers when he was staying at Angoulême and Zulma had written this one. Balzac at once ascended into fiction:

You were afraid you were being laughed at. By whom? By a poor child, the victim of yesterday as he will be tomorrow, of his feminine modesty, his shyness, his trustfulness. You ask me suspiciously to account for my two different handwritings; but I have as many handwritings as there are days in the year, without being in the least versatile on that account. This changeability is born of an imagination which may still conceive anything and yet remain pure.

She had evidently been writing at the same time to Polish friends in Paris for all the gossip they could give her – hadn't she said that his 'outward semblance probably did not reveal his brilliant imagination'.

The interchange warmed. Soon the correspondents became autobiographical. However crushing the hours of his work, Balzac found time to write letters of enormous length and detail. To him life had become the habit of writing. Mme Hanska said she had once known love but it had come to nothing; and she made the correspondence more piquant by telling him that there were personal, practical difficulties in her life – a watchful older sister and a husband. The confessional correspondents would have to use an intermediary – the Swiss governess of Mme Hanska's daughter. The older sister was the scandal of the family: she had been the mistress of Pushkin, whereas Mme Hanska was the pious one. In his replies Balzac built up the familiar self-portrait: the unloved son, the man battling with financial misfortunes, writing sixteen hours a day, frustrated and unfortunate in love. He is a mixture of the innocent, the cunning, and the self-dramatizing. He was always recklessly given to describing one woman to another and was soon obliged to recoil into dismissive explanations. The Berny story was loyally told, but now *she* was an old woman; he had been maltreated by a heartless creature, the Marquise, and now was driven back to the monkish life of a man who, failing to find love, had drowned his frustrations in work. He finished a very early letter with the now-permanent fantasy that he was working on *La Bataille*, a novel, he artfully pointed out, that had no women in it. He compared *Le Médecin de Campagne* on which he was working to *The Imitation of Christ*. He sent her a copy of the fourth volume of *Scènes de la Vie Privée*, which he had dedicated to her – that is to say he had placed her initials at the beginning of the final scene. But there had been a difficulty, Mme de Berny had seen the new initials and had objected, so he had to remove them. Here he spoke out with daring honesty – his feeling for Mme de Berny was one he scarcely ever belittled:

Someone who is a mother to me and whose wishes and even jealousies I am bound to respect, has asked that this minute expression of my feelings shall be removed. I do not fear to tell you of the dedication and its deletion because I think you have sufficient greatness of soul not to desire an act of homage which would have pained a person as noble and as great as the one who bore me, for she protected me amid the distresses and disasters which nearly caused me to die young.

Alas, greatness of soul was not one of the pious Mme Hanska's virtues. She was to turn out to be a woman of demanding temperament. She was accustomed to absolute rule of past and present.

Mme Hanska was a very great lady indeed: the Faubourg Saint-Germain could offer nothing to equal in its recent history – and only remotely in its past – the primitive feudalism in which Mme Hanska had been brought up. She was a Rzewuski, a family famous in Polish and Russian wars from the tenth century. The family were not noted for stability of temperament; they were explosive, proud, rebellious, eccentric, and appeared to transmit from generation to generation a constitutional melancholy. Her great-uncle was a Radziwill who had supported an army of 10,000 at his own cost. Her father had been ambassador in Holland and Denmark for a time. She had been brought up in isolation with her brothers and sisters by a severely Catholic mother – Balzac said he and she were united by having mothers who had injured them – and a father who was very much the eighteenth-century rationalist. She and her sisters were noted for their beauty, their education, and command of languages: their intelligence was said to 'glitter like stalactites'.

There is a vivid account of her upbringing in Sophie de Korwin-Piotrowski's *Balzac et le Monde Slave*. At nineteen she was married to Count Hanski, a rich landowner, a patient, gentle Freemason who, as she said, did nothing but 'plant his cabbages' and was a bit of a pedant. They moved to his mansion at Wierzchownia, under the government of Kiev – a damp country of small valleys dotted with windmills. Corn stretched to the horizon. The mansion was an impressive place, built by French and Italian architects at the turn of the century and approached by a long avenue of poplars. It was faced by Corinthian columns and when eventually he saw it Balzac compared it with the Louvre. It was virtually a small self-contained, self-sufficient town populated by the family relations and three hundred servants, and had its own bakers, carpetmakers, bootmakers. Except for an annual journey to Kiev on official business the family rarely moved. In reflecting on the character of Mme Hanska as a young wife, one thinks of her first four children: they died. Only one child, a daughter, was left. One can understand her despondency. She embroidered, gardened, stared out of the window of the château. She read the Polish poets, who said over and over again that the endless plain of corn was a hell of isolation. So she half turned to the erotic mysticism that was the religion of the Romantics. George Sand's declaration that a woman had a right to her own life made her restless, though she objected that a woman should not put all her faith in treasure on earth. She had entered the dreadful thirties which Balzac alone had shown to be the age when mature love at last appears to women.

The correspondence was long, but for Balzac it was alraedy a vow of love. She was a genuine 'princesse lointaine'.

She had read *Les Chouans* – it had everything to stir a Rzewuski – revolution, civil war, violent personalities: as we have seen, she had read *La Physiologie du Mariage*, a book so immoral in its cynicism about marriage and yet so indulgent to women and containing that attractive idea that the happy marriages are those in which a wife has all the arts of the mistress. Much to reproach the witty Frenchman there: Mme Hanska had a taste for reprimand – indeed Balzac drew out this stern maternal trait in women. In *La Peau de Chagrin* she noted, with patriotic irritation, that Balzac did not realize when he drew the character of Foedora that there is a world of difference between the Russians and the Poles. What, like every other lady, she wanted to know was whether he had ever known such a woman? Had he in fact stood hidden in the bedroom as the icy beauty undressed? Had he loved her? Balzac had his stock reply to this question. He describes the process of artistic creation and at the same time takes pride in the rumours: but he varies the tale. Some say, he writes, that she was drawn from the Russian Princess Bagration who was in Paris. Even Mme Récamier had tried to 'foedorize'. He reduces the number of claimants from seventy-two to sixty-five.

I drew Foedora from two women I have known, although not intimately. Observation was enough and a few confidences that have been made. Some kind souls say that I was courting one of the most beautiful courtesans in Paris and that I hid in the curtains. Calumnies. I have indeed met one Foedora, but I shall never draw her portrait – and that was a long time after *La Peau de Chagrin* was written.

He was thinking of the Marquise de Castries: foolishly, he had told Mme Hanska about her – or Mme Hanska's spies had told her. There was lifelong fuel for jealousy here. Still, extra-sensory perception was at work: hadn't she sent him a copy of *The Imitation of Christ* just at the moment when he was writing the story of the Christly Médecin de Campagne! He burst out:

I love you, unknown woman, and this strange thing is simply the natural effect of a life that is empty and unhappy, which has been sustained only by ideas and in which I have met misfortune by imaginary delights . . . I am a prisoner in his cell who hears in the distance that delicious voice of a woman . . . My virile imagination which has never been prostituted or worn out, is really my enemy; it plays upon a young pure heart, violent with repressed desires, so that the smallest feeling ravages my solitude. I love you already without having seen you. There are pleasures in your letters that start my heart beating; and if you only knew how ardently I hurl myself towards what I have desired so long or what worship I am capable of. What bliss it would be for me to surrender my life for a single day. To remain, without seeing a living soul, for an hour like that!

The desire for submission in a man preoccupied with dominance is curious.

Presently, in 1833, Mme Hanska announced that she and her husband would be travelling in Switzerland and would shortly be in Neuchâtel, chiefly because the Swiss governess (who had saved the life of Mme Hanska's surviving daughter) had relatives there and because M. Hanski was in poor health. The news came when Balzac was at law with his publisher for failure to deliver his manuscript. In a rage he had gone to the printers and smashed up the type of the part that had been set: he lost his case and had to pay. What excuse could he find for covering his journey to Neuchâtel? He was once more toying with the old scheme of publishing cheap editions of the classics and the only suitable paper was to be had at a mill near Besançon on the road to Neuchâtel. He knew there was no hope for the scheme because he could not raise the money, but he had to throw dust in the eyes of Mme de Berny, the Marquise, and Zulma Carraud, watching him in France, and the eyes of his creditors too. He went.

Told to put up at the Hôtel du Faubourg, by accident, confusion, or design he stayed at the Hôtel du Faucon where the Hanskis were staying. Below was the blue Lake of Bienne, beyond it rose the mountains – a poetic scene. The Hanskis travelled like a migrating tribe. They arrived with the governess, the child, two elderly relatives, and a large selection from their three hundred servants.

How exactly Mme Hanska and Balzac met and recognized each other is told in many versions. The one certain thing is that she was dressed in violet and that she was, at first, as alarmed as he was. *He* had pictured her as slender: she was dark and abundant. *She* was taken aback by his short fat figure, his untidy clothes and hair, and the gaps in his teeth. When he ate he scraped his plate with his knife and shovelled the food in gluttonously. She was shocked: he had not been gently brought up. On his side, he found a young, handsome woman who combined an air of imperial dignity and loftiness with naïve abandon and lasciviousness. Her fine swelling forehead suggested to him the mystic, but the superb neck was smooth and solid, the mouth shapely, if liable to contract, the nose was delicate but dominant and there was a slight cast in her splendid eyes. The voice was soft and low and she spoke excellent French with a pretty foreign accent.

Balzac's brilliance, his fame, his energy, conquered her. She had long been in love with his mind; now she was passionately drawn to his person. Balzac took care to captivate the husband by his conversation and the Count too was so entranced that he followed him everywhere, as Balzac complained. For the Count, Balzac was a great delightful Western European. Balzac went on in his letter to his sister:

God, but the Val de Travers is beautiful and the Lac de Bienne is ravishing. This is where we sent the husband to order luncheon. But we were exposed to view. So, in the shadow of a great oak tree we exchanged our first quick kiss of love. Then, since her husband is getting on for sixty, I swore to wait and she to keep her hand and heart for me. Was it not delicious to have dragged a husband, who looks to me like a tower, all the way from the Ukraine and travel six hundred leagues to meet his wife's lover who had only had to come a hundred and fifty, the monster!

It was not only delicious: it was Napoleonic. Balzac had travelled under the name of the Marquis d'Entragues: he did this, he explained, so that there would be no scandal. Mme Hanska was a little piqued that he stopped at a kiss. His room, he explained, was awkwardly placed but in Geneva, he said, he would show her that he had more enterprise in love than ten men. The time was October.

After three or four days he had to leave for Paris. Four days of jolting in the rumbling diligence and, as always in his love affairs, he had to borrow money from the woman he was courting. She gave him 1000 francs. She had to be careful: her husband held the purse. And then she could not but be aware – though she made the gift shyly and delicately – that she was a woman of rank dealing with an artist. The difference was to become important: it made her high handed materially and spiritually, but that was in the future. They had promised to meet again in Geneva in December and, while he was away, her mind alternated between the inborn suspicion that all Frenchmen were libertines and the joy of having found a Byron in her life at last – a nobler Byron.

Balzac took six days getting back to Paris because there were crowds fighting for places on the diligences. The Marquis d'Entragues had to travel *Impérial* and was jostled and shoved by six peasants from the Vaud who treated him like an animal being driven to market – but travel always distracted the writer whose brain did not stop working. He arrived at the rue Cassini worn out and (he told her) had a bath at once. He said she was his angel, his wife, his idol. He told no one about her: she was sacred. He went down into Paris to see publishers and get a new contract. He landed an excellent one with a widow called Mme Béchet; and excitedly he wrote to say he'd pay off all his debts in six months. It was always six months for him. But there were costs and indemnities to pay. He dismissed from his mind his large debts to his mother and to Mme Berny but, when he faced the facts of his situation, he found he had somehow enormously increased his debts once more; and he still had *Eugénie Grandet* and the *Duchesse de Langeais* to finish. There was the pile of corrected proofs to re-correct, that is to expand, for the widow had bought a new edition of his collected *Etudes de Mœurs*. He had promised to keep a journal for the exacting Countess for she insisted on knowing everything he did, but when he had to postpone his journey to Geneva until Christmas she became impatient. Uneasy jealousies and accusations started at once and were very marked. Maddened by neuralgia and distressed by her reproaches, he wrote that she had been an angel of deliverance in his eyes, but now he understood she was a real woman. Forgetting Marie de Fresnaye's child, he repeated that for three years he had lived in chastity. However, he was writing well: 'My whole being feels that it is being raised to a higher pitch. Animated by this hope I shall undoubtedly do the finest work I have ever done.'

He arrived at last in the snows of Geneva on Christmas Day in 1833 and her doubts melted. He found a ring waiting for him and a lock of her black hair. He stayed there forty-four days but each day spent twelve hours at work from midnight to noon. It was a savage pleasure to finish the *Duchesse de Langeais* in Geneva. There his hopes had been ecstatic as he had walked by the superb lake and paused in the Villa Diodati with the Marquise de Castries; but now, in this company, in the company of Evelina Hanska, he danced *le galop* like a child down the long salon; and when he had to be with M. Hanski, he kept them all in fits of laughter. Now he was having a most exquisite revenge – as he said, the privilege of the artist. If there is a cult of ugliness to match his idealism, in much of his work a feeling for revenge may be at the bottom of it.

When his work was done they went for enchanting walks, not always with M. Hanski. The Hanskis had taken a villa and Balzac had got a room at the Hôtel de l'Arc. Diplomatically perhaps he caught a cold so that she had the excuse of bringing medicines to his room. He never forgot the swish of her grey dress over the creaking boards in the room where she became his mistress. She promised that 'if anything happened' to her ailing husband she would marry her lover. In the meantime she gave him an inkstand and a piece of the grey dress she had taken off. (The following year he bound one of his books in it and sent it to her.) Ecstatic sexual love stimulated Balzac's other appetite for talismans and furnishings. It was he who suggested that they should keep their letters in specially made caskets; it was he who suggested the inkstand. This was to be in malachite, hexagonal in shape and to be engraved with the device *Adoremus in aeturnum*. On three of the sides of the hexagon there was to be a star; on the other three, the inscription *Exaudit Vox Angeli*, a phrase that contains the initials EVA. And –

always wanting more of everything – he asked as an afterthought for a malachite paper knife.

What did Mme Hanska and Balzac talk about as they found opportunities to walk alone together in the narrow streets of Geneva, or beside the lake that seemed like a sea washing its promontories and within sight of the majestic Alps? The miracle, no doubt, that annulled the sufferings of their lives. The *Almanach de Gotha* also! That bible of European nobility and royalty bewitched Balzac and she could add heady 'inside' stories about her family's connections with its princes. She captivated the story-teller in Balzac by her tales of the exploits of the Rzewuskis. One in particular stuck in his head and in *La Recherche de l'Absolu*, written the following year, Polish critics have seen traits of Evelina's uncle, General Chodkiewicz, who wrote seven volumes on chemistry and the search for the philosopher's stone, in the portrait of Balthazar Claes. And the moral earnestness of his reckless mistress had a perhaps awe-inspiring effect: to be so sexually passionate and yet to appear virginal and innocent! We must allow for Balzac's romantic habit of always seeing angels of purity in the married ladies who shared his bed – it was the fashion of the time – but there was something in Evelina that did exact this hardy tribute. The more voluptuous her adventure, the more moral her mind. Balzac was a novelist through and through: as metaphysician he had the alacrity of the magpie. If he could postulate the divine, he also 'sparkled like the wine of Vouvray' in his *Contes Drolatiques*, and the effect of successful love on Balzac was to fill him with ideas for more stories. There were two novels, of extreme difference from each other, which seem to owe something – though never everything – to their talks. The first is the novel *Séraphita*. Great beauty in women often has its masculine tones and Mme Hanska strikes one as belonging to that category and it is interesting that the central character of *Séraphita*, which was written for her, is an exalted and winged androgynous being who appears to two young lovers. This being has risen above the flesh and is on the point of becoming an angel; as Séraphita she is female to the young man and she is Séraphitus, a male, to the young woman. The lovers are too sensual to rise yet to heavenly love, but Séraphita points out the mystic's path ahead:

The seraph lightly spread his wings to take his flight and did not look back to them – he had nothing now in common with the earth. He sprang upwards; the vast span of his dazzling pinions covered the two watchers like a beneficent shade, allowing them to raise ther eyes and see him borne away in his glory, escorted by the rejoicing archangels.

But as he disappeared from the sight of the two lovers:

Death and impurity were repossessing themselves of their prey.

The story was to be dedicated to Mme Hanska. Wildly, but by the mysterious necessity which makes the idea for a story come to life when the milieu is changed, Balzac moved the scene from the Alpine peaks to the snowfields and ice-caps of Norway, a country he had never visited, and had to get a Genevan botanist to instruct him on Norwegian flowers. Balzac always documented. *Séraphita* was a flattering tribute to Mme Hanska's Northern mysticism and it was so notable for its poetic or impassioned style that some critics have thought Gautier polished the book for him. The awkward tribute cost Balzac more than a year's hard work; in fact a later book, *La Recherche de l'Absolu* came out first. The publisher was in despair when he read them, but he was wrong about *Séraphita*. To the modern reader the book is tedious and when the publisher read it he thought so too. Yet it was a popular success in book form though not when serialized. Balzac had proved himself to be at one with the public who, shaken in their religious faith, were as fascinated as Balzac and Mme Hanska were by the demi-gods of religiosity. The century would produce many more.

The other tale that can be traced to these weeks of sexual ferment is *La Fille aux Yeux d'Or*. It is said also to have been inspired by a picture by Delacroix, *The Girl with the Perroquet*. It is the story of a young Creole beauty shut up in a secret, luxurious seraglio by her lesbian lover, an older woman. A young dandy discovers the girl – he will reappear in *La Comédie Humaine* as Marsay, the cynical politician – they become lovers. The lesbian finds out and murders the girl and the young dandy discovers that he is the brother of the lesbian. Balzac appears to have slipped back into one of his early melodramas. There is more to be said about this story later on; all we need note now is that triumph with Mme Hanska stirred his fancy to two extremes: piety and Oriental orgy.

Balzac was received warmly by the impressive intellectual society of Geneva. The Hanskis could be proud of their genius. What is astonishing is that for the first time in his love affairs he utters the word 'marriage'. It is true that living in the presence of a husband he was safe in making the rhapsodic vow; even so, his behaviour and his letters show that he felt he had met a destiny. She was the ideal mistress-wife, a rich beautiful woman of intellect, yet also something out of the *Arabian Nights*. And she had what every Balzac dreamed of: vast property. In time, after they were obliged to part, he would have a painting of her mansion in his study in the rue Cassini and gaze with child-like greed and wonder at the romantic place. Not only a woman but an estate had panted in his arms. It would stir him to the proud statement that he too had a mansion to match it: *La Comédie Humaine*. But there was another aspect of the case which had a strange appeal to the man, though not to the writer who was an 'exceptional' creature and set apart. Until now he had been set on dominance; yet she had made the advances. It was she who dominated. It amused him with a mingling of irony and awe to call himself her 'moujik' and address her as 'the Maréchale'. French gallantry? She was young and no mother-figure, but she did inspire awe.

And on her side – what did she feel? Fear that, having made the advances, she would be despised by him. And that having got her so easily, he would tire quickly of her. She shared the common feeling that vanity ruled the French and that they could not be trusted in love. Even at the first meeting she had suspected he was already married and there had been a tiff because her flirtatious aunt, Marie Potocka, had amused him. Balzac himself said of the Poles that if you showed a Pole a precipice he would jump over it. She *was*, in a sense, innocent, and had made the leap. She had leaped at his genius, but she could not really grasp the realities of his life. She could understand that writers are harnessed in the work that absorbs them; and it went hard with her to hear him say he was 'obliged' to get back to it. No one but herself had the right to impose an obligation! If she pledged, both as a proud and cautious woman and troubled Catholic, she was nervous.

The day of parting came. M. Hanski gave the order to his tribe and their carriages took them over the Alps to Italy. For Mme Hanska the delightful journey was a distraction from her loss and her fears and may have taken her mind off any guilt she felt; guilt may even have attached her to her husband. It does not seem to have occurred to Balzac at any time that she might feel this guilt. Their vows had necessarily a pleasant spiritual vagueness, half hope, half melancholy. Letters came fast from him, addressed formally to husband and wife; and secret, passionate ones for herself alone. There were few letters from her. Perhaps in new scenes the affair was fading in her mind; perhaps he was alarmingly eloquent. They arranged to meet in Italy later on, or in Vienna when the holiday would be over and the Hanskis shut themselves up in the Ukraine once more.

Balzac set off vigorously, like a conqueror, on the first part of his journey back to Paris on foot across the Jura. The conditions of travel required stamina and he was in excellent form for the long, rumbling coach ride to Paris. He described it all and insinuated 'drolatique' hints of their private bedroom language. His 'Bengali', the little bird of Asia, longed for her 'little cage of delights' and he tells her how enchanting her face is when it goes pale at the crisis of love. It seems that they had talked about their figures by the lake and he suggests she give up tea and coffee, eat only dark meats and try sea bathing and washing in cold water. It is all very domestic.

La Comédie Humaine

Back Balzac went to 'that hellish Paris', that second Rome, that scene of 'mud studded with diamonds', where everyone was still going mad dancing the *cancan*, dressing up for masked balls, giving rowdy parties in restaurants like Le Rocher de Cancale, and where the aristocracy of the Faubourg Saint-Germain met the celebrities who went to the grand soirées of the Austrian Embassy. Balzac wrote to Mme Hanska that he was once more a galley slave and that there was nothing but trouble in the family: his mother had made one more bad deal on the Bourse and had been obliged to sell her house and go and lodge with friends in Chantilly. His deplorable brother Henri had failed in the West Indies and had brought his wife home; he had, of course, run through her fortune which in any case was not as large as he had imagined. Balzac repeated piously that his mother's sins were coming home to roost: they were an unsparing family. Laure, the sister, as ambitious as Honoré, was nagging her husband to improve his position: the expert on canals had moved on to an interest in railways which were being built in England and had invented a shunting 'hump' for the sidings and was trying to persuade Balzac to go with him to England to sell the idea: Balzac kept the suggestion in mind. It might be useful if he was obliged to go off on one of his secret flights.

And there was tragic news. Mme de Berny was dying slowly of an aneurysm of the heart. He went to see her at La Bouleaunière where sadly she corrected proofs for him. Her children were around her. She was sixty now and very weak. Mme Hanska was moving from Naples to Rome, Florence and Milan, and Balzac wrote to her again and again about his old love for Mme de Berny. It was one of the direct challenges to the Polish lady's grievances: 'My affection for her is doubled . . . Generous feelings are so rich; why go in search of the bad?' He was firm that Mme de Berny had been his conscience, his mother-mistress and insisted on his name for her, La Dilecta. Evelina was to be the Predilecta, the inspiration and guardian of his future. One can see in this insistence that he was trying to show the mistrustful Countess that he was capable of sustaining a single love above all others. He was, he said, a man whose imagination was made active by feeling rather than by thought. If he was moved by remorse at the sight of the gentle Dilecta, he planned to make amends by writing a novel that would celebrate the love that she had given him.

But flushed and energized by the new love, he soon threw himself into the Parisian swim. He was hauled off to the balls at the Opéra and to his friends in the so-called *loge infernale* at the Italiens – though he professed in his letters to be bored by it all. He gave a wild dinner party for Rossini and for 'the tigers' of the *loge* – 'stupid people'. The ravishing and good-natured Olympe Pélissier presided. He had his dining room redecorated and bought new furniture for the occasion – all on credit. He owed the butcher alone 850 francs. 'My dinner!' he wrote to Evelina, 'It is still a sensation.' Rossini had been amazed by his silver, his bronzes, his dishes, his furniture, and his carpets and clocks. Above all by the carpets!

And, building up the theme that anything the nasty gossips said about his life would be untrue:

I must say that my cane, my engraved buttons and varnished boots have persuaded literary gossips that I am the lover of an old Englishwoman (Lady Anelsy if that is how you spell it) whom I met with the Duchesse d'Abrantès who was two *loges* away from me and Mme Delphine Potocka's *loge* was between us and that I waved to her and that, unable to keep the old English lady's face in my heart, I had it carved in the knob of my cane.

He had, he said, seen the Marquise de Castries and had been presented by the dangerous Potocka at the Austrian Embassy where all the brains, beauty, and fashion gathered. These reports were a daring attempt to show Mme Hanska how truthful he was and that he sailed blamelessly among the women she feared, that all the rumours spread about him were normal Parisian scandal which her noble spirit would know how to ignore. His excited manner showed that he enjoyed this whirl of irony and back-biting: it was the general pleasure of the city. He was telling her he was a success. And he loved the publicity: it might be idiotic, but authors needed it. Like a child, the artist joins the game. But Mme Hanska's noble spirit shrivelled at the news.

His success was a reward for the triumph in 1833 of *Eugénie Grandet*. His other novels had been admired, but their sales were small. This new book was a best-seller. It contained passing fragments of his own life – the heroine might have a touch of the girl who had fallen like a flower from heaven:

The poor child did not do herself justice; but humility, or more truly, fear, is born with love. Eugénie's beauty was of a robust type often found among the lower middle classes, a type which may seem somewhat wanting in refinement, but in her the beauty of the Venus de Milo was ennobled by the beauty of Christian sentiment which invests women with a dignity unknown to ancient sculptors. Her head was very large; the masculine but direct outline of her forehead recalled the Jupiter of Phidias; all the radiance of her pure life seemed to shine from the clear grey eyes.

She had slight smallpox marks on her skin; they blurred but had not spoiled her complexion. Her nose was a trifle large, her tall frame was strong rather than lissom – but 'this was not without its charm for judges of beauty'. But novelists take a little here, a little there, from two or three models: the forehead is Mme Hanska's as he saw it at Neuchâtel; and the incident in the novel where Eugénie shyly gives some of her money to her penniless lover echoes Mme Hanska's parting gift to him. The other characters, the provincial talk and business came from the notebook he had carried about with him when he was staying with the Carrauds at Angoulême. Every time he heard a curious sentence he pulled out the book then and there, gave a shout of laughter and wrote it down to the astonishment of the local people.

Old Grandet is the ruthless type of countryman – a wine-grower of Saumur – who appears in the reign of Louis-Philippe, buying up the sequestered or bankrupt estates of the aristocracy of the *ancien régime*. We see him in the market breaking price agreements and manipulating bankers and lawyers and Balzac knows this kind of thing inside out. At the same time, Grandet retains the peasant's rooted belief in coin – indeed gold coin – as both the only safe wealth and the miser's mystical treasure: Balzac enlarges it by inflating Grandet with his own monomania. Zulma Carraud rightly thought that Balzac exaggerated Grandet's fortune – he always exaggerated literal amounts of money: there was not *that* amount of gold coin in circulation in the whole of France, she said, let alone in Saumur. She objected that there was nothing worthy of dramatic symbolism in the lives of the innumerable misers of provincial France. Misers are mean little people. The miser near Angoulême, she said, does not cut the joint: he lets it go bad! A neighbour of hers goes picking up straw for his fire and makes his own coffin of rough wood in advance, knowing well that his family will simply wrap his corpse in newspaper. Another burns the figs his wife has bought at the market in case the family should get the habit of such luxuries. All very true, but it is not artistically Balzac's point. He was one of those novelists who adds himself to what he sees. For him the artist was a monomaniac projecting a dynamic self which is really the unconscious.

When one turns from Balzac's follies in Paris to the work he was doing, one sees his prodigious energy. He was working on *Séraphita, La Recherche de l'Absolu*, the beginnings of *César Birotteau*, the revisions of other works, all at once. There were months of solitude – and one can believe him, for the work is there. The year before when he had finished *Le Médecin de Campagne* and moved at once on to *Eugénie Grandet*, he had rushed over to his sister's flat and had shouted with excitement 'I am about to become a genius.' She was the first to hear the plan of *La Comédie Humaine*. Mme Hanska was the second to hear of it. He had indeed matched her mansion with one of his own in their talks in Geneva. He expanded the idea in a letter:

I will send you the first batch of the Etudes Philosophiques, and I think you'll see the enormous adjustments that will have to be made in my entire project: the social studies.

The brilliant title, *La Comédie Humaine*, had not yet been invented; the mass of interconnecting novels was at present called *Etudes des Mœurs*.

They will portray all aspects of society, so that not a single situation of life, not a face, not the character of any man or woman, not a way of life, not a profession, not a social group, will be missing. Not an aspect of childhood, maturity, old age, politics, justice, war, will be left out. On this foundation I shall examine every thread of the human heart, every social factor and it will be real.

On the second storey I shall place the philosophical stories, for after portraying effects, I shall deal with what has caused them . . . Finally I shall turn to an analysis of principles . . . *Les Mœurs* are the play, the causes go behind the scenes, and the principle – he's the novelist himself . . . The whole will be an *Arabian Nights* of the West.

It would be his Madeleine and round its base he will trace like a laughing child the arabesques of his *Contes Drolatiques.* He ends, directing his words to her jealousies:

After this how much time will be left for pursuing the women of Paris? . . . I have chosen. Today I reveal to you my sole mistress. I have taken away the veil. There she is, the woman who will share my nights and my days – it has even cost me time from her to write you this letter, but it is delightful to pay that price . . . You can see for yourself that my wings are spread.

The great plan had grown out of the necessities of his haphazard methods of work, his constant need of money, and his incurable extravagances and obsessions. The vanishing man who must be pursued from the rue Cassini to his tailors, to many other addresses under assumed names to escape his creditors, who slipped off to the Margonnes at Saché, the Carrauds at Angoulême and Le Frapesle, to Mme de Berny at La Bouleaunière and would soon turn up in Versailles, Ville d'Avray, Italy, and Vienna can construct a settled dwelling only in his work. *La Comédie Humaine* is a collection. By his nature Balzac was profoundly, incurably, essentially a collector. He had to rearrange and alter his collection of fictions into a whole, change the names of some characters, fill in the gaps, extend the area of acquisition. An irrepressible furnisher, he was now furnishing history. He was making a powerful effort of will to bring into a whole what had been dissipated. He had always been a man of promises, lagging on his contracts, getting money for what he had not done, promising his mother and all the women in his life. In the end the one unbroken promise is this vast structure of seventy novels and more than two thousand characters.

The brilliant idea of the recurring character was born of his disorderly habits. An orderly *roman fleuve* that follows each character chronologically from cradle to grave becomes shallower as it proceeds; but now, free of the tyranny of time (as in a different way Proust was to make himself), he could show a character in middle age in one novel, in another story go back to an earlier, or forward to a later unexpected view of the same character in circumstances totally different, yet living out the logic or accident of his historical life story. Historical studies, he said, inevitably omit the place of the accidental in life. Each book of *Le Comédie Humaine* stands alone and the reader can say – as one does about one's friends in real life – Ah, that is a side of Rastignac or Lucien de Rubempré or Félix de Vandenesse or d'Arthez we did not know! This is what he was like before this fate or that altered him. Who, knowing Marsay as a political figure, would guess that at one time he could have been capable of the daring and terrible adventure of *La Fille aux Yeux d'Or*? Balzac's greed for people was fulfilled by his plan.

In his prose and as a psychologist Balzac is far less accomplished and sensitive than Stendhal. He is rudimentary, but Proust, who admired him, went to him as a master. Balzac is no poet; his lyrical writing is conventional and sentimental; and he can be too journalistically knowing. But his fecundity throbs, his power of documentation, his ubiquity as a novelist are extraordinary. There is the spry, pungent, and pervasive sense that, in any scene, he was *there* and in the flesh. This comes a good deal from the gifts of the talker whose voice imposes a spell. We are constantly aware of his person for he writes as one seriously possessed.

There is, for the critic and biographer, a certain comedy in this personal presence of Balzac in his scenes which has been pleasantly observed by Félicien Marceau in *Balzac and his World*, one of the most penetrating books on the novelist. He emphasizes one curious trait of the two thousand characters of *La Comédie Humaine*: they are subject to Balzac's extremely convenient dogma that 'in Paris, as in any country town everyone knows everyone else's love affairs and financial business and utters them'. Like Expressionists they declaim at once:

No one for example is unaware that Cardot gives Florentine 500 francs a month, or that Camusot allows Coralie two thousand for the same period. Lucien de Rubempré goes to see the money-lender Samanon. They have never seen each other before. 'You live with Coralie', Samanon tells him, 'and your effects have been seized.' How does he know? Frasier is an obscure neighbourhood solicitor yet he knows all about the misfortunes that have befallen President Camusot's wife as well as exactly who her family are and the role she played in the d'Espard affair . . . Rastignac starts paying court to Mme de Nucingen and there is immediately not one tenant in the Pension Vauquer who isn't aware of it.

On the surface this does not strike the modern reader as so very extraordinary. Balzac was writing at the formative period of a new kind of life: the life of the big city which started, after all, as a collection of small villages gummed together. No doubt 'everyone' did know everyone. Groups interlock. The same interlocking of rich and poor, vice and virtue, decency and crime can be seen in Dickens's picture of Victorian London. But what M. Marceau calls the 'remarkable indiscretion and extraordinary frankness of Balzac's heroes' is part of nature in such circumstances. Very convenient for the plotting of the novelist that they are so explanatory! But note: it is in Balzac's own reckless nature to be so in his personal life. Whether that indiscretion is historically justified or not, it is unquestionably his and out of indiscretion he enables us to hear the voice of the big city telling its own shameless story. He becomes Paris itself because he talks for it.

For within this dominating and tactless voice which jumps the ordinary limits of behaviour – that confesses but also releases, there is another voice that utters its unconscious in flights of self-imagination, in allegory, fantasy, and in melodrama. Melodrama in a novel is a way of covering up, or of getting round an emotional block or conflict which the novelist and perhaps his society are unable to face or resolve. In *Le Père Goriot*, one of the best constructed and therefore one of the most satisfying of his full-length novels, he hears this allegory-producing inner voice in certain passages referring to old Goriot himself and above all in the portrait of Vautrin. Goriot is not simply a vermicelli manufacturer who has become rich and who, like any bourgeois of the period, longs for a vicarious rise into higher circles by making good marriages for his daughters. (This is what Balzac's father had done, tragically, for his daughter Laurence.) Goriot is more. He is also a sort of Lear. He has felt in himself a prophetic destiny. He sacrifices his fortune, is reduced to misery, will even be proud of the adulteries of his 'daughters and eventually die penniless because of their ingratitude and his self-sacrifice. Balzac's other voice calls Goriot 'the Jesus Christ of paternity'. He says:

When I became a father I knew God. He is everywhere since creation came from Him: I am the same with my daughters except that I love my daughters more than God loves the world, because the world is not as powerful as God is, and my daughters are finer than myself.

His attitude is also almost as erotic as a lover's. He adores his daughters even for the evils they do to him. The words go back to

Balzac's mystical strain and his double vision. (Certainly Balzac had no conscious interest in fatherhood: it was deeply repressed until very near the end of his life.) Some critics have suggested that in rhetorical cries, like old Goriot's, Balzac expresses the 'alienation' that has its roots in the impersonal life of the big city where, because people are alone, their buried passions are enlarged.

Vautrin is a more powerful example of this enlargement. He is notoriously drawn, a good deal, from François-Eugène Vidocq, the convict who became chief of what was later called the Sûreté in Paris: Balzac dined with him more than once and learned many odd things about criminals. (For example, that prison affects the voice because it slowly dries up the throat.) As the silent, watchful intriguer of the Pension Vauquer, Vautrin is an apparently ordinary if suspect man. If he is shady, he is mysteriously acceptable: 'He was the kind of man who calls forth the remark "He looks a jovial sort".' He has dyed red whiskers, broad shoulders, well-developed chest, muscular arms, strong square-fisted hands. His face is furrowed and hard in spite of an insinuating manner. He is a boisterous laugher, very practical with his hands, especially with locks that have gone wrong. He has travelled all over the world. He lends money to anyone who asks. But what disturbs is something underlying his manner. He seems to know everything and secrete power. He is – as Balzac wished to be – encyclopedic and resilient because unattached. He has ' . . . an imperturbable coolness which seemed to indicate that this was a man who would not stick at a crime to extricate himself from a false position . . . ' He knew or divined the concerns of everyone about him.

There is always a part of Balzac – almost a part of his flesh – in all the men and women of his novels. One can see that Vautrin is a double image – a man and yet also a new consciousness of power for its own sake that was growing in the nineteenth century: power in science, machinery, colonization. Balzac was always fascinated by ruthless will: the figures known as 'the lion' or 'the dandy' are predators. Unlike Stendhal's characters they do not set out to maintain their self-esteem. They want money and power and they state it openly.

Vautrin plays a Satanic part in his relations with the young Rastignac:

Paris you see is like a forest in the New World where you have to deal with a score of varieties of savages who live off the proceeds of their social hunting. You are a hunter of millions. To catch your millions you set your snares. Some hunt heiresses, others a legacy; some fish for souls, yet others sell their clients hand and foot. The man who brings home most game will be praised, fêted and received into good society.

Or:

A man who prides himself on following a straight line through life is an idiot who believes in infallibility. There are no such things as principles: there are only events, there are no laws but those of expediency . . . A man is not obliged to be more particular than the nation.

Crime and justice are opposite sides of the same coin. And, always with his eye to the sexual life of his people, Balzac made Vautrin, the rebel against society, homosexual. He says to Rastignac: 'But I, I love you: a man is a god who looks like you.' This love is the single remnant of virtue in a harsh nature. Only in that can he be wounded. Vautrin certainly hates women. He says 'I know you as if I had made you' – the homosexual has a craving for paternity.

It has, of course, been argued that Balzac was homosexual or had been homosexual at some time. There is no evidence of this, but he often said that the artist was a man-woman. He was a good-natured animal and enjoyed the natural open affection that men normally feel for each other and that seems (to a male) rare between woman and woman. He correctly described himself as a half-child. We come back to the main point: that he spoke out loudly from the different parts of himself. Heterosexual or homosexual, love is the same passion to this analyst. When he gave Vautrin magnetic eyes he was describing his own. To George Sand he wrote:

I like exceptional beings. I myself am one. Moreover I need them to throw my commonplace characters into relief and I never sacrifice them unnecessarily. But the commonplace characters interest me more than they do you. I enlarge them; I idealize them in reverse, their ugliness and their stupidity; I bring to their deformities an added dimension of the horrifying or the grotesque.

We shall meet Goriot's daughters, one as the wife of Comte de Restaud. Delphine is married to the banker, Nucingen, of great importance later. We have already met Rastignac briefly in *La Peau de Chagrin* and Mme Beauséant who has already appeared in *La Femme Abandonnée*: in *Le Père Goriot* we see the earlier dramatic intrigue which has led to her unhappiness. Henri de Marsay – to become Prime Minister eventually in the chopping and changing of governments under the unsteady reign of Louis-Philippe – the lover in *La Fille aux Yeux d'Or*, will eventually be the lover of Delphine de Nucingen. It is in *Le Père Goriot* that the pieces of *La Comédie Humaine* begin to interlock.

To the pleasure of the caricaturists Balzac was now not simply stout: the sedentary life and the gourmandizing had given him a heavy belly. The journalists made fun of his coat of arms and his aristocratic pretensions and had their revenge for the condescending airs he put on when he met the press. The canes were a gift to them. He bought three more: one had a knob of cornelian, another was encrusted with turquoise, another was made of rhinoceros horn. He was drawn as a pot-bellied tavern-keeper putting on the solemn, self-satisfied act of a pasha. He wrote to Mme Hanska:

You cannot exaggerate the success my latest cane has had in Paris. It threatens to create a European fashion. People are talking about it in Naples and Rome. All the dandies are jealous.

Delphine de Girardon, whose husband serialized his work in *La Presse* and for whom he wrote articles, brought out a witty book, *La Canne de M. Balzac*. He was often at her salon and she, though suspected by Mme Hanska, was one of his innocent friends. She charmed everyone. In the course of her book she made a very acute remark about the cane: she saw the magic in it. He carried it, Mme de Girardon said, to make himself invisible.

Invisibility he badly needed: invisibility, in his dubious moments, from the friends of Mme Hanska, of course; invisibility from his creditors, too; but also invisibility from the eyes of the State. Because of the threat of civil revolt Louis-Philippe had founded a militia, the Garde National, and all male citizens were on a rota for duty. It infuriated workers who could not afford to lose two or three days' work; and it infuriated writers particularly. When the knock at the door came Balzac joked, parleyed, gave the sergeant a bottle of wine or bribed him; but this no longer worked. Balzac did what one would expect: he gave one more sensational dinner party, left his keys with Jules Sandeau and nailed a notice to his door saying Apartment to Let and vanished to another place on the outskirts of Paris, across the river, at the rue des Batailles. It was on the site of the present avenue d'Iéna, overlooking the Seine, a tumbledown empty house. It stood on waste land where farm animals and chickens wandered about and he rented it in the name of an imaginary widow called Mme Durant, said to be a melancholy recluse. There were rumours that she went out only at night for a walk by the river – the figure was undoubtedly Balzac in his monk's robe. The house was empty except for his room on the second floor and an attic at the top where he worked and to get into the place (according to Gautier who has given a comical account of it), one had to give a password, such as 'The plum season has begun', or 'I am bringing some Belgian lace', or 'Mme Bertrand is very well.' Fact and fantasy rose together in Balzac's mind. There were many conspiratorial groups and secret societies in Paris and a good deal of Balzac's love of masks and secretiveness and lying, jocular or serious, was rooted in a childish love of fiction as well as a need for it. One went up bare staircases in the house, down empty passages and through unfurnished rooms, until one came to a closed door. What was behind the door? The Orient: a boudoir of a sultan of the *Arabian Nights*. There are many descriptions of it, but Balzac's own in *La Fille aux Yeux d'Or*, begun in Geneva and finished in the rue des Batailles in 1835, matches Gautier's. Balzac's life fertilized his fictions. It was exactly the setting for the sensational tale of hidden love and perversity in high life, brought to a murderous climax by a girl's lesbian lover. Balzac has gone back to his Gothic phase: the girl is a Creole, Paquita Valdès. There was a Turkey carpet – one remembers that carpets were a luxury known only to the very rich – a round table covered by a cashmere shawl – the latest expensive thing, a fine mirror over the chimney-piece, a picture of Leda and the Swan by Boulanger and a circular divan fifty feet round:

The back of this immense bed rose several inches above the cushions which further enriched it by the manner of their trimmings. The divan was covered with red material over which was draped Indian muslin, ribbed like a Corinthian column with raised and sunken ridges and adorned at the top and bottom with a band of poppy-red embroidered with black arabesques. Beneath the muslin the poppy turned to rose, the colour of love, reflected by the window curtains, and decorated with fringes of poppy and black. Six silver-gilt arms, each carrying two candles, were fixed to the walls at equal distances over the divan. The ceiling from which hung a silver chandelier sparkled with whiteness and the cornices were gilt. The carpet was like an Eastern shawl, with designs recalling the poems of Persia, where it had been worked by the hands of slaves. The chairs were upholstered in white cashmere with black and poppy-red adornments. The clock and the candelabra were of white and gold.

The whole is in Balzac's notorious bad taste – he was not for nothing the son of a mother whose family had made their money in the embroidery trade – and for him the place shimmered like snow. He spiritualized the scene:

The soul has I know not what attachment for white; love takes pleasure in red and gold heightens the passions, giving the power to realize love's fantasy. Thus everything that is vague and mysterious in man, all his unexplained affinities, were indulged in their unwitting predilections. There was in this perfect harmony a mingling of colours which evoked in the spirit a sensual response, random and undecided . . .

Random and undecided: it hints at a new dream as yet undisclosed.

The walls were quilted. He and Gautier stood there screaming and posted someone outside in order to find out whether the cries could be heard. What cries? the imaginary screams of Paquita Valdès when she was being slashed to death? Or other cries, more personally interesting? Who was to occupy the bed? A mysterious lady called Louise, very persistent and pressing, a painter who sent him sketches? Unlikely: he wrote her tender letters but refused to see her; he had become wary of female correspondents. The flirtatious Countess Potocka? At all costs his hiding place must be kept from her. He also guessed that, with others in the Polish and Austrian colonies in Paris, Marie was one of the Predilecta's spies. Mme de Castries? Surely not that cold cruel woman who had humiliated him? Still, he was anxious not to make too much of an enemy of her because of the savage portrait of her in the *Duchesse de Langeais*. Balzac was a realist in intrigue. Who could tell *when* M. Hanski would consent to die? Mme de Castries and he were on bickering terms: when he hated, she was all coquettish ingratiation; when he responded, they quarrelled again. The hostess who rummaged out all secrets had heard rumours of a secret seraglio. He indignantly denied her insinuations. He has worked like a slave. He told her austerely that one must love in order to live, but 'you don't love'. He was in remorseful mood and distilling his remorse about Mme de Berny in a new novel, *Le Lys dans la Vallée*. But he heard that the teasing Mme de Castries had moved to the district and so he had one more try. He had fifty pages of proofs to correct on top of everything else, he said, so that people who said he had five or six mistresses were lying. ('I'd have to be a Hercules!') But he could do with a little femine distraction on the fifty-foot divan. Why (he asked) didn't she come round to see it? When he got up in the morning – between eleven and one – alone? No one would know – and perch for an hour on the divan like a bird, where she would have an hour of poetic and mysterious life?

She did not do so. For the moment, the fifty-foot divan was waiting. For whom? Unhappily not for Mme Hanska. M. Hanski's health had improved in Italy. The angel of his dreams was turning into an impatient woman. She was irritated when, in one letter after another, he was obliged to postpone the promise to join her in Italy because of his work and because he had no money. How could he be penniless, she asked, when *Eugénie Grandet* and *Le Père Goriot* had earned him so much? The Hanskis moved on to Vienna and he swore he would come to her there; but there were more delays and she complained that instead of writing her a full account of his doings once a week, he had cut it to twice a month. Then as she glared across the frontiers at him and tapped her foot an awkward thing happened. He was, as we have seen, in the habit of writing two kinds of letters to her: those which were suitable reading for a husband; and, through the Swiss governess, secret and passionate letters. By accident M. Hanski got two of these secret letters. There was a scene between husband and wife. The accident seemed fatal. It called for an act of Napoleonic deception on Balzac's part. He brought to bear all his skills as a novelist, all the coolness of a Vautrin. He wrote a long letter to M. Hanski saying that Mme Hanska, a woman of intense literary curiosity and the purest and most innocent woman in the world, had in her innocence many times asked him what sort of love letters de Monteran and Marie de Verneuil (the lovers in *Les Chouans*) would have written to each other. Balzac had not taken her seriously but she had persisted and, at last, he had written them. But (he told M. Hanski), he had now heard from her that she was outraged by the letters. She had thought them shocking and he feared she would never speak to him again. They had destroyed, he feared, the confidence of the innocent lady whose mind was so elevated and philosophical. One could hardly expect M. Hanski to swallow such a tale; but now Balzac became, as he was fond of saying, 'sublime'. As a novelist he knew how important it is to turn the tables on one's characters: he hit upon the subtle idea of begging M. Hanski to plead for him and to get

Mme Hanska to forgive him. He would die, if, by an act of stupidity, he lost the noblest friendship of his life. We do not know what happened exactly between husband and wife, but M. Hanski calmed down. Like everyone else he had been charmed by Balzac and was vain of knowing a man so famous in Europe, especially among the Austrian aristocracy to whom he had no doubt boasted of Balzac's coming visit. He also knew that he and his wife would soon be far away in the Ukraine and there was nothing to worry about.

For Mme Hanska the accident was unpleasant not only because of the quarrel with her husband and her exposure to censure in the field where she regarded herself as impregnable by nature: the moral and the respectable. (One can see from a letter M. Hanski wrote to Balzac a year later, when he sent him the present of an inkstand, that his friendly feelings for Balzac and his pride in knowing him and reading him, were unchanged: perhaps *he* too had reserves about his wife's hot temper. She had the high art of transferring guilt to others.) But having settled with her husband she was now struck by the inventive resources of Balzac. He had lied only too brilliantly on her behalf: it was a revelation. She re-read his letters and compared rumour with text. She came to things like his description of the evening at the Italiens when he had met that 'old Englishwoman, Lady Anelsy if that is how you spell it' – did she exist or was that a cover for another Englishwoman, young and beautiful, married to an Italian, the Contessa Guidaboni-Visconti? She had heard from Mme de Potocka that he had met such a lady at one of those famous parties at the Austrian Embassy. Balzac said that the Guidaboni-Viscontis were a kind couple who let him share their *loge*. She wondered if he really laboured as hard as he said and even set to working out how many books he had written, and in which particular months in order to check. She seems to have pushed out of her mind the fact that she had the consolation of a husband, with whom she shared a bed. She shuddered when Balzac said that after intense work he should use that so ambiguous French word, *distractions*.

She wrote acidly to Balzac that she could not wait in Vienna much longer. They were about to pack up and return to the Ukraine. Mme Hanska was Ideal and Fortune. When he got this ultimatum Balzac turned in alarm to his new publisher, Werdet, who was trying to lure him for his list. Balzac had treated him with contempt, but now in desperation his mood changed.

He left the rue des Batailles by *coucou*, one of the uncomfortable little buses of the city. He went to see Werdet in his office in the rue de Seine. Werdet wrote an account of the interview with the novelist:

'I am exhausted. My head is empty, my imagination has dried up. I have drunk hundreds of cups of coffee; I have taken two baths a day – nothing works. I've got to travel to Vienna.'

'Go to Azay le Rideau [near Saché]. You always work well there.' Balzac roared. 'No. Vienna!'

'You will ruin me', Werdet said.

'On the contrary I shall save you. I shall finish *Séraphita* and send you also the complete manuscript of *Mémoires de deux Mariées*. Once in Vienna my imagination will wake up again . . . I shall rediscover it in the company of the dear angel, the Carissima I have often told you about, and who is waiting for me . . . I want 200 francs. You haven't got it? You can easily raise it – sign a note. Get it. I shall start from my sister's house and at eight o'clock, clic-clac.'

And, Werdet says, he said it like a child, imitating the click of a whip. He fixed Werdet with his gold-flecked eyes and he got the money.

Up to now Balzac had always taken the diligence when he travelled, but that would not do in 1835 for a decisive visit to the fabulous Polish Countess who was staying with her retinue in the grandest court of Europe. He would be surrounded by princes and dukes. The great Metternich was there and Balzac's superstitious mind, convinced that coincidences were foreordained, must have reflected that Metternich and he had shared a mistress in the Duchesse d'Abrantès and they were thereby almost related; and not only that, Mme de Castries had been the mistress of Metternich's son. Balzac was not travelling as a pirated novelist and bourgeois, but as a fellow aristocrat. He hired a private coach for 400 francs, plus 10 francs to get the lamps repaired. He ordered new gold buttons for his blue coat and 'a divine lorgnon', had the arms of the Marquis d'Entragues engraved on his luggage and dressed his servant, Auguste, in new livery. The whole equipment cost him 5000 francs; half a year's income. Not until a year or so later did he realize that his appearance made him ridiculous. They drove through Germany with Balzac shouting 'Faster, faster!' out of the windows. Perpetual small payments had to be made at the posting houses, at the *octrois* and frontiers: neither he nor his servant spoke a word of German.

It took them seven days to travel through five countries and at Vienna he was put to stay in the expensive quarter. Balzac, who had not slept for three nights, rushed to Mme Hanska who was staying near by. She was mistrustful and now she had to be circumspect. He found she would rarely meet him and then only in drawing-rooms. If they met privately the pleasure was destroyed for him by her jealousy. She still sulked about Mme de Berny; about every other woman he had met, mistress or not, she was suspicious and violent.

In Vienna he stuck as best he could to his sacred routine of work – twelve hours a day. To bed at nine in order to start work at three a.m. A concession. In Paris he went to bed (he now said) at six p.m. He had weakened, he said, to the extent of giving her an extra three hours of his time. The late hours kept by Viennese society did not suit him. He sent her notes. They were wretched. One he called 'Note from a dirty and untidy man.' She had complained of his appearance. She herself was taking foot baths for she had begun to suffer from gout. And she had lost her voice. They went for walks in the Prater but the walks were ruined by disputes. Still swearing love and innocence, he was even driven to say he loved her for her jealousy.

There is not an hour or a minute we can call our own . . . I have never been so happy or suffered so much . . . I knew how unhappy I should be before I came, and unhappiness is what I have found . . . If I did not know that we are bound to each other for ever I should die of misery. Do not leave me: it would kill me . . . The wretched are always faithful, their feelings are their only treasure . . . What have you to fear? My work proves my love for you.

Still, she softened to the extent of agreeing to pose with Balzac for Daffinger, the miniaturist – she was an inveterate collector of autographs and literary items that would establish her importance. When he got back to Paris he put the original in his boudoir at the rue des Batailles. He fancied his powers as a reader of character by the face and wrote to her:

Your mouth is one of the softest creations that I know; it has the expression which your aunt [an enemy of his] so often reproaches you with; but this is superficial of her. Without your mouth your swelling forehead would seem hydrocephalic. There is in it a balance between the sensitivity and ideas, between heart and brain. . . . The last time I watched you with detachment at Daffinger's, I thought I saw some slight signs of cruel anger.

Don't be offended; this is something your aunt also has noticed, but the movements of your mouth are full of good nature. You have something violent in your first impulse, and then thoughtfulness, good nature, sweetness and nobility quickly take their place. I don't think of such things as defects . . . If you were exclusively good, you would be no more than a sheep . . .

With *La Bataille* in mind – his fantasy of escape persisted – he went on a trip to Napoleon's near disaster at Essling to see the battlefield.

He also looked up the booksellers to encourage his sales. And he saw Metternich, the Chancellor, the political conqueror of Napoleon. Metternich said, 'Monsieur, I have never read any of your books' (untrue – Balzac knew that he had 'devoured' *L'Histoire des Treize*) and went on:

But I know you and it is obvious that you are mad or that you live by making fools of other lunatics and set out to cure them by a madness greater than theirs.

They talked politics. And Metternich gave him the plot of a story.

Balzac was fêted in Vienna. If the trip was a failure for him as a lover, a failure for him as the would-be man of fashion – the aristocracy took his clothes and manners as a private lark – he was a triumph as a man of genius. At a concert the audience stood up to acclaim him when he came into the hall. But for the traveller Vienna was a disaster. It cost him 15,000 francs and he had to borrow a small sum of money to tip the porter when he left for Paris.

He returned to more and more disaster. He had run up bills in Vienna in Werdet's name and Werdet could not meet them. Indeed, as Balzac had jokingly foretold, he soon bankrupted his publisher. Cornered by her brother's creditors, Laure had pawned all his silver, those proud pieces engraved with the crest of the Marquis d'Entragues. The tale of trouble is unending.

This will teach you, Evelina, to force a penniless writer to leave Paris and his desk to run to Vienna, to defend himself against the stupid reproaches of a jealous woman.

There is an estimate, made by him in 1836, that in addition to the 40,000 francs he owed to his family, there was still another 118,000 outstanding – 53,000 more than in the previous year. For once more he had plunged into a money-making scheme: he had borrowed heavily to invest in a new paper he was editing, the *Chronique de Paris*.

Once more a dream of fortune had failed and, for him, incomprehensibly. For in Vienna he had met the historian, Baron Joseph de Hammer-Purgstall, a polyglot who had written an eighteen-volume history of the Ottoman Empire. He had given Balzac a talisman, in the form of a ring on which Arabic characters were engraved. Balzac called this lucky stone 'Bedouck'. Balzac swore that when he saw the stone the Turkish Ambassador had cried that it was a ring that had belonged to the Prophet and that the English had stolen it a hundred years before. 'Let us go at once to the realm of the Grand Mogul who has offered a reward of tons of gold and diamonds for its recovery.'

Balzac proposed to his friends that they should go at once and when they laughed and refused he got into a rage, and then fell down on the floor and went fast asleep.

The Monk with the
Jewelled Cane

Balzac hated England because it had defeated the god of his youth, but he could not contain his unrest and envy at the spectacle of English wealth and power. It was natural to feel a boy's patriotic dislike of the enemies of his country during the wars. He longed, he said, 'to sink an English ship'. But there had been two thousand English residents restricted to the outskirts of Tours during the wars and they brought with them an allaying sense of the exotic and romantic to him. Like his father he read deeply in English literature – and not only Shakespeare, Sterne, Richardson, and Byron and the Gothic novelists. As we have seen his first pseudonym on his trashy novels was the ennobled anagram of Honoré – Lord R'Hoone. In his twenties and thirties he was carried away by the general craze for English fashions and imperturbability in behaviour, the passion for English horses, carriages, and clothes. Visiting English aristocracy were setting the tone. The most exclusive of Parisian clubs – Le Jockey – was founded by Lord Henry Seymour, the illegitimate son of the Marchioness of Hertford who, herself indifferent to the starchiness of the Faubourg Saint-Germain, let off the ground floor of her house to the Café de Paris. It must be said that whether they settled in Paris for pleasure or to economize, English visitors let themselves go and became figures of notoriety or wonder to the French.

This was not a matter which Balzac could pass over. He had as reckless a weakness for generalizations on national character as he had for everything else. And this for him of course meant a study of the women. He wrote (in *Le Lys dans la Vallée*) that the English deified matter. The divine spirituality of the Catholic soul was lacking in them. They possessed in the highest degree the science of living which adorns the most trifling material objects, which makes your bedroom slippers the most beautiful in the world, which endows your linen with an indescribable quality, which perfumes your wardrobe and lines it with cedar, which at given times pours out tea, elegantly served, which banishes dust, nails down carpets from the lowest stair to the furthest corner of the house, etc., etc., so that the soul dies under the weight of comfort, the terrible monotony of well-being and lack of spontaneity. He proceeds to explain the character of the Englishwoman. She is an object.

These fortifications of polished steel built up round an Englishwoman, caged by golden wires into her home, where her feeding trough and drinking cup, her perches and her food are all perfection, lend her irresistible attractions. Never did a nation more elaborately scheme for the hypocrisy of a married woman by placing her always midway between social life and death. For her there is no compromise between shame and honour; the fall is utter, or there is no slip; it is all or nothing – the To be or Not to Be of Hamlet. This alternative, combined with the habits of disdain to which manners accustom her, makes an Englishwoman a creature apart in the world. She is but a poor creature, virtuous perforce, and ready to abandon herself, condemned to perpetual despair buried in the soul; but she is enchanting in form because the race has thrown everything into form. Hence the beauties peculiar to the woman of that country: the exaltation of an affection in which life is compulsorily summed up, their extravagant care of their person, the refinement of their love . . .

As sirens they appear impenetrable, but in reality they are quickly known. They long for the conspicuous and extraordinary; their hearts crave for spice and pepper.

What are these words doing in the novel written in 1836 while Mme de Berny was dying at La Bouleaunière and which was to be a monument to her? How does it come about that such a novel has the very English title of Le Lys dans la Vallée? The answer is that during the previous year while he was quarrelling with Mme Hanska in Vienna, his mind drifted off to thoughts of Fanny, wife of the Conte Guidaboni-Visconti: this was the couple who had been sharing the expense of a box at the Italiens with him. He called her, for his usual reasons of romantic mystification, by her second name, Sarah. He imagined her coming to him in the rue des Batailles: perhaps he had originally prepared it for her.

The Contessa had not pursued him. She was not one of his letter-writing women nor are there any letters, except on matters of business, from him to her – at least they have not been preserved. She was not a collector of autographs and had no desire to be a literary celebrity, although she made much of having met the Contessa Guiccioli in Venice and envied her life with Byron. So in her long liaison with Balzac she is an uncertain figure, vivid for a moment and then disappearing. The labours of a later biographer, L. J. Arrigon, have at any rate freed her character from the slanders and inaccuracies of one of her neighbours at Versailles, the sneering magistrate Lambinet who, as we have seen, libelled the Duchesse d'Abrantès. He regarded Fanny as depraved, drunken, and transparently dishonest. Like the rest of the Parisian English she certainly paid little attention to public opinion.

She came of a solid, well-connected, dashing gentry family in Wiltshire, the Lovells of Cole Park, and her grandfather was a bishop. They were the sort of people who went to Jane Austen's Bath and there she had met her husband who came from the Italian nobility in Milan. They had a house in the Champs-Elysées, now beginning to be laid out, other houses at Versailles and Vienna. (The last connection was dangerous for Balzac: Mme Hanska had relations in Vienna.) He had managed at last to get an invitation to the Austrian Embassy and that was when he first met the Contessa. The short man stood before a tall, voluptuous, ash-blonde Juno with the greenish eyes of an Oriental princess – any woman for whom Balzac fell became Oriental at once. She had small ears and the English rose complexion and the candid, laughing manner of one practised in headlong seduction. She had one curious habit: she took care to hide her feet – decorum? Or were they large? In addition to being Oriental, he found her 'athletic'. Her laughter – it turned out – was caused by the sight he presented. He was of course over-dressed: he was wearing a green frock-coat with gold buttons, a white waistcoat with coral studs, and his fingers were pimpled with rings. But when her friends joined her laughter and said he was *appallingly* fat, she turned on them and said with sudden naïvety that she liked fat men: her previous lover, the Prince Kowlowski, by whom she had had a son, had been very fat and had made her happy. Balzac took care to tone down his appearance at their next meeting and his talk soon charmed her. When he went off he cut off a lock of his hair and left it in a box for her: women always respond to a surprise. Perhaps this incident explains a devious aside in one of his letters to Mme Hanska: 'Would you still love me if my hair was long? Everyone says I look ridiculous as I am. But I stick to it. I haven't had my hair cut since those dear days at Geneva.'

The Contessa was notorious for her love affairs. She was conveniently equipped with an unnoticing husband who in no way restrained her. A kind but boring man, he had two modest and absorbing hobbies and perhaps their eccentricity appealed to her English nature. One was for concocting, bottling, and labelling medicines in pretty bottles. Balzac called him a character out of Hoffmann and thought the Contessa came out of *Romeo and Juliet*. The other hobby was playing in orchestras. He liked to slip out of his house in Versailles into the orchestra pit and play the violin there. He was more than affable to his English wife's lovers.

Balzac made no progress with the Contessa at first. The story is that she became his mistress after a dispute at a party. One of the Contessa's distinguished lovers, Louis de Bonneval, was present, a man celebrated for his elegance, and he made the mistake of hinting to the Contessa that Balzac was linked with Mme Hanska. How often news of a rival is the beginning of love! It was quite enough for the fighting Contessa: she changed lovers at once, that evening. There is another story – doubtful because it comes from Victor Lambinet – of Bonneval's revenge. Balzac had talked of *La Comédie Humaine*:

My work will embrace all classes in France in the nineteenth century: the scholars of the future will consult it.

Bonneval replied, according to Lambinet, in *Balzac Mis à Nu*:

For descriptions of streets where decent people never go, for brothels, for furniture and dirty clothes – low life, in short, I agree. But in good society I have never met anyone who spoke the language you give them. Where can you have found your models?

Bonneval was right. One can, by a process of dilution, detect certain traits of the Contessa from Balzac's portrait of Lady Dudley in *Le Lys dans la Vallée*. The realistic descriptions of ordinary people in his novels give way to hyperbole when he meets the upper classes. She is a huntress who lets no man escape and when she gets him is again Oriental in self-sacrifice and yielding; but she has the wiry foot of the doe, 'a sinewy wrist no horse can defy'. Her briliance is phosphorescent, she does not perspire but 'lives in water'; yet her sexual demands are 'a tornado like the sand-spouts of the desert'. Her soul expires and she creates a terrible monotony of ease. It is rather unnerving and rather blackmailing to hear her say she will die for you. It is true, he added, that after the tornado has passed she 'infuses tedium into physicl pleasures by never varying them'.

In fact the Contessa was a good-natured Wiltshire girl who proved time and time again that she would do anything for her 'Bally', as she called him in her hearty, sexy way. She was no intellectual, as Mme Hanska claimed to be, though like everyone else she had dabbled in Swedenborg and played for a time at spiritualism – both subjects congenial to Balzac's pretensions. Even the magistrate Lambinet half admired her. He accused her of greed when in fact her financial generosity to Balzac, when she could ill afford it, was continuous. Lambinet called her an actress, when she simply had the downright English manner. He said she was stupid 'in giving herself away', that is, she was without the French formal ingenuity. She was probably flushed with excitement. He said she drank a lot – she probably did – and ate too much. She reprimanded Balzac's Rabelaisian talk, but in her cups was apt to be shocking herself. By the end of their first years she gave birth to a son, said to be Balzac's – he grew up to have Balzac's unmistakable nose with its flattened tip. Those who argue that the child was not Balzac's note that he never boasted about it. But he would surely for once have kept quiet, for Mme Hanska knew the Contessa's relations in Vienna.

There is a letter from one of her friends, quoted by Maurois, which brings out what Balzac always sought in women besides their sexual attraction. He sought the story-teller:

It is simply that Mme Visconti is full of wit and imagination and fresh, bright ideas, and M. de Balzac who is also a superior person, enjoys her conversation, and since he has written a great deal and is still writing, he often makes use of the original fancies which so constantly occur to her . . .

And, beyond the stories she could tell? The Contessa was as grand as the women of the Faubourg Saint-Germain, but more careless. She was not a mother-figure, for she was young; rather she had some of the amorality of his sister Laure: artists must do what they like. The Contessa's independence probably was a relief to him though also a puzzle, for he more than once complained that the vice of the English was their individualism. In his habit of keeping two love affairs going at a time, in different secret compartments, there was a certain orderliness and precision. It is conceivable that she shocked him. She could not equal Mme de Berny as a critic and admirer, nor vie with the high-sounding utterances of Mme Hanska, but (as biographers have noted) she looked after him as a man, thought up excuses to help him in his disappearances and was amused by his love affairs. He may not have loved her deeply, but his affections were always strong and he found almost a domestic refuge in her company and an escape from jealousy. Their liaison lasted for five years and they were the years when he was doing his best work, when he wrote *Le Père Goriot, Les Illusions Perdues, César Birotteau*, and brilliant short things like *La Messe de l'Athée* and *Facino Cane*. The couple met rather than lived together.

During this time Balzac kept up his flow of letters to Mme Hanska. There were gaps in them which had to be explained. His brother-in-law's shunting invention was useful: he was going to Boulogne. In fact he was on a trip with the Contessa. Mme Hanska was still his *épouse d'amour* but, after the violent scenes in Vienna, the tone is lower and he wrote in the voice of long-suffering and anxious friendship, clogging the pages with long, confusing accounts of his work and the new financial messes that were piling up. The vision of being eternally united to her was fading. M. Hanski refused to die.

I long to escape from this crater which is burning up my spirit and fly to the end of the earth. I am the Wandering Jew of the mind, always on my feet, tramping without rest or happiness in the heart.

It was true and untrue: there was distant ideal love and there was the love at hand that passes.

Mme Hanska was convinced that he was with the Contessa; he used every subterfuge in denying it. He was protecting the independence of the multifarious persons inside him. The 'moujik' was in terror of his tyrant: the disciple of Molière loved intrigue, the imitator of Napoleon regarded Napoleon's use of dissimulation as the great virtue of exceptional men. Then Balzac felt in his chosen slavery as a writer that he was entitled to sexual pleasure and its undoubted reviving power. He and Mme Hanska had had long frowning wrangles about fidelity. She had a husband; how could he, Balzac, be expected to live for years in chastity? Like any woman of her class she could not bear the suspicion – indeed it was knowledge now – that he was going to bed with a woman of her own class: why did he not do what all men were permitted to do by upper-class women – go with prostitutes or wenches if they must? The argument dragged on openly or by insinuation for years. As late as 1843 he was still writing to her:

A man is not a woman. Can he remain from 1834 to 1843 without a woman? You know enough medically speaking that a man would be driven to impotence and imbecility. You say 'Take prostitutes'. If I had I would be in the state X got himself into in Rome. And also put in the scales the overwhelming need for distraction which any mature creature has when he is bound by perpetual care, misery and weariness.

It is possible that in her careless encouragement of any idea that came into Balzac's head, the Contessa had an indirect responsibility for the next big financial disaster of his life: the attempt to make a fortune by reviving the moribund paper *La Chronique de Paris* which came out twice a week.

The idea of founding and editing a paper of his own was glorious to him. The pursuit of capital turned into a series of riotous dinner parties. He still rented under another name the house in the rue Cassini – if he never quite gave up a woman he also never quite gave up a house, nor indeed a piece of furniture voluntarily – and one of the most lavish of these parties, given at a time when he was trying to sell shares in the paper, was given at that address. Sturgeon, hams, plovers, asparagus, and pineapple fritters were ordered from a famous chef. The Vouvray flowed. Balzac's figures are never to be trusted but he wrote to Mme Hanska that his own interest in the *Chronique* amounted to 32,000 francs – borrowed money, of course; publishers were in on the deal. If he could only get 2000 subscribers he would make 20,000 francs straight off, besides what he got as a director and for the articles and stories he wrote. The old story of Balzac as a businessman was repeated.

There were only 288 subscribers: receipts were 800 francs, expenses 7900 francs. He hoped to resell his own shares, but could not find a buyer. The crash turned into farce: the officers of the Garde National broke the monotony of their deals with him and nabbed him at the rue Cassini. He was marched off to the prison nicknamed 'Les Haricots' on the charge of failing to report for duty. The caricaturists let themselves go for a week. To Mme Hanska, in one of those long letters of his that go on protesting and dissembling from day to day, he wrote:

This prison is frightful; we are all packed in together; it is cold, there is no fire. The prisoners are of the lowest class, they spend their time gambling and shouting, not a moment's peace. There are poor working-class fellows who can't afford, for their families' sake, to give up two days' wages; and a few artists and writers who at any rate prefer prison to the Garde. The beds are awful. I have a table, a chair, a pallet and here I am, trying to get to the end of *Le Lys dans la Vallée*.

Balzac soon settled down. Werdet, his publisher, and a crowd of friends came to see him. He was much put out by seeing his rival Eugène Sue – also jailed – arrive with a servant and fine food, and was stirred to compete. Balzac sent for his own servant, dressed splendidly in maroon uniform with the coat of arms on it, and wearing white gloves. Balzac too held a feast. He boasted that at any rate he would leave behind him the legend of how to live well, even in jail. Flowers arrived and a lock of fair hair from a woman with a note in English saying 'From an Unknown Friend'. Perhaps she was the Contessa. The whole week cost Werdet, 'that feather-brained child' as Balzac called his publisher, a lot of money. In the meantime the collapse of the *Chronique* had added 45,000 francs to his debts; and he was threatened by another publisher with legal action and fines if he did not deliver two novels on an outstanding contract in two months. Werdet and Balzac screamed that one had bankrupted the other. Werdet was certainly bankrupt. Balzac went off once more to Saché, to look out on the trees and the little valley he knew so well, to get at last to the end of *Le Lys dans la Vallée* and in twenty days – so he said – to write the first volume of *Les Illusions Perdues* which, with *Le Père Goriot*, stands at the head of his best work. It is usually said that an artist needs peace: Balzac needed the turmoil he provoked.

His letters to Mme Hanska at all times – but particularly now – were long and garrulously sustain the drama. It is as if his hand and brain were machines that could not stop writing, moving from novels to letters and from letters to novels, almost without putting the pen down. But Mme Hanska evidently wrote him one of her black letters, accusing him not only of childishness in business, and debauchery in private life, but of a new vice: his enemy, her Aunt Rosalie, 'had proofs' that he went to casinos and had become an inveterate gambler. So he was, but not in the Contesse Rosalie's sense. He wrote back defending himself. If once or twice in his life he had gone to a gambling house it was simply to watch and this is true:

I am down but I am not out. My energy alone is left. Really the sense of loneliness is more afflicting than my other troubles. What a long sad farewell I have made to the last year, swallowed up without return. It has brought me neither complete happiness, nor complete unhappiness; I have lived frozen on one side, burned up on the other; and I feel attached to life only by the feeling of obligation . . . I am in my attic expecting to die there exhausted by work: I thought I would be able to endure it better than I do. For a month now I have been getting up at midnight and going to bed at six in the morning, and I am living on the merest diet enough to keep me alive, so as not to ruin my digestion. Not only do I often feel too weak to write, but so much life swarms in my brain that I have nasty turns. I have fits of giddiness, even when I'm lying down . . . I feel there is an enormous weight on my head.

And nimbly he moves on to pronounce his favourite fantasy, that he is chaste:

I understand now how the absolute continence of Pascal and his huge labour made him feel there was a deep abyss on either side of him and why he had to have two chairs at his side . . .

His health was beginning to give: his breathing became bad; he collapsed on a walk at Saché after receiving her letter, from 'a rush of blood to the head'.

In Paris, the Contessa was persuading her husband to rescue him. The only way to save Bally – she told her husband – was to get him out of the country. The Guidaboni-Viscontis were involved in an old legal squabble in Turin about an inheritance. Balzac was an efficient lawyer and the couple sent him to Turin as their agent. The gossip was that in this period she was nursing his child.

Travel was always good for Balzac's health; he recovered at once: indeed so dramatically that he took a girl on the journey, a pretty and exhibitionist young journalist, Caroline Marbouty. She was to pass as his secretary and being one of the many women who adored the image of George Sand, she travelled with Balzac dressed up as a young man. Balzac got his tailor to fit her out. She wrote to her mother: 'It suits my original turn of mind.' She had long before disposed of a husband.

Like all men of superior intellect, she said, Balzac is very much preoccupied with his ideas and not very lovable . . . His physique is poor and his face, though wonderfully expressive, is bizarre.

One need hardly say she paid for the trip. Only one thing marred the journey – 'my wretched ailment has returned, worse than ever' when they crossed the Alps. In Turin they occupied separate rooms, lived gaily in luxury, and met the distinguished figures of Italian society. Caroline Marbouty was believed to be George Sand in person. Some of this comes out in his novel *le Secret des Ruggieri*, written in 1836. With his knowledge of law, Balzac enjoyed his negotiations – he was always sounder on other people's business affairs than his own – but the matter could not be concluded. He and the girl both swore they had not been lovers on the journey; afterwards the girl boasted that they spent three nights together before it started, but that afterwards she had kept her distance. She had taken up with Balzac in order to push her career and she told her mother that Balzac was kind and frank, but only interested in the future and not with the love of women. He was interested, she said, only in the physical act of sex and that would not satisfy *her* needs.

They returned gaily to Paris after Balzac had taken her to all the spots in Switzerland sacred to his love for Mme Hanska, for he was a man who liked going over old emotional ground. But back in Paris he was shaken by tragedy and remorse: Mme de Berny had died. Her life had been wretched in the last two years. She had left her husband; one of her daughters had gone mad; her favourite son, Armand, had died. She had refused to allow Balzac to come to her becuase of her physical collapse: she hated to be seen as a ravaged dropsical woman, scarcely able to breathe. She had the comfort of reading the idealized portrait of herself he had written in *Le Lys dans la Vallée*. Mme de Montsauf, he wrote, is 'but the pale reflection of the least of her qualities, a distant reflection of her'. (Paris gossip was strangely wrong: it said the original of Mme de Montsauf was the Contessa.) Two days before she died Mme de Berny sent her remaining son to call Balzac to her, but he had already left for Italy with Caroline Marbouty. He was ashamed of his frivolity and shocked when he heard this later. There is a desperate note in his plea to Mme Hanska to stop nagging and believing all the gossip her Aunt Rosalie picks up in Paris privately and in the press. He begs Evelina Hanska to become Mme de Berny's heiress: 'You who have all her noble qualities, you who might have written that letter by Mme de Montsauf, which is an imperfect echo of her invariable wisdom.' He sealed the letter with the seal he used when he wrote to Mme de Berny and if this was a stupid thing to do in his relations with a woman as touchy as Mme Hanska was, it was a sign of his theatrical but nevertheless earnest fervour. The act sprang also from his story-telling instinct – what a dramatic detail! A tale in, say, the love of Dante for Beatrice!

But the shock was greater than he had imagined it would be because it was a shock to the artist as well as to the man. *Le Lys dans la Vallée* is a failure, for the most part, as a poem to Mme de Berny in which the scenes of natural beauty in the valley of the Indre were to be reflected in the souls of the hero and the heroine; the prose was meant to be a kind of music and that, though he struggled to achieve it, was outside his natural gift, which is brusque and explanatory. He must have known that half-falsified reminiscence and confused emotion had put the subject out of focus. He was forcing himself to draw from life, and from his own immediate life and *that* he could not consent to see clearly. He was intelligent enough to see the difference between dissimulation and act. But for the biographer one or two curious facts about Mme de Berny are revealed: as Mme de Montsauf she is a bit of a Polonius in her protectiveness and also the woman of business; she is more agitated by her children than has appeared and there is the extraordinary fact – confirming something in her early letters – that at one time, when she realized she was too old for Balzac, she had proposed that he should marry her daughter. The one perception which seems to have come to Balzac as he looked back upon his romance with the Dilecta is that he and she were, emotionally, children. This seems likely to have been so, and it forces a cloying sentimentality on the book; but clearly from Mme de Berny's protest about the end of the tale she saw the falsity of the passage where the pure Mme de Montsauf is said before her end to feel the fury of repressed sexual desire. After all, Mme de Berny *had* been his mistress. One can see Balzac attempting to face his personal situation with three women in the letter Félix de Vandenesse receives from a woman he is pursuing when Mme de Montsauf is dead:

Poor woman! She suffered much; and you, when you have made a few sentimental speeches, think you have paid your debt over the bier. This is, no doubt, the prize that awaits my affection for you. Thank you, dear Count, but I have no desire for a rival on either side of the grave . . . I asked you a foolish question, it was my part as a woman, as a daughter of Eve. It was your part to calculate the results of the answer. You ought to have deceived me; I would have thanked you for it later . . . Do you know nothing of women? They must have the defects of their qualities . . . We are not such simpletons as you think.

For long afterwards, Balzac speaks of the sudden emptiness in his life and in his unavailing letters to Mme Hanska one sees the desperate appeal of the egotist who is at a total loss. From real life came a very different utterance. Zulma Carraud wrote to him:

I saw a deep wound in your heart and wept with you for the angelic being whose greatest sufferings you ignored. Has there been no reaction in you, Honoré, in your soul? I possess none of her right to speak to you, but on the one hand I am restrained by none of the diffidence which has so often caused her to keep silent. Although you have begged me not to refer to the subject, I must ask you whether, on the day you suffered this mortal blow, you did not realize that there are other things in life besides a pocket knife costing 800 francs and a stick has no other virtue than to attract notice. What a celebrity for the author of *Eugénie Grandet* . . . The life you have betrayed, Honoré, the talent you are stifling at its source . . .

Yet she was wrong: he might be throwing his life away, but his talent thrived on that. It arose from his greed. His imagination was itself a greed. He had come back from Italy recharged with stories good and bad. He was writing *La Vieille Fille* – an addition to his gallery of monstrous virgins – and several other stories.

Balzac's creditors were getting cleverer. One remorseless fellow discovered that the tilbury had been carelessly left in a shed in the rue Cassini and seized it. There was a housekeeper there and her book contains pathetic entries. She had preserved a humble vestige of genuine accountancy:

Feb.	5	To the porter of the Mont de Piété extra money for rush job	1 franc
	6	Carriage to Mont de Piété	4 frcs
		Tip for porter	2 frcs
	7	Porter's fare for message saying tilbury had been seized	1 fr 25
	12	Dinner party, repaid Buisson [the tailor] 20 frcs borrowed.	

The Contessa persuaded her husband to send Balzac to Italy for a second time to continue their negotiations in Milan. The Guidaboni-Viscontis didn't get anything like the sum of 73,760 Milanese livres; but Balzac managed to get them 13,000 less lawyers' fees – and his own expenses. A pickpocket stole his watch.

There were no accompanying ladies this time. Balzac blossomed once more. He was popular in Milan; he was compared with the aurora borealis; a sculptor did a statuette of him in his monk's robe which was intended for Mme Hanska, and Balzac gave it to the Contessa instead. But he offended the Venetians; he spoke unfavourably of Manzoni. They were shocked that he talked continuously of his money affairs. He left for Genoa and there, held up by quarantine, he had one of his fatal encounters. He ran into a speculator called Pezzi who told him that the Romans had left heaps of slag on the surface at their silver mines in Sardinia. All you had to do was to extract the silver from the slag. Fortune! Balzac was captivated. He was now agog to travel to Sardinia the next year; but before that he had to return to Paris. He nearly died getting back across the St Gothard in fifteen feet of snow. One sees the short fat man puffing and freezing with his guides. He wrote about it to Evelina Hanska and added that once he had finished *Les Illusions Perdues* and written a play he would come to the Ukraine. She did not welcome this. She was unwilling to let go of her genius, but she wanted him at arm's length.

The Guidaboni-Viscontis hid him in the Champs-Elysées when he got back, but after a few blessed months of peace, the remorseless creditor who had seized the tilbury made another ingenious move. He sent round his bailiff who pretended that he was a messenger who had come with a valuable Etruscan vase. When the novelist came eagerly to the door, the bailiff grabbed him by the arm: 'I've been nabbed', shouted Balzac. He faced five years in prison. It was serious, for a judge and gendarmes were waiting outside. The Contessa rushed forward and paid up, some say 10,000 francs.

He had had a terrible fright. To show his gratitude to the Contessa he bought a carved and tasselled walking stick for her husband. At this time he was writing *La Femme Supérieur* and *La Maison Nucingen*, also the story called *Massimilla Doni*, the result of his short time in Venice. It is a story about singers and here Balzac had to mug up – there is no other word for it – a number of ideas about music and the relation of the voice to sexual passion. The theme is that excess of passion in an artist may render him impotent with the woman he loves; he can only recover his powers with a woman who loves him but whom he doesn't love. Some tale he had picked up in Venice? Some passing comment on his personal life at the Contessa's? One cannot tell for in his habit of using every drop of himself and mixing it with other persons he became the multifarious novelist and, as Delphine de Girardin said, became less and less visible as a man.

I have got through thirty nights of this damned month [he wrote to Mme Hanska] without, I think, having slept more than sixty hours during the whole time. I haven't been able to shave and now I am against all affection. I have a goat's beard like the young men . . . I must start work again on *César Birotteau* . . . it is ten months since the Figaro paid me for it.

In addition to this a story suggested by his ambitious sister's attempt to push the declining career of her husband had to be done. In the novel the husband is turned into a civil servant and this was quite enough to drive Balzac with his passion for detail to go into the whole question of reorganizing the French civil service. It was a typical expansion of a simple subject into a study of social groups, this time the bureaucrats. That the man who wrote *Massimilla Doni* and the picture of Venice in decline should be capable *at the same time* of going in depth into the question of French bureaucracy is fantastic. His friend Léno Gozlan, in *Balzac en Pantoufles*, said of his novels what was true of Balzac himself:

He was the human encyclopedia by instinct . . . he did not want any fact taken by itself; for him it was part of another fact, and that fact part of a thousand more.

The Novelist Becomes
a Fiction

He was nearing forty and he was exhausting himself. The fits of giddiness came oftener; his hair was greying, his lungs were weakened. He coughed, he said, like an old man and excess of coffee gave him stomach cramps. He told Mme Hanska what a success he had had with the aristocracy in Milan and Venice. Mme Hanska replied meaningly that his Italian friends in Paris were very fortunate to be able to have such a secretary as himself whom they could send anywhere they wished to look after their affairs. How the Hanskis wished they had such an obliging friend. Balzac allowed himself irony in his replies. He rubbed in her piety as a prim Catholic and sent her ten new *Contes Drolatiques* but told her not to read them, for they were not suitable for women, but to hand them to her husband: 'They will cheer him up when he has the "blue devils".'

But if self-induced misfortune shattered the man it always fertilized the novelist. He wrote *Histoire de la Grandeur et de la Décadence de César Birotteau* which is the story of his own case transferred to the life of the simple old perfumer who loses his head, goes into land speculation and is soon ruined by financial rogues. Balzac has gone back to what he knew best: the life of the tradesman and his family. He was paid a huge sum for the book: it was soon swallowed up. One might expect that César Birotteau would have purged him of the insane projects that came into his head; but once the book was written the fever returned and in the very form that had ruined the perfumer: speculation in land.

The idea came out of a very moral decision to change his manner of life. He had now three addresses in Paris, all too hot for him. He must cut Paris out and retire to the simple country life. The thing to do was to sink the Birotteau money in land and to build. After a few years the increase in property values would enable him to pay off what he owed to his mother who was living in poverty: land lies still, one cannot spend it.

Where to find a tranquil but promising spot? Balzac's calculations became astute. He went off to Touraine, but prices were too high. The Railway Age had begun; the value of suburban property was going up. There was a new line in construction from Paris to Ville d'Avray on the route to Versailles. In a month or so the dream budded. Just as the credulous Birotteau had bought land near the Madeleine, Balzac plunged and in 1837 bought a rocky, inaccessible hillside plot for 18,000 francs with a cottage on it, putting 1500 francs down. Who put up the rest? The Guidaboni-Viscontis, of course: the Contessa would do anything for her great and amusing Bally. And in her English way she was practical. A small house at Ville d'Avray would be useful to her and the children in the summer and it was convenient for her husband's orchestra at Versailles. The idea was even more seductive to the lovers: Balzac would put most of his books and furniture into the cottage occasionally occupied by her husband and herself: the bailiffs could not touch what appeared to be theirs. Twenty yards away, he got an architect to build a small, ugly place, scarcely furnished, where he himself could live and work. Later on there are tales that when bailiff-like people were thought to be prowling in the trees, Balzac would rush some of his own valuables into the Guidaboni-Viscontis' place. It was called Les Jardies. On what remained of his earnings from *César Birotteau* he could afford it.

For years, if he had not been Balzac, he could have lived easily on his earnings though, considering his success, he was ill-paid by the standards of the time. (It is reckoned that his books brought him no more than 15,000 francs a year.) The dream of Les Jardies began to blossom and blossoming time was always fatal to his imagination. The little holding was bare. Balzac had visions of it as a large estate planted with fruit trees. He had the notion that he could put down, of all fantastic things, a pineapple plantation on the sunny slopes – but a plantation under glass. Why had no one in France ever thought of a plantation under glass? He became an instant gardener and builder:

I shall buy twenty-year-old magnolias, sixteen-year-old limes, twelve-year-old birches, poplars and so on with clods of earth round.

A new furnishing operation on the scale of the rue des Batailles began, if in a rural manner. Luxuriant and useful Nature was to replace divans and carpets. The place would be another Eden:

I shall also have vines which are brought over in baskets, and will produce grapes this year. Yes, civilization is a wonderful thing! It is true that today the ground is as bare as the palm of one's hand, but by May there will be an amazing transformation. I must acquire another two acres nearby for kitchen gardens, fruit trees and so on, for which I need 30,000 francs, but this sum I propose to earn in the winter.

He described the house he was building as having three storeys:

A staircase almost like a ladder leads from one storey to the next. Right round the house runs a covered gallery . . . supported on brick pilasters. The whole of this little pavilion has an Italian look . . . There is just room for me in this house of mine.

But there comes word of servants' quarters, sixty paces away, stables, harness rooms, guest rooms. The place is getting larger. There was going to be a stone gate and a green arcade leading to the front door. Walls – for defence – had to be built round the property.

People who came to see him during the long building period could hardly hide their laughter. His ugly little house stuck up out of the clay, among two or three skinny trees, like an empty birdcage. It was noted that the staircase was outside! The clay soil softened in the rain: his retaining wall fell down. And when rebuilt fell down again. The ground had not been properly surveyed. The hill was steep. No trees would take root. Yet he stuck to his scheme for the pineapple plantation and Gautier and he even searched for a shop in Montmartre where he would sell the pineapples at 5 francs a time and make 400,000 francs on the crop. If ever a great novelist was a shopkeeper it was this descendant of shopkeepers. His furnishings of his birdcage took a new form. On the walls he wrote in charcoal: here an Aubusson tapestry; here a ceiling painted by Delacroix; here a fireplace in cipollino marble; here a Trianon mirror.

Suddenly he realized he was poor again: he had sunk his large earnings in property. Property is not cash. He had added 50,000 francs to his debts. This astonishing discovery came to him while the workmen were still building his hermitage. He went off to work at Saché or with the Carrauds at Le Frapesle. But instantly he saw, in a new vision, the solution to his difficulty. The old lesson of his failure as a printer came back to him: to save the printing business he had doubled his stake and started the type-foundry. Always expand; always extend. If he could not corner the pineapple market, there were always those Sardinian silver mines he had heard about in Genoa, at his meeting with the strange fellow called Pezzi.

At the Carrauds, where he was still working on *Les Illusions Perdues*, he got Carraud's opinion. He supported Balzac's plan, which was to join Pezzi and take over a group of the silver slag-heaps. Mad as the idea sounds, it was really excellent and – in other more patient hands, of course – was bound to be very profitable. The enterprise followed Balzac's usual course. He scraped together a few hundred francs by the sale of some jewellery, crawled to his mother who, poor though she was, was always ready for a specu-lation. (Honoré was her only hope now.) And he got 100 francs out of her. Once more he climbed on the luggage-seat of the diligence for Marseilles. The journey took five days. In March 1838 he was in the city. He wrote to Zulma Carraud:

In a day I shall unfortunately lose one more illusion, for the moment one reaches the point of success, one loses faith in it . . . It appears that what one suffers from being energetic is far greater than what one suffers from a sluggish liver.

To his mother from Marseilles:

Now I am nearly there [Sardinia], I begin to have a thousand doubts, but one cannot risk less if one needs more. I am in a terrible hotel – if I fail, a very few nights of writing will make up my losses.

He sailed to Ajaccio where he was stuck without a boat to get across to the other island. He spent his time sketching out the plot of a play called *La Première Demoiselle* and reading *Clarissa Har-lowe* and *Grandison* in the public library. The books bored him. One day he rushed into the street – dressed in a sort of cloak and red velvet knickerbockers – to rescue a donkey that was being attacked by dogs and some Army officers had to rescue him. The local garrison asked him to dinner: conversation was, of course, about Napoleon. At last he found a crew of coral fishermen who took him on a little fishing-boat to Alghiero – it took five days and he slept on deck. They lived on the fish they caught and ate horrible bread that tasted like clay. At Alghiero there was a four-day quarantine for anyone coming from Marseilles – cholera had broken out there – and he lay on deck eaten alive by mosquitoes. The poverty, the lack of food depressed him, as he went first on an awful diligence and then rode thirty miles on horseback across the mountains to the site of the Roman mines. He arrived to see the entrances to the mines blocked in by vegetation and landslides: the depressed and exhausted novelist realized he was no mining engineer, despite the good report on his samples. Worse, Pezzi had long before got a licence to open the mines and had even formed a syndicate. Balzac was once more shown to be an incompetent businessman in practice. He had forgotten about licences and called Pezzi a rogue. Pezzi, not Balzac, made the fortune. He crawled back to Milan where the Guidaboni-Visconti bankers rescued him and a Prince Procia compassionately gave him a little room to work in: he had returned to be the secretary of history.

He was approaching forty, worn out, in low spirits. The Duchesse d'Abrantès, to whom he had occasionally written when she implored him, and who had been his chief source of inspiration for his Napoleonic tales, having in this a direct influence on his writing, had died in poverty and misery. There is a curious passage in one of his letters after hearing the news:

What I need is a priest's life, simple and quiet. A woman of thirty with three or four thousand francs and who liked me, provided she was gentle and nice to look at, would suit me as a wife. She would have to pay off my debts and in five years my work would pay her back. This calls for an enormous sacrifice, but it would be better to marry than to perish and my life span is uncertain ... it is impossible at my age to do the enormous amount of work I have to do, without turning to other forms of exhaustion and this amounts to death.

But back at Les Jardies he fussed with the builders and recovered. He finished the second part of *Les Illusions Perdues*.

Mme Hanska wrote asking for George Sand's autograph and was very alarmed when Balzac – no sooner home than restless – went to stay with the novelist at Nohant. He and she had been on uneasy terms because he had taken in Jules Sandeau at the rue Cassini, but that was now smoothed over. Balzac went to Nohant because he had a nose for a story. What had really happened when George Sand had seen Liszt go off with Marie d'Agoult? His gift for worming the intimate secrets out of women was reawakened. What was the secret of the dedicated Republican Comrade George Sand? He found her alone smoking a cigar by her fireside, wearing embroidered yellow slippers and red trousers. She had a double chin, like a cathedral canon's, fine eyes, but a look of stupidity when she was thinking. They sat up talking till five in the morning. The tête-à-tête went on for three days and Balzac hastened to tell Mme Hanska that George Sand was essentially a man: tall, generous, devout, chaste – 'ergo, not a woman'. He pointed out – a hint to Mme Hanska – that she had paid off all the debts Musset had piled up before he became her lover. 'People who have great and beautiful souls recognize that her follies are really her claim to fame.'

She taught him – though he hated tobacco – to smoke Latakia in a hookah and it put him into a dream-like state in which he was instantly acquisitive. He asked Mme Hanska to send him one of these pipes and five or six pounds of Latakia 'for I have few opportunities for getting it direct from Constantinople'. And, always wanting something extra, he added:

If the hookah is decorated with turquoise so much the better, I'll send you a pearl necklace in exchange. How about it? If you love me, you'll say Yes.

He got George Sand's permission to write the story of her involvement in the Liszt-Marie d'Agoult affair: George Sand wanted revenge on Marie d'Agoult. The novel called *Béatrix* was the result. It is one of Balzac's unbelievable exercises in sophistication; it also splits in two. For between finishing the first part and the second, six years went by; and Balzac's love affair with a new lady, Hélène de la Valette, is dragged in. She had visited him several times at Les Jardies and they went off to Brittany together. Hélène, of course, lent him 10,000 francs. The affair seems to have stopped and started again, and lasted on and off for years. She was a nymphomaniac and a liar, but although he half-detested her, it drifted on.

Béatrix is dedicated to Sarah. What the Contessa thought about such escapades is not known. She is said to have been an inexhaustibly good-humoured woman and to have been mostly concerned with the practical business of helping him and asked no questions. She was certainly a refuge in that long period when the Hanska dream had almost faded away. And although careless of appearances, she knew how to be discreet and how much, like a woman, Balzac enjoyed secrets – her enemies called her cunning. She certainly schemed for him. In dedicating the book to her, he wrote:

Under the shelter of this brief concealment, your superb hands may bless it, your noble brow may bend and dream over it, your eyes, full of motherly love, may smile on it since you are here present and veiled ... Like that gem of the ocean garden you will dwell on the fine, white level sand, hidden by a wave that is transparent only to certain friendly and reticent eyes.

He says he is

... gratifying one of your instincts by offering you something to protect.

Balzac knew how to please women. He was always appreciative of their clothes and flattered them by openly coveting their furnishings. After the visit to Nohant he saw George Sand many times in Paris in the company of Chopin – whose playing bored him – and was enraptured by her dark, carved oak dining room, her *café-au-lait* boudoir, her pictures by Delacroix, and her bric-à-brac: she was a best-seller.

He had spent wildly at Les Jardies. He turned to write for the theatre: that was where successful contemporaries like Dumas and Hugo had made their fortunes. But if he knew how to write novels he did not know how to write plays. His plots and situations were theatrical enough, especially when he was writing badly, but his discursiveness, his passion for detail, his endless dialogue got in the way. He was a born explainer and lacked the gift of omission and suggestion. Also his reckless promising and his methods of work were against him. In a five-act play the fourth would be missing. He was annoyed when asked for it and would deliver nothing but scribbled-out notes. Still, he was a learner. One subject seemed a certain winner – *Vautrin*. This reached performance, but the leading actor took it into his head to caricature Louis-Philippe and the police closed the show down. It was followed by the *Ressources de Quinola* and here – brazenly out for the money – Balzac intervened in the sale of tickets. He bought up whole blocks himself in order to resell them at a profit! The first act succeeded, but in the following nights the theatre was a riot of cat-calls and hisses. As for the ticket-selling intrigue, he soon lost what profit there was in it. He had been too grasping – or was it that he was simply arrogant and thought that since he was famous Paris owed him a fortune?

The dream of Les Jardies was coming to an end. The Guidaboni-

Viscontis began to spend more time *en famille* at what was, after all, their house. The 'superb hands' of the Contessa perhaps became too caressing in the long evenings of suburban life and in her daily caresses – Balzac said – a woman is the enemy of the Muse. A wife or mistress always ended by being jealous of the time he spends on his works. She knows that work is the real mistress. There is a suspicion that boredom settled on Balzac and the Contessa when at last life at Les Jardies became domestic. The excitement had been in secret meetings and absences.

And then Balzac's extravagance at the place brought about a decisive crisis. The Contessa rescued him again and again but nothing could save him. He was, to put it mildly, tricky about money and even *her* devotion was strained. The butchers' and bakers' and servants' bills were unpaid. The inevitable carpets had cost him 5600 francs. He owed his tailor 11,700. His advances from the Mont de Piété were 3000 francs. He still owed 12,000 francs on the débâcle of the *Chronique de Paris*. Les Jardies now cost 55,000. He owed 15,000 to the Guidaboni-Viscontis; 30,000 to old Mme Delannoy, 2500 to his sister; 500 to Dablin; 40,000 to his mother. Well over 200,000 francs. And there was 30 francs to the watchman. Balzac used to hide behind bushes to avoid paying him. He hated small debts.

Seizures began. A bailiff who had managed to creep up the rocky slopes surrounding the property got in and managed to snatch some chairs, a candelabra, bedding, a table, a hat, and three pairs of boots which had not been smuggled in time into the Guidaboni-Visconti house. There were other comedies. Balzac was unmoved. Debt was really activity; it simply inspired him. But at last a tougher and more ingenious creditor saw that the Conte Guidaboni-Visconti was the vulnerable point in Balzac's defences. He brought an action against the Conte for concealing Balzac's belongings in his own house and depriving the creditors of their security. This was too much for the Contessa. It was not fair play to drag her husband into trouble with the law. She broke with her Bally – though, a long time afterwards, the couple again lent him a large sum. The sale of Les Jardies was inevitable. He tricked again. The place on which he had spent altogether 100,000 francs fetched 17,550. But the buyer was Balzac's proxy called Claret. The creditors had to accept what they could get and Balzac now remained the secret owner – in debt to the Guidaboni-Viscontis who did not ask yet for their money.

There was nothing for it but to vanish again. This time he fled to Passy. To find him at the little chalet on the hill in the rue Basse one knocked at the door and asked for Mme de Brugnol, a housekeeper, who would always deny that a M. de Balzac lived there.

Love as Destiny and Railway Shares

Balzac had shown himself to be a man who never willingly let go of anything: he kept pages of writing against a rainy day, he corrected, recorrected, patched, added, brought old things up to date. No tapestry was more dense, more expanding than his. He dropped women, but somehow kept a connecting thread. And, above all, he held on for years to his hiding places. While he was at Les Jardies he had not only his room at Saché, but some sort of lien on the rue des Batailles, and the room at his tailor's in the rue de Richelieu. Even now when he had to get out of Les Jardies he left his furniture, books, and bibelots with the Contessa. At first the new hiding place in the rue Basse on the outskirts of Paris at Passy – it is now the rue Raynouard and the house is the Balzac Museum – was scantily furnished. It is the only house of his that survives. The chalet, surrounded by trees and gardens, had belonged to the patron of Watteau. It appears to hang like a half-concealed cage from the cliff overlooking the Seine, between an upper and lower street; with the classic Balzacian convenience of entrances in the two streets, it is a discreet symbol of Balzac's talent for the double life.

He occupied the top floor approached from the rue Basse. One can still see the concealed door by which he escaped down steep stairs to the back door; in his day the smells of suds and the noise of a laundry came up from below him and there were families of shouting children in the slummy lane. It was common to see him puffing and stumbling over the stones of the lane when he came back by the ramshackle local bus along the quays from Paris. In the room where he worked was the portrait of Mme Hanska, a painting of her house at Wierzchownia, some picture-frames and unframed pictures stacked against the wall, two bookcases with one or two reference books, and a small work-table with a dictionary on it. Luxury no more. And no sign of titled ladies. Printers' boys, publishers, theatre people who found out where he was were met by Mme Brugnol, the housekeeper, a tall woman of forty who looked like a robust and rosy nun and had a peasant's sly smile. She was a homely, busy, stubborn soul who had made a profession of being the housekeeper-mistress of writers down on their luck. Compared with the other ladies who had been in his bed, Mme Brugnol had the distinction of being penniless. At the time when he fled from Les Jardies, leaving heavy debts to the butcher, the grocer and the stonemason and gardener, he had gone off to buy Mme Brugnol a brooch. So a transaction was settled. And, to keep up his standards, he added the 'de' to her name. She expected to be his mistress for life or so, she said, he led her to believe. Very little is known about her except that in the course of time she fought for her rights, contributed something to the pathos of social history, and emerged victorious from her troubles. But in the early Passy days she was a devoted servant. Devotion to Balzac did not pay.

Mme Balzac could not get on with her when she came to stay, but approved of her. She said: 'I hope that Honoré will make her life secure as soon as he can do so. It will only be fair, because she curbs his spending and saves him from many follies.'

What Mme Brugnol thought of the portrait of Mme Hanska was yet to be seen. For Balzac the picture had hardened into a memory to which he had become almost indifferent. He wrote fitfully to her; she, deceived so often, had written only once in 1841. That year he was forty-two and he was frightened by the loss of his youth. He had still not succeeded in the theatre. Pulling himself together he saw that the best thing he could do was to reorganize the collected edition of his novels and stabilize the idea of eight years ago: *La Comédie Humaine*. Before he had not hit upon a good general title, but now a friend who had been reading Dante's *Divine Comedy* returned from Italy and gave him the superb idea. Not the divine, but the human. It was an exact definition.

The pressing impulse behind the revived idea was commercial. It was a means of getting a good price for a reissued work, for he had been careful to keep his copyrights – and of being paid well for the novels still needed to fill the large gaps in the design. He found an eager publisher and a good lawyer. Severe restrictions were placed in his contracts on the cost of corrections – even so, out of a first advance of 15,000 francs he had to pay out over 5000 for these. His spirits quickened and, ever a man for programmes since his printing days, he wrote the famous *Avant-Propos* for the work. There were gaps in the edifice and also oddities: he had written all kinds of stories, often in response to the needs of editors. Now he would have to change more names, write linking stories. His studies of provincial and Parisian life, his philosophical tales, his studies of the passions, had certainly been the work of a social biologist who 'is drawing in infinite detail the true history of the morals and beliefs of our modern society . . . ', the history ignored by the historians, but now he was emboldened to state the usefulness of Catholicism, his firm, conservative belief in monarchy, his support of the rights of property, and his theories relating to the mysterious electric or magnetic fluid that binds animal and spiritual creation. The document was a manifesto, for once more the opportunist was tempted by political life. He had the passing hope of being elected to the Chamber of Deputies and he was putting himself forward as a tentative candidate to possible backers. They did not appear. But he checked the note of exorbitance in the *Avant-Propos* – his publishers told him to be modest – and the temperament of the artist emerges with dignity and insight:

Chance is the greatest of all novelists. In order to be creative one has only to study it. French society is the real historian, and I have merely tried to guide its pen.

But ambition could not be kept out:

. . . to produce for the France of the nineteenth century, a work such as has unfortunately not been bequeathed to posterity by Rome, Athens, Memphis, Persia or India.

Mme de Balzac was sixty-two and as restless as her son. She moved from pensions to her daughter's house; then took rooms with friends and went back to pensions. She wrote a pathetic letter of appeal to her son: she did not know where to turn and had received no money for twenty-seven months. He took her in at the rue Basse, but she could not 'stand the daily upsets and storms' of his life there. Nor could he stand her and she quarrelled with Mme Brugnol. His mother was a borrower too. She owed a large sum to her old lover,

M. de Margonne. She left the rue Basse trying to get a promise from her son that he would pay at least the arrears of interest on his long debt – all she had received over the years was 600 francs.

At this time Balzac was working on four books more or less at once: one was a politico-historical work, *Une Ténébreuse Affaire*, and another, much closer in one respect to the kind of domestic conflict about money which he knew by heart, *La Rabouilleuse*. It is one of his stories of sexual exploitation: the corrupting of a young girl who in turn corrupts and destroys the impotent son of the man who has corrupted her. She and a new lover rob him of everything and she ends her life eaten up by disease on the streets of Paris. But the whole is contained by a situation similar to Balzac's in his relations with his mother and his brother Henri. The widow Agathe Bridau has two sons: one, Philippe, the favourite who drifts into dissipation and villainy when he leaves the Army, and unable to get a job, ruins his mother; the other, a puritanic and dedicated artist, whom his mother despises. He reminds one a little of Delacroix in his puritan reserve. The gradual development of Philippe's character from that of the young Napoleonic veteran trained to kill in war, into the profligate remittance man who in peace becomes a villain, is wonderfully done, for Balzac is a master of showing how the climate of society works upon private passions. Brave as a soldier, Philippe is demoralized by peace and the new order. Vice and virtue are shown springing from the same source. There is compassion in Balzac's impartial words about Agathe Bridau: 'Nous avons tous notre passion malheureuse.' The bearing of contemporary history is conveyed with Balzac's sardonic, abrupt precision. For example, when he stayed with the Carrauds he found out everything about a group of half-pay officers who, after the Restoration, played lawless and cunning practical jokes on the town of Issoudun – farces that ended in murder. Balzac understands the difference between ingenious local hooligans and the master scoundrel down from Paris. The episode is brilliant as a piece of story-telling and is close observation of post-war anarchy.

When one looks from Balzac's life to his novels, one sees that his sense of what life is like is far, far stronger in them. In his own life, neither himself nor the people he moves among make more than a shifting general impression; once he left that little work-table he was no more than a bizarre occurrence or, so to say, a human 'untruth' who has no sense of the reality of people about him unless they are useful to him. In the interest of his genius they had to be squeezed dry. The famous impatient sentence – spoken to someone who had talked about a tragic family death: 'Let's get back to reality – Who is going to marry Eugénie Grandet?' is no joke. The only reality (*his* only reality) was his appetite for what he could imagine.

In Passy he was subdued but stoical. His lawyer was trying to sort out his affairs. He was still hoping that success in the theatre would bring him the fortune other writers were making there, and in one way Passy was better than Les Jardies. It was closer to Paris. This was important because in order to fulfil the grandiose plan of *La Comédie Humaine* to which, apart from revisions, he had to add four new works a year, he was obliged to go out to Laguy and work at the printers. They were a lazy, genial body of men and one had to be on the spot and even bribe them to get the work done. Mme Brugnol was not only a housekeeper: she had to deal with editors and publishers for him as well.

But he never lost belief in Bedouck, the talisman. Magic was not really superstition to him; he enacted it as a novelist every day. But why did the mysterious fluids of magic not offer him Fortune out of the skies? Why never the coup? He was in the habit of going to fortune-tellers in Paris and some time in this grinding year he went off on the impulse to see Balthazar, the fashionable crystal-gazer. The man was also in the abortion business, as it ultimately turned out, and had not yet foreseen his own bad end. He amazed Balzac by the accuracy of an account of his past life and struggles. Soon – Balthazar said – the tale of defeat was going to end. A sensational event would change his fortunes completely. It could happen 'in a six' – six days, weeks, or months. Sure enough (though like anyone else Balzac squared the dates) the sensation came. In the freezing February of 1842 Balzac suddenly felt a blaze of fire in his body. A black-bordered envelope arrived from the Ukraine. He opened it to find a formal announcement saying M. Hanski was dead.

He gazed, stunned, at the portrait of Mme Hanska on the wall and on the little picture of the great house at Wierzchownia. He was incapable of speech all day. He rushed out at last dazed into the bitter cold and yet he was still throbbing with heat. Ten years had passed since he and Mme Hanska had made their vow: eight years since they had met in Vienna. The portrait that contained a memory gone flat now suddenly came to life. She was the *épouse d'amour*, the mistress-wife at last. The dream was reborn.

He wrote a letter of sympathy. Now, he said, he could write to her freely, with open heart. Their misunderstanding would vanish. But he noticed there was no personal word for him in the message.

Oh write and tell me that you are now mine totally, that we shall be happy and nothing will cloud our happiness . . . How often, in the midst of my bitterest moments, in my struggles and misfortunes, I have turned toward the North – which is for me the Orient, peace and happiness . . . My angel, my heavenly flower, in everything you want me to do I will follow your wishes.

In a few weeks his work will be over and then he will go at once to Germany to lessen the distance between them and wait until she calls him to her. He changes from the semi-invalid of his last letters to a man with only one or two grey hairs: heart and body are young – due to his monastic life! – and he can look forward to another fifteen years of vigour.

The effect of her news was overwhelming. For years he had rarely needed to sleep more than five hours a day: now, every day, he fell fast asleep for fourteen hours. Work did not interest him. He was too dazed to think: he simply thought of nothing but the life that would be his and hers.

Her next letter was a shock. Curtly she told him that neither he nor she had any further obligation to each other. She had no wish to see him. Year after year, she said, he had deceived her with other women and had lied to her. He could easily have visited her but instead he had gone off to Italy with other women. He had bound himself to that hateful English Contessa. His troubles were due to extravagance and debauchery.

The shock, terrible though it was, might have been shrugged off by a libertine, but for the first time since the death of Mme de Berny, Balzac was fatally in love. That is to say, the whole of his nature was engaged. A man of strong sexual appetite and susceptible imagination, he easily felt desire; his many love affairs released his energies as a man and an artist. They both distracted him and united him, while they lasted, to the common human experience, until the time came to shut the study door. They did not weld together his whole nature; for (as he constantly said in letters and in the scenes of his novels) if artists are dangerous to women – although artists alone understand them – women are intolerable in the end because they are by nature jealous of any interest that is not directed exclusively to themselves. Love for Balzac until now was sexual desire, supreme while it lasted, but no more than ordinary necessity. To be transcendent, to fulfil the whole man love meant the fulfilment of desire *and* ambition. Love was not love unless it was destiny, with all the possibly tragic overtones of that word. One was made strong and dominant when one was ruled by a power stronger than oneself. Distance and wealth had given Mme Hanska the force of a vision. To lose her now she had become free, near, and real would be a catastrophic failure.

Balzac turned to his great exemplar: Napoleon. Napoleon, the strategist, the diplomat, the master who had magnetized Europe and conquered by the sword. Balzac would have to magnetize by the pen, but not in fiction: this time, exhaustively committed, in real life. He settled down to a campaign which, in its way, is a personal counterpart to *La Comédie Humaine*. It took the form of a ceaseless and ever-resourceful barrage of scores, indeed hundreds of letters. They were not simply love letters, sent to entangle the fancy and ram feeling home; they were directed to her interests as a harassed widow; they went into the detail of her life at Wierzchownia, as if he had planted himself there domestically and as of right. He placed himself beside her in her difficulties. He no longer denied his infidelities. He had broken with the Contessa before her letter came – though he did not tell her of the unbroken financial entanglement which would go on for years. He flattered Mme Hanska's prejudices, warned her of the dangers of mysticism to a Catholic soul. He enormously flattered her desire to rule, and even absurdly overdid it by comparing their relationship to that of Prince Albert and Queen Victoria; fortunately she had little sense of the ridiculous. Once more – but now without the old irony of the gallant – he called himself her serf. He humbled himself, agreed, teased in a fashion that strikes one, and may have struck her, as unmanly: this in the long run may have been fatal to his complete success. However, his presumption, or what he thought of as 'taking the ascendancy' in any conflict, did enable him to make himself seem necessary and impartial in the unexpected difficulties of her position. There was in Balzac that solid core of common sense. But his confessions did not allay her jealousies. She exacted more and Balzac was driven not only to destroy the images of the women who had been his mistresses, but even to turn on Mme de Berny and his mother. Mme de Berny, he said, had avenged all the sufferings inflicted on her by her Corsican lover by inflicting them on him! Once more one sees how naturally the preoccupation with revenge comes out. It is disturbing to see him crawling in this treacherous way in order to placate his torturer. He went even further when, adding to the familiar tale that he had neither mother nor childhood, he said, 'My mother ruined me in 1827', when it was he who had ruined his mother, had never paid his capital debt and had, in his wild career of extravagance, scarcely paid anything to keep her alive.

If you only knew what my mother is like. She is a monster and a monstrosity. At this very moment she is killing my sister, Laure, as she killed Laurence . . . We have often thought her insane but a doctor who has been treating her for the last thirty-three years saw her the other day and said 'No she is not insane. She is just wicked' . . . My mother has been the cause of all the evils that have fallen on me.

One is used to the fantastic Balzac; but at the beginning of the siege of Mme Hanska, a sickness appears. One is at the beginning of a long suspicion that the diagnosis in *La Peau de Chagrin* is true: those who live entirely by intellect and imagination destroy themselves.

Why did Mme Hanska not break? Why did she waver? Was she torturing him? Did the campaign weaken her? Did she love him at all? Had she loved him at all? Two years passed before she consented to see him. About the love there has always been a question. In the years of separation from Balzac what love she had she gave to her only daughter. Her initial coldness was perhaps due to a natural grief at her husband's death, and to the difficulties of her position. Her family in the Ukraine knew all about the affair with Balzac and were afraid that she was going to be mad enough to throw herself away on the vulgar little Frenchman who was obviously after her money. And one of their first acts was to see that she had no control of her property. They succeeded in getting the marriage settlement annulled, and put her possessions in the administration of the Court of Nobles. To Balzac this was medieval barbarism and he urged her to appeal to the Supreme Court in St Petersburg, for Poland was under the absolute rule of the Tsar. The sensible plan, Balzac the lawyer wrote, was to separate her part of the estate from that of her brothers and her daughter and for her to live on the still very large income that would be left. He advised her to preserve and increase her personal savings; and since the rich are commonly frightened by money, she saw the force of that. So, still evading him, still accusing, but now involved in his campaign and, to that extent, weakened by a master of diplomacy even if wryly amused and confused by it, she took her case to St Petersburg.

It was central to Balzac's method as a propagandist to assume that, once the difficulties are removed, he and she will be married, as *equals*, that is his contracts will have paid off his own debts. His letters drift into his familiar day-dream accountancy, and if one speculates on Balzac's sanity or, at any rate, on the fevered anxiety in his mind, it is because the master of documentation now rambles almost to the point of salivation when he is playing with figures. He imagines her living in Paris:

Listen, dearest soul of my soul, I am not a man of extravagant tastes; for the great – and I consider myself great – there is a choice between two ways of life. Live in style, like people who have 100,000 a year or simply what I can't stand – nor could you – the half-and-half middle-class style. You can live in a suburb on 12,000 a year, with only two servants and be respectable. But when I say 12,000 a year I mean, add to this a house, setting it up and running it. However, I have 80,000 francs of furniture myself. [Where? At the Guidaboni-Viscontis – that is to say what had not been seized by creditors.] Between 12,000 francs a year and 60,000 for two people, husband and wife, there are of course other possibilities, but they have their vexations: one is liable to sink to the level of those middle-class people who hanker after luxury and float uncomfortably between economy and extravagance. Life really is without worries in Paris on 60,000 a year providing you run things properly . . . Let us suppose you have 800,000 francs in cash and you intend to live in France, this is what you would have to do to live well and at your ease. First you buy a small property for 300,000 francs where you spend seven months of the year which will bring you in 10,000 income; but you and your family will be able to live on 7,000 francs for seven months. You sink 100,000 francs into a house in Paris and live there five months in the winter; and having done that you put the 400,000 that is left into French funds to cover your four winter months which will cost you 15,000 francs.

Happiness and security for 800,000 francs: the subject entrances him, as it might have entranced Micawber. He drifts on into detail. In the winter it costs 5000 francs to keep a carriage; meals 5000, clothes and amusements 5000. General expenses 2000 and 2000 left for exceptional expenses. Still:

May be the best thing is to have a house in the country, as Lamartine does and his income is only 50,000.

Mme Hanska pondered the love: she was alarmed by the accountancy which was now mentioned in almost every letter. It too was a
passion. The love, though pleasant enough to listen to, could be
rather too blatant. She was annoyed by his latest novel, *Albert
Savarus*, which gave an obvious and intimate account of their early
days by the lake in Geneva. That was taking propaganda too far.
The family were appalled by the publicity. She had written to her
brother, before her husband's death and before she knew about the
Contessa, a statement of her confused feelings. She loved Balzac, she
said at this time, but she was glad she was not compelled to decide:

His letters are the great event in my life of solitude. I await them
impatiently, I want to read in their pages all the admiration with which
they are filled, and I am proud of being something which no woman has
ever been to him before. For he is a genius, one of the greatest that
France has produced; and when I remember this, every other consideration
disappears and melts into the pride which suffuses my soul at the thought
of having won his love, though I am so unworthy of him. When we are
alone together I cannot avoid noticing certain incongruities and suffering
from the thought that others too may observe them and draw their own
conclusions . . . but perhaps I am glad I do not have to make up my mind.

If M. Hanski were to die, she hoped, she said, that she would know
how to do her duty. She felt this all the more strongly now. While
Balzac slaved at books he no longer wanted to write very much and
was afflicted by neuralgia, breathlessness, and headaches, she went
to St Petersburg and forbade him to come there.

Unwisely Balzac had given Liszt, who was then performing in St
Petersburg, an introduction to her, forgetting that Liszt made love
to every woman he met. Liszt at once began a courtship that startled
her and impressed her, though she rejected him; but an odd thing
happened. Hearing love spoken by a man of genius in person fav-
oured Balzac's cause. Liszt stirred her senses, the current of desire
began to flow. Suddenly she sent for Balzac. He was mad with
excitement and penniless, of course. The Secretary of the Russian
Embassy reported his application for a passport. 'Enter', he said, 'a
little fat man, greasy, with the face of a baker, the clothes of a
cobbler, the hide of a cooper, the manners of a stocking salesman
and the smock of an innkeeper.' Balzac scraped together some money
from his publishers and took the boat from Dunkirk. The month
was July. Buisson, the tailor, had disguised the innkeeper: Balzac was
dressed in a black frock-coat, a brown jacket, black satin trousers, a

white satin waistcoat. (This raised his debt to Buisson by 800 francs to 14,000, unpaid for seven years.) In addition, he had spent 800 francs on several rings, tie-pins, and a good watch-chain.

Bedouck had a sense of humour. Balzac found Mme Hanska was staying with her daughter in grandeur in the street called Grande Millionne. He arrived with a migraine, worn out, and was put in a modest lodging where he was eaten alive by bed bugs. What happened when the lovers met at last, after ten years? No one knows. All we know is that she had grown stout and he swore she was as young as ever. And he was very fat indeed. A disillusion? No. He wrote a charming compliment in her album and his voice had its effect on her. They went little into society so that she would not be affected by his 'incongruities'; here, outside her own country and home, she could gather the tributes paid to his genius as somehow part of his tribute to her. The recriminations of Vienna did not recur; they both read Goethe and Balzac could rely on his physical presence having its effect. Physical love was decisive; it was only when she was away from him that the spell went and irritability and suspicion returned.

He called her his Loup. They called themselves the Loup-Loups. When he worked up an enthusiasm for despotism and the Russian Tsar she had to remind him she was a Pole and a Catholic. They agreed that once she had won her case – which she eventually did – and once she had got her adored daughter married, their own marriage might be considered. He had to be content with that and went off dressed up in Russian furs, after twelve days. On his way home he stopped at Dresden to look at the Rubens 'because they remind me of a certain Eve'. Not altogether tactful. The only bad thing to happen to him in Russia was that he had got sunstroke at a military review and this had consequences. It revived the mysterious symptoms of his boyhood illness at Vendôme. During his breakdown at school he had had 'congestion of the brain' that had affected his powers of speech and given him hallucinations. Was that illness at the bottom of a congenital instability of mind or body? Years of overwork had made him liable to an inflammation of the membranes that enclose the brain. When he got back to Paris the old family doctor recommended leeches. Balzac's digestion was disordered too. He was glad to do no work for a month.

The Last Orgy of a
Spendthrift

It has been said that neither overwork nor the poisoning of the body by overdoses of coffee that kept him going at night, nor the pursuit of money, killed Balzac; that he was a man who was killed by love. In 1844, the year following the reunion in St Petersburg, he was forty-five and the strange, tragic pattern of the grand love affair was established. It is a story of ecstatic meetings and (for him) of absences that drained the will to live. In his love affairs of the past, even in his love for Mme de Berny, it was he who had evaded and had gone off; in this grand passion, Mme Hanska evaded him, always at the moment when he thought everything was on the point of being settled. The sign of his total committal was that henceforth there would be no line drawn between the realities of his life and the obsessive imagination of the novelist: his life became completely a fiction. The five years after St Petersburg are a novel by Balzac in every detail – even, in the end, the melodrama was not excluded. He invented and wrote best when his erotic impulses were roused and satisfied. Now, in the crisis of middle age, when Mme Hanska's absences deprived him and when he was uncertain of her love, he became so sexually obsessed that the imagination was paralysed.

When he got back to Paris from Russia, if there were any letters from Mme Hanska, they were once more short and without tenderness. Balzac was baffled by her coldness and he wrote:

The long wait in my heart and the dream of happiness has destroyed more in me than I could have believed . . . I am torn at the very root of my life to the point of dying of it. Uncertainty works into every detail of my life:

there is only one word to describe my situation: 'I am burning myself up' – *je me consume.*

Mme Hanska had gone to Dresden with her daughter and she ordered him not to join her there. 'As roughly as a Cossack', he said. She was annoyed to be compared to 'such savages' and he had to take it back. So a battle of rare letters, vague invitations and curt refusals of anything he proposed began once more. Mme Hanska has been accused of cruelty and of unfeeling coquetry and there was indeed a vein of cruelty in her, as Balzac had seen: she went from languor to temper in a flash. Perhaps like him she was sexually greedy and, once satisfied, went dead. She was a prudent and orderly widow, harassed by her relatives and by no means free. She had – one must remember – a swarm of powerful relatives in Dresden, a city full of Poles and notoriously given to gossip and ridicule, and she was nervous of public opinion. She was looking for an aristocratic husband for her daughter, a matter she took earnestly for she had put all her feeling into seeing that her daughter's marriage should not be as unhappy as her own had been. She had found a young man, Count Mniszech, who seemed possible and in this critical moment in which family prestige and councils were important she was afraid that the loud, unrestrained Balzac, who knew nothing of Polish susceptibilities, would interfere and spoil everything. After all he was not a rich landowner; only the rich understand the values and practices of the rich.

In the rue Basse, Balzac was left to his tortures. Now by an effort of will he turned once more to the congested burden of the fictions in his head. He sweated through the final and dullest part of *Les Illusions Perdues* – the troubles of the inventor, the most minutely documented part of that book, and concerned with the manufacture of paper. The novel, at any rate, reconnected him with his early life as a printer and he dragged in the melodramatic figure of Vautrin to liven things up. He was also writing his *Splendeurs et Misères des Courtisanes* (pure sensational Eugène Sue, he said), but it was more agreeable, he said, to write about the Parisian demi-monde than his other subject, *Les Paysans*, a long complex novel about the greed and corruption of the land-hungry French peasantry. They were the Grandets of France. In all these novels human rapacity and desire for power is the subject. *Les Paysans* had been in his head for years; it was an important part of *La Comédie Humaine* and he had reckoned it would run to eight volumes. He had often listened carefully to M. Hanski on the habits of the Polish peasantry and what Balzac heard he infallibly stored in his mind. The book was being serialized quite profitably and he was struggling, but without the old *élan*, to compress it into three volumes. Already the first instalments were boring the readers of *La Presse* in which it was appearing. (It was never finished by him, though Mme Hanska patched it together, very conscientiously, after his death.) Every night the load of words, scenes, and people filled the emptiness of his own life with an imaginary society that poured through him and entangled him in its relationships:

That worthy magistrate, Sarcus by name, having a stipend of 1500 francs, has married a penniless girl, the oldest sister of the Soulanges apothecary, M. Vernuit. Mlle Sarcus was an only daughter, but her beauty was her only dowry, and she could not be said to live on the salary of a country notary's clerk. Young Sibelet was related to Gambertin (his precise degree of relationship would have been rather difficult to trace among the family ramifications of a small town where all the middle-class people were cousins). Adolphe Sibelet, surpassingly ill-favoured . . . belonged to that class of man whose only way to a woman's heart lies through the mayor's office or the church . . . With something of the suppleness of a steel spring, he would relinquish his idea to seize it again on another day, a shifty disposition of mind closely resembling baseness, but in the course of apprenticeship in a country notary's office Sibelet had learned to hide this defect beneath a gruff manner, which simulated a strength he did not possess . . . His grumbling manner was taken for the result of an honest outspoken nature, a capacity much praised by his employer, and an upright integrity which had never been put to the proof. Sometimes a man's defects are as useful to him as better qualities to his neighbour . . . Adolphe was fond of his wife but he constantly said to himself 'I have made a mistake. I have three sets of shackles: (a wife and two children) and only one pair of legs. I ought to have made my way before I married.'

Because Balzac's sexual ambition was frustrated – for Mme Brugnol can only have satisfied necessity – he fell back on the lust for things. In the *Cabinet des Antiques* written years before, Balzac had already dealt with the boom in the antique trade which had become general in France. The parvenu society coveted the things of the past either because it had been deprived or simply because this craze was one of the side effects of the popularity of Scott's novels, and of the historical bent of the Romantic movement: as in everything else,

Balzac contained the lusts of his age. He had always been a buyer and had bought in the belief that everything would go up in price. He was instinctively commercial and, anticipating the wealth of Mme Hanska, he began to buy recklessly in all directions. Dealers could sell him anything. What, years before, in the rue Cassini, the rue des Batailles, or Les Jardies had been a sportive, wilful extravagance, now became a systematic lust that begins to look like an uncontrollable disease. Mme Brugnol had been given a 'de'; now he discovered a royal connection in Mme Hanska. She was the grand-niece of the Queen of France. Objects worthy of such an ancestor must be found and soon were. In 1843 he had come across an escritoire and chest which he said had been made for Maria de' Medici in Florence. He gave 1300 francs for it.

I have made a marvellous historical discovery and shall ascertain the details this very morning. It is only the chest which belonged to Maria de' Medici. The escritoire bears the coat of arms of Concini or the Duc d'Epernon, but it also has the two letters M in a charmingly entwined border. This proves that there was an intimate relationship between Maria de' Medici and one or other of her favourites . . .

But, always a dealer, he added that he would offer it to the King for 4000 francs. Or to the Louvre. They turned it down. He would try the Duke of Sutherland, Robert Peel, Rothschild. With every rejection the price went up – to 10,000, then 20,000, and finally 60,000 francs. In the end he had to keep it and when it was sold after his death if fetched next to nothing, like pretty well everything else in his collection. In 1845 and 1846 he bought, among a mass of objects, two Sèvres vases – 'they must have cost between 5 and 600 francs. Don't whisper a word to anyone I got them for 35' – and a set of armchairs. There were quantities of pictures: a Ruysdael, a Natoire, a Holbein – all fakes; and a chandelier of solid brass that had belonged to the German Emperor and weighed two hundred pounds – the metal alone was worth 2 francs a kilo. He was becoming a fantastic scrap merchant. The little house in the rue Basse looked like a dealer's store. A journalist went to interview him. Balzac said:

See this cup. It is a masterpiece by Watteau. I found the cup in Germany and the saucer in Paris. I wouldn't take less than 2000 francs for them. Look at this *Judgment of Paris*, one of the best things of Giorgione. I've refused an offer of 12,000 francs from a museum. I've got more than

400,000 francs worth of pictures and objets d'art here. Look at this portrait of Mme Greuze by Greuze: Diderot wrote 20 of his most polished and sublime pages on this little sketch. If this picture is not by Raphael, then Raphael is not the greatest painter in the world. These statues are by Cellini. I had these Chinese vases sent over from Pekin . . .

In fact they had been manufactured in Holland: Balzac had stepped into the shoes of his own illustrious Gaudissart, the super-salesman. In the meantime he had not paid his mother's tiny pension and he called her a Shylock; but he sent her 3 louis for her birthday.

Suddenly Mme Hanska, having settled on Count Mniszech for her daughter, told Balzac he could come now to Dresden. He went full of joy once more. The visit started awkwardly because the young couple never let Mme Hanska out of their sight for a moment. The gossips of Dresden giggled at the sight of the two fat middle-aged lovers admiring the Rubens in the museum. So the four of them left for a long European tour. This was perhaps the happiest year of his life with her: he did no work at all. Naturally Mme Hanska bore the cost and seems to have formed a fund called the *Trésor Loup* from her private savings to the tune of 100,000 francs. That sounded very promising. The four travellers called themselves the *saltimbanques* and went gaily to Hamburg and Cannstatt where Mme Hanska, suffering from gout again, took the waters. Count George Mniszech, the wealthy young fiancé, was a feeble young man in Balzac's opinion, with a pale face, red-rimmed eyes, a bad stomach, and a scrofulous complexion. He was something of an artist and a collector of insects. Balzac thought him 'unformed' in his manners. The party gave themselves nicknames. Balzac became Bilboquet after a comic punster at a Cirque they went to see in Cologne. Nicknames for the others were taken from the show: Atala for Mme Hanska, Zephrine for her daughter, and Gringalet for the Count — Balzac's merry notion. Loup-Loup was pleasant for intimacy but Bilboquet, *en famille*, was a considerable improvement on Mme Hanska's condescending 'le bon Balzac' — as it were the 'nice little man' not quite of her class. Bilboquet was ingenious. They all longed for Paris but Poles were not permitted to travel in France because of the diplomatic quarrel of the time: he smuggled the four of them in on his own passport. He also liked costing the trip in detail — outside of purchases on the way! Mme Brugnol was told to find a discreet flat in the rue de la Tour in Passy and was commanded to move the most deeply personal of his possessions there: his sacred blue carpet.

He announced he was going to sleep at the rue de la Tour, so in the rue Basse Mme Brugnol firmly moved into Balzac's bed while he was away. Whether it was this manoeuvre that opened Mme Hanska's eyes to Balzac's relations with his housekeeper is uncertain; but the two women were instantly on hostile terms and Mme Hanska said Mme Brugnol must go. Civil war began in the rue Basse; it was to end in tears and blackmail, with Balzac's mother and sister taking Mme Brugnol's side.

Balzac insisted on the two Polish ladies being in Paris incognito and went to great lengths to keep the visit a mystery. He enjoyed that. After a while the party set off on a grand tour of France, especially in Touraine where they visited scenes of his childhood and they looked for châteaux for sale. Then they went north to The Hague and Amsterdam, buying antiques all the time. Mme Hanska had caught the craze. But at Rotterdam there was a quarrel about an ebony wardrobe costing 375 florins. Quite a serious quarrel. Both parties took it badly – Balzac with all the violence that shows how deep the obsession with furniture went:

What I suffered on the quay at Rotterdam only God and I know – still I say again – nothing can change a heart that has loved for fourteen years, which until then had never known love, passionate love . . .

He would put up with any humiliation.

There was a break in the trip. Mme Hanska went on to Baden repeating that Mme Brugnol must be given six months' notice: Balzac had to face that storm in Paris. Then, once more, the four *saltimbanques* were united in a journey to Lyons by river and on to Naples and Rome. The 'Bengali' was at the top of its form, but the metaphors now became gastronomic:

Cannstatt – all the delicious trifles of dessert, the gourmet trying to accustom himself to a loaded plate but not being able to . . . Karlsruhe – alms bestowed on the poor, but Strasbourg – ah, at Strasbourg it was expert love, a Louis XIV feast . . .

Lyons was 'sublime'.

A peasant rising had taken place in Poland and Mme Hanska decided to sit it out in Rome. The longed-for marriage was no nearer because Anna and Mniszech had to wait until they came into the fortune of Mniszech's father. Balzac went back to Paris to deal with his publishers, his debts, and Mme Brugnol. If frustration in love had paralysed his imagination, triumph also had so intoxicated him that he did not want to write a line more. With the longed-for happiness almost in his grasp he could settle to nothing. He let *Les Paysans* drift: the passion for objects and property now governed him entirely. New lawyers were bringing his debts to order and were reducing them, but that of course was fatal. He started spending again – with Mme Hanska's money, the *Trésor Loup*. One of his lunatic acts was to buy a 10,000-franc share in a ship which the admiring shipbuilder had called the *Balzac*: no more was heard of it. He was puffing about all over Paris, considering houses and plots of land. He also put a great deal of Mme Hanska's money into railway shares. They were now falling in value – as everything he touched did – and as they got lower he was, of course, anxious to buy more and more for the inevitable rise. (It occurred, but not for many years.) One would have thought he might have made a generous settlement on Mme de Brugnol – but no. He was proposing to get rid of this woman who had slaved for him – as women did – without giving her a penny. She was very attached to him and had imagined herself secure for life. There were tears of sorrow, screams of rage. She suddenly became a Balzac character, as rapacious and incalculable as he. She demanded to be set up in a tobacco shop, then in a stamp shop, then she demanded cash: at every discussion, the price of his freedom went up. While she bargained, she looked about for a husband, the most promising candidate being an ornamental sculptor called Eschoet. A relentless punster, Balzac-Bilboquet at once called her *la chouette*, screech owl. The mild nun-like peasant was fighting back. Balzac knew his French peasants – as he showed in *Les Paysans* in 1844 and later, in 1846, in the portrait of *La Cousine Bette*: they are people of one idea, he said; the desire for revenge builds up slowly in them from birth. Bette would work quietly for years to encompass the ruin of the cousin who had become rich and of whom she was the humiliated poor relation: the parallel with Mme Brugnol is close, also with the terrifying Mme Cibot, the concierge who turns from caring for Cousin Pons to robbing him; and it must be said that to the novelist the wretched trouble with Mme Brugnol was worth more (for it was an irritant) than the bliss of loving Mme Hanska. In many ways hate met the needs of Balzac as an artist far more intimately than did love.

About this time Mme Hanska exasperated him – and therefore

provided him with another source of traits for Bette – by sending him Mlle Borel, the Swiss governess who had been the intermediary while M. Hanski was alive. The girl wished to enter a convent in Paris. Was Mme Hanska testing Balzac by sending him a young woman? Or trying to turn his mind to piety? He was very impatient at having to endure even for a short time the presence of a moralizing, newly converted Catholic in his house and he had always hated doing services for his friends. He resented the interruption. Mlle Borel was in an intolerable state of virginal exaltation – he regarded virginity as a monstrosity – and she rather presumed on her moral condition. Emotions are easily reversed: her remorse in deceiving M. Hanski had been transmuted into sensations of flirtatious spiritual superiority. She rather took to Balzac and he nervously rushed her into the convent where she could become a bride of Christ. 'You are Madame at last', he drily said. Her case revealed to him the atmosphere at Wierzchownia: Mme Hanska had appeased her own Catholic guilt by making Mlle Borel into a nun and no longer needed her as a governess. Another poor relation or 'hanger-on' to be studied; and for the acidulated variety of the type there was Mme Hanska's aunt, the Countess Rosalie, the inveterate enemy who never missed a chance of collecting malicious gossip about him.

In one more of her sudden changes of mind, Mme Hanska called him to Rome. He dropped work at once, let his publishers and readers down, and went to get new clothes at his tailor's and fell over in the street afterwards in his excitement – one more of those falls he was liable to when in love, if it was love. Mme Brugnol screamed at him 'You love no one but yourself.' In Rome, Mme Hanska was amorous. The four *saltimbanques* renewed their cheerful journeys. The lovers went to visit the spots sacred to their love, Neuchâtel and Geneva, then on to Germany. Balzac returned to Paris with money to buy more railway shares, with plans for a new meeting soon, for the time of the marriage of the young couple – the necessary preliminary to his own – was now getting near; and he went down to consider the Château de Moncontour that stood above its mirror-like reflection in the waters of the Loire. To crown this excitement came a piece of news that awed him: Mme Hanska was pregnant. He would have a son, to be called Victor-Honoré. He was certain it would be a son. Nature had conquered Mme Hanska: she would be forced to marry him! He had attained ascendancy at last. In the past he had been perforce deprived of acknowledged paternity by the existence of husbands: now there was no husband. If old Goriot had been called the Jesus Christ of fatherhood, Balzac saw himself in no such martyred role, but rather as the Napoleon of the condition. The only difficulty was that – because of the relations in the Ukraine – the necessary marriage which would legitimize the child would have to be secret.

When anything secret had to be done Balzac was in his element. He plotted all kinds of moves, including suborning mayors, priests, high officials, moving the scene from Germany to Metz, from Metz to Passy. There was to be a good deal of bribery and the sly shuffling of documents in darkened alcoves: two things he did not reckon with. One could get round the fact that Mme Hanska had no certificate of the death of her husband, but a birth certificate was indispensable. Mme Hanska refused to provide one: she was not going to reveal to Balzac, or indeed anyone, that she was six years older than she had pretended. She had been born in 1800 and was only a year younger than himself. As for her reputation, a Rzewuski had no need to bother about that. A year's time would be time enough for marriage: the child could be 'recognized' afterwards. The second point was more serious: pregnancy brings its own 'moment of truth'. She could manage Balzac intermittently as a lover; as a husband he would be hopelessly untrustworthy with money and property – a far more serious matter even than infidelity. Once more she told him to stay away.

Souvent femme varie – Balzac was stunned. No man, he knew, could change the mind of a pregnant woman. But similarly no woman could do anything with a man who, at Balzac's age, ascends into the higher monomania of paternity. We know exactly what Balzac's concept of responsibility was: more responsibility meant more extravagant promises and expense. Marriage was now certain. He took drastic action. Without warning Mme Hanska he made her the owner of a large house off the half-built wealthy suburb near the Etoile in the Champs-Elysées. The place looked as grim as a barracks or lunatic asylum, people said. It had two windows on the street, thirty-nine in all looking on to a courtyard. It was in the rue Fortunée – happy name – and was part of a park-like property known as the 'Folie Beaujon'. The original builder in the 1780s had been a gay fellow who wanted a very private place for *fêtes galantes*; during the Revolution the grounds had become a public pleasure gardens. After its value went down the land was broken up into lots. What appealed to Balzac was the prison-like secrecy of the house. There were only those two windows on the street, the rest were concealed behind the high walls of a courtyard; and from the upper floor one could walk along a passage into the gallery of a church which adjoined at the back: a pious version of the doorway of escape at the chalet in the rue Basse. A woman could live here incognito, he told Mme Hanska, indeed there was a secret apartment which the happy M. Beaujon had built for the purpose. To relieve any remorse a lady might feel in the morning she had only to pass straight from the bedroom to the gallery of the church to hear the Holy Office – unseen.

'Your religious habits', he wrote to Mme Hanska, 'and your piety are to me the most beautiful qualities of your beloved soul.'

He concentrated on the chapel to take her mind off the fact that the dilapidated place would cost a fortune to put in order. Another advantage: property was booming in this neighbourhood now becoming fashionable. One could live there for five or six years, then sell for 120,000 francs what had cost only 32,000.

Mme Hanska was horrified. She saw herself trapped by a monster. He announced that he was going to transform the barracks into an Oriental palace. Into the house trooped the builders and decorators; carts drew up with cargoes of antiques, loads of malachite and bronzes, sculptures, coats of arms, marble, quantities of Boule. In time there would be Smyrna carpets, curtains for nineteen windows at 300 francs a window – 'we must have the best: it lasts longer'. He bought what was said to be the bed of Mme de Pompadour, while workers installed the central heating. He was continually in cabs, studying plans, between the rue Basse and the rue Fortunée. There was an *octroi* at Passy and the officials nudged each other knowingly when the peculiar fellow always carrying catalogues went by in his floppy hat. He was forty-seven.

In the meantime Mme Brugnol was still at the rue Basse, quietly going through his letters and discovering Mme Hanska was pregnant. What news to send to the Ukraine! She decided on blackmail. It cost Balzac 7500 francs to get the letters back – but she still concealed one or two – and Mme Hanska had to order him to burn every letter of hers he had kept. Too frightened to disobey, he wept as he burned the lot. A melancholy evening. But a happier time for Mme Brugnol: she turned down Eschoet, the sculptor, and benefiting by the 'de' Balzac had given her, married the rich brother-in-law of a peer of France and ended in the bliss of fashionable life. Her waiting had paid off: Balzac's had not.

One could travel by rail to Germany now. He went off to the marriage of Anna. The furnishing mania had not exhausted the new power that had come to him now he was going to be a father. Naturally he was very short of cash and openly asked Mme Hanska 'to make an effort' in that department. She refused, although he called her 'his white plump voluptuous love'. And Balzac was experiencing couvade – he had offered to take charge of the baby when it was born and he too was pregnant – with furniture. He returned to Paris to finish *La Cousine Bette* and to hear dreadful news. The child was born prematurely and dead. He broke down and could not stop crying. He said he would come to Dresden even though he had to earn 16,000 francs in two months. Mme Hanska was too distressed, she said, to see him. There was nothing to do, he said, but wait and wait, as for eighteen years he had waited. Everything that had gone wrong, he said, was his own fault. He knew it. But there was something of pride and glory in this abasement. His instinct of *engrossissement* or magnification was at work as infallibly in this as it was in everything else, making even slavery larger and more spectacular.

The ecstasies and anti-climaxes of these past years of living in fire one month and in ice the next had brought Balzac's mind to its extremity. He was no longer restrained by his natural humour and common sense. He was no longer living in the foreground of his observation and experience, but was on the edge of its extreme horizon. The evidence of this is the sudden yet strange revival of his genius at its best. After *Les Illusions Perdues* and parts of *La Rabouilleuse* he had been less productive and certainly in a rut, but now, with astonishing speed he was writing two masterpieces, *La Cousine Bette* and *Le Cousin Pons*, the two studies together called *Les Parents Pauvres*. In the former we see Balzac creating characters who are outside the control of his realism. It is as if, unable rationally to face certain emotions, he is forced to inflate them to mythical dimensions. The portrait of Bette in the early chapters is the excellent Balzac we know; but when emotional shock brings out her jealousy of her cousin, she becomes a figure of absolute evil. She becomes incredible as a person, but credible as allegory.

The peasant woman's face was terrible; her piercing black eyes had the glare of a tiger's; her face was like that we ascribe to a pythoness: she set her teeth to keep them from chattering and her whole frame quivered convulsively. She had pushed her clenched fingers under her cap to clutch her hair and support her head which felt too heavy; she was on fire. The smoke of the flame that scorched her seemed to emanate from her wrinkles, as from the crevasses rent by a volcanic eruption . . .

. . . Thus in one moment Lisbeth Fischer had become the Mohican whose snares none can escape, whose dissimulation is inscrutable, whose swift decisiveness is the outcome of the incredible perfection of every organ of sense. She was Hatred and Revenge as implacable as they are in Italy and Spain.

This is melodrama such as one finds in the portraits of Vautrin and it is bad writing; and melodrama is always a sign of evasion, of experience undigested. From the view of a biographer *La Cousine Bette* seems to contain signs of personal disintegration. In excess the life force is making its last bursts as if it rushes to death. And, in the end, the awful death of Mme Marneffe and Crevel her lover by poison – a mysterious poison concocted by Brazilian Indians – and Bette's own death from tuberculosis, too, mark the sense of something mystical in doom. In detail after detail Balzac's own drive to excess pervades. As a rule, Balzac's novels had looked back twenty or thirty years but now, in putting his subject close to the time of writing, his own person seems to burst out.

These comments are far from being a commendation of this element in the novel but are, rather, notes on the new unrest that ferments in Balzac and matures his impartial observation of life elsewhere. The excess in the character of Bette frees Balzac in his treatment of the other characters and allows him to go without rage into the marvellous variety of scenes and people. The sexual excesses of Baron Hulot are not in the least melodramatic: the comedy of shame is packed with observable incident and variety of feeling. The use of topicality – the Baron ruins himself as a man of honour by getting hold of Army funds in Algeria – is brilliant. Hulot is seen for what he is, yet with compassion, so that we feel him to be the victim of his vices and very nearly their hero. Hulot has been identified to some extent with Victor Hugo, who was indeed caught in bed with his mistress by the police, just as Hulot was caught with La Marneffe; but Hulot is Balzac in self-portrait in one particular aspect: naïvely shameless but compelled; easily deceived in his losing struggle with passably good intentions:

The Baron, once started on this path of reform, gave up his leather waist-coat and stays; he threw off his bracing. His stomach fell and increased in size . . . His eyebrows were still black and left a ghostly reminiscence of Handsome Hulot . . . This discordant detail made his eyes, still bright and youthful, all the more remarkable in his tanned face, because it had so long been ruddy with the florid hues of a Rubens; and now a certain discoloration and the deep tension of the wrinkles betrayed the efforts of a passion at odds with natural decay.

When Hulot is finally ruined and goes for help to Josepha, his old mistress, we hear perhaps the words in which Balzac as a man and artist would be willing to be judged. Josepha says:

'And is it a fact, old man, that you have killed your brother and your uncle, ruined your family, mortgaged your children's house over and over again, and robbed the government till in Africa, all for your princess?'
Hulot sadly bent his head.
'Well, I admire that! It's a general flare up. It is Sardanapalus! Splendid, thoroughly complete. I may be a hussy, but I have a soul I tell you, I like a spendthrift, like you, crazy over a woman, a thousand times better than those torpid, heartless bankers, who are supposed to be so good and who ruin no end of families with their railway lines – gold for them and iron for their victims. You have only ruined those who belong to you, you have sold no one but yourself; and there you have excuses, physical and moral, "C'est Vénus toute entière à sa proie attachée."'

Here, remarks Balzac, as if he were before a jury, the magnitude of the crime was an extenuating circumstance.

Great novelists use every part of their natures. In *La Cousine Bette* he had shown the vengeance of the poor female relation and Hulot brought to disgrace; in *Le Cousin Pons* he turns to the male poor relation, the harmless hanger-on who is the victim and who believes ill of no one. He gave Pons two of his passions: the greed of the gourmet and the mania of the collector. The manias of the man fed the novelist. There is the warm tenderness of resignation in this novel which is free of his exaggerations. Pons, like the curé of Tours, is the most delicate of his creations and he comes from the firm centre of Balzac's imagination. But once he put his pen down, and as if only in the act of writing words was he alive, he immediately took it up again, without a pause, to write to Mme Hanska. The letters are fiction, too, but the weary fiction of one to whom facts have become meaningless. They stream out in dreadful monotone and are, in a painful way, absurd as if he were talking in his sleep.

The fiction is that he is paying off his debts and he and she will live as equals:

So you see in the first three months of 1847 I shall have my plate full because add to the 12,000 francs, 3000 for carpets, that's 15,000. I have already paid off 15,000 plus what remains to be paid in the present month. Looking back on it, I have bought 50,000 francs worth of furniture in the last eighteen months and I have receipted invoices for 28,000 francs, and in the last six years I have bought to the tune of 30,000. So, 30,000, 28,000 and 50,000 adds up to 108,000 francs without reckoning in my silver, my library and my own personal furniture.

It is impossible to know what he meant; it was certainly impossible for Mme Hanska. And, he added, words that reduce one to despair:

I am sure if you reckon it all by weight, there is 3000 kilogrammes of copper and gilded bronze. The amount of bronze is almost frightening. The house – as you rightly say – is a mine of gilded copper – for as my cabinet-maker says – there must be 100 kilos of it. At 8 francs a kilo it would fetch 32,000 francs at the coppersmith. So you can see the value of it – I say nothing of its value as art.

The drawing room alone had 1800 francs worth of woodwork.

At last Mme Hanska came to Paris to see the Oriental palace he had prepared for her. He lodged her in an apartment in the Champs-Elysées which they shared and she paid for. Creditors got wind of the presence of the rich woman. Buisson, the tailor, wanted his 14,000 francs, but settled for 8800. Mme Hanska insisted on cheap living – warmed-up stews; rather touchingly she left the fresh meat for him. But when she went to see the house she was shattered. What a hole! What a prison, decked up with appallingly ugly junk, obviously worthless! She harangued and accused. She stayed two or three months with him in Paris. The high words that passed between them when she saw the mass of scaffolding, paint, and half-unpacked antiques ruined the visit. In the intervals of truce he took her to the Italiens – delightful, but reminding her he had shared a *loge* there with the Guidaboni-Viscontis. To Very's – reminding her again of what he had told her of his wild dinners. As far as one can tell they met none of his friends. Suddenly she decided to go back to the Ukraine. Still no marriage.

The Price of a Dream
Achieved

Her letters were rare. He had moved into the house and sat in the smell of paint and plaster among the scaffolding, like a caretaker. He had come after their quarrels to detest the place: it was a mistress, indeed an infidelity, he had tired of. Once one achieves one's desire, he had often said, it means nothing. Often he simply sat and wept about the lost child and the muddle of his life. He feared her love had gone. He tried to stir her interest in the house. He pleaded, for example, to be allowed to install a pretty and expensive water-closet, speaking of its marble, its consoles, flowers, and candlesticks as if it were the most adorable little boudoir! She refused the permission. Sulkily he ventured a touch of humour! Would Her Majesty, he whimpered, permit him to buy a cheap mahogany box for his shoes – if not he'd go on keeping them in the window-boxes on the stairs. Nothing was to be bought! Even so he managed to sneak in two door-knockers for the main gate that cost more than the gate itself. Couldn't he come to the Ukraine? 'I realize that you don't want me and I fall prey to a double despair, that of not being expected and of not having written anything.'

Suddenly her mood changed; perhaps now she was in her own home she was bored. After Western Europe life in the Ukraine was dull. She told him to come.

Balzac set off as one travelling at last to the Promised Land. He was equipped like an explorer. In 1847 railways were sketchy in France and Germany; much of the journey would be by road. He took provisions for eight days: ship's biscuit, coffee concentrate, sugar, a package of tongue, and a bottle of anisette. For a man with

171

a bad stomach, a damaged heart, and who suffered from neuralgia, the journey was awful. He was in nothing like the sound condition he had been in on his rough expedition to the silver mines of Sardinia. The train journey to Brussels was fairly easy. But then on to Hanover he had to take the out-of-date German diligence – style 1820. Rather grand passengers were with him part of the way: an embassy man taking messages to Metternich, a collector of porcelain, and a lady known as the 'queen of Hamburg'. He changed into a train at Hanover for Berlin; next day, Breslau. At every change Balzac became demented because he thought his luggage was lost or stolen. People humoured him, treating him as a drunk. On to Cracow, in a wood-burning train. At Gleiwitz, the frontier, a row with the Austrian customs. The terrible journey crawled on. At Dubno he slept for the first time for nine days. The last 100 leagues of the journey took 30 hours in a *kilitka*, a rough vehicle that hit every rut on the awful road, in clouds of dust as it crossed the cornlands of the steppe. The driver drank his anisette.

The steppe, he said, was the silent prairie of Fenimore Cooper. One more night on the road and then, as the sun was setting, Wierzchownia appeared out of a fold in the ground suddenly like a mirage. The vast place looked, he said, like another Louvre or Greek temple. The month was September. He arrived with a terrible migraine.

The house was said to be the most luxurious in the Ukraine and the estate was larger than a French department. Yet inside the walls were noticeably bare except for mirrors ten feet high. There was one Carcel oil lamp for the whole patriarchal mansion. The place was heated by straw stuffed into the stoves. The night Balzac arrived a number of outlying barns and houses were burned down in a terrible fire. The estate numbered 40,000 souls and there were 300 domestic servants. He was given a suite of three luxurious rooms – the rugs and the silver amazed him and also the fact that there were five or six other suites like his. From the windows he looked out at the endless miles of corn, broken here and there by a forest of oak.

The family were excited by his arrival. He was their adored Bilboquet. He was stupefied to see the servants prostrate themselves before him, flat on their stomachs, knocking their heads three times on the floor and kissing the toe of his slipper – as he had kissed the toe of the Pope in Rome the year before. Spectacular wealth, but – it soon turned out – all the Polish landowners were up to their ears in debt: Mme Hanska's daughter, now married, had been given her share of the estate and was already spending it fast; Balzac was bewildered. But he announced proudly that he would pay off all he owed by his pen. He set to work on a novel, the last part of *L'Envers de l'Histoire Contemporaine* (The Seamy Side of Contemporary History), to show that he intended not to sponge, but to support his future wife by his own efforts. He worked by the country time-table he had followed at Saché – writing all day, coming down to dinner in the evening. In the vast drawing-room with its columns, lit by groups of candles, there was a Van Dyck, a Rembrandt, and a Guercino, Balzac's own smoke-blackened portrait by Boulanger – rather gratifying – and to greet the writer in proper state, the young Mniszechs brought over from their place some miles away a Greuze, two Watteaus, and three Canalettos – every Polish landowner had his stock of Canalettos. The evening passed with the gentlemen playing chess and the ladies doing embroidery. Some biographers say that they treated Balzac as a court jester and that he did little work, but in fact he worked well and at any rate not self-destruc-tively. He was famous in the Ukraine. He travelled. They took him to Kiev and the Governor gave a banquet for him, though in fact he had been instructed by the Russian secret police to keep him under strict vigilance: what disturbed the Russians was that this great visitor from the West was enormously popular and this might be dangerous because of the Russian-Polish tension and the semi-revolutionary peasant rising of the previous year. He was in a land where suspicion was king.

The instinctive businessman in Balzac could not be repressed. Seeing the neglected oak forests and being an investor in railways, Balzac soon saw a colossal profit in this timber. Within a month of his arrival he outlined one of his grandiose schemes in a letter to his sister: cut down the trees and sell the timber in France for railway sleepers. Transport would be a problem. Accountancy revived. Sup-pose one exported 60,000 thirty-foot cords at 10 francs and allowed 20 francs for transport, at a profit of, say, 20 francs, one would make 120,000 francs. Even supposing one made only 5 francs profit, one would net 420,000 francs.

Balzac told his sister to consult her husband, the engineer. He is talking, he says, only of trunks of trees, but possibly there was usable wood in the heavier branches; and there would be the profit on firewood. So he went on. But the longer he stayed the more he understood the realities of Mme Hanska's life: dealing with losses of crops, sacking dishonest managers, the ruling of an estate. He saw that he had at least two years of hard writing before he or she could disentangle themselves from their respective obligations. But life was peaceful and timeless. He felt he could stay there for ever, with only one serious care: that of keeping his mother up to scratch in supervising what was going on in the rue Fortunée and in seeing no burglars got in to steal his treasure. He lived like a pampered but fretful sultan, but he had also seen the trials of an owner of a feudal estate. The servants might bow to the ground before one: but Mme Hanska, her son-in-law, and her effusive daughter, who addressed her parent as 'my idolized angel of a mother', were tangled in lawsuits about their inheritances. The Polish aristocracy behaved with the avarice and venom of the French petit bourgeoisie. There was little ready money; and indeed cash was rarely used in this patriarchal life. There was quite a fuss when it came to paying for the franking of letters received. As for outgoing mail, a Cossack simply rode off with it once every week or so. Hailstorms destroyed the crops; fires burned down the barns; and all Mme Hanska could be certain of was an annuity of 20,000 francs. Or so she moaned. It was illegal to transfer her inheritance abroad. If she sold off her share of the estate it would have to go to her daughter who already had her own share. The money she put into railway shares and the payments on the house came from her personal savings during her marriage. As things were going, Balzac told her wryly, they would be a white-haired old couple before they married. He was intuitive enough to see she was half-hearted, even hostile; but he brushed this aside. He seems, to judge by their letters, to have had allies in the young Mniszechs. They obviously thought he was good for the mother; also the daughter was a budding spendthrift and longed to settle in Paris close to the rue Fortunée. Their manner of writing is so ecstatic and fond that one can only conclude they had contracted the fever of their dear Bilboquet; they regarded the Ukraine as barbaric.

But a demand for payment of a new instalment on Mme Hanska's allotment of railway shares came from Paris. Bankers charged 12 per cent for transferring moneys, so Balzac left with 90,000 francs in his pocket to make the payment personally. No more 'squandering' Mme Hanska warned him and no more bric-à-brac. In the January of 1848, when the snow was hard enough for the sleigh that would take him on the long jingling ride to Cracow, he set off wrapped up in furs on top of his overcoat. When he got to Paris in February rain was falling.

He was depressed. When he got to the rue Fortunée he understood that he had made a mistake: he had bought the place too soon. What he had reckoned would cost him at most 125,000 francs had in fact cost 400,000. Still everything in his life had always cost more and in fact loss excited him and, in his mind, turned into heroic incidents in his struggles, forcing him to drive the work of *La Comédie Humaine* further. As he said to his sister, the situation at Wierzchownia was touch and go: the stakes were high; indeed they had reached the point of double or quits. He redoubled his campaign to maintain his fiction:

Listen, Laure, isn't it something to have it in one's power, just for the wishing, to create a salon where only the élite of society will meet, ruled by a woman with the polish and presence of a queen, high born, educated, a woman of wit and beauty. One's position is unassailable . . . I have sought nothing less for eighteen years . . . Don't think that I am infatuated with luxury for its own sake. I love the luxury of the rue Fortunée for what goes with it: a superb well-born woman of great family and who – putting her fortune aside for the moment – brings with her every social advantage the world can offer.

If he is defeated in this, he says, he will vanish into some hole. Indeed it will kill him.

Always on his returns from his pursuit of the mirage he was brought to earth by a shock; and this time it was from a quarter to which he had rarely paid attention. Intent as always on the details of his accountancy, he had known that Mme Hanska's railway shares had lost half their value: what he had not seen in this misfortune was its connection with politics. The railway fever in France, England, all Europe, had overshot its mark: there were 50,000 unemployed workers in France alone, and in France this was one of the crucial items in the beginnings of the revolution of 1848. He had always been one of those sage, middle-of-the-road bourgeois who baulked at any attack on property and who took a paternalistic attitude to the working classes. They must be gently led; but since his visit to St Petersburg and the sight of the Tsar, and perhaps also because Mme Hanska shared with the Poles and himself a hero-worship of Napoleon, he leaned more and more to the mystical attractions of despotism. Domination was an idea that fascinated his mind. No one had described so intimately the lust for money and the corruption of the upper bourgeoisie who had ruled French society under Louis-Philippe and his minister Guizot with his famous slogan 'Get rich'; yet no one, when it came to the show-down was more suspicious of democracy, socialism, or even the new cry for an extension of the suffrage. It threatened the very basis of the profession to which he had appointed himself – to be the overworked secretary of history. Now history seemed to be saying that it had no room for secretaries: he was so self-absorbed in his task that he had not noticed that the industrial revolution had come late to France and that the disturbance was profound. He had often mocked the lethargy of Louis-Philippe; he had also seen that that lethargy had hardened into a fierce resistance to reform of any kind. He had always been a monarchist, and a Catholic too, and now he feared the call for a republic. It would lead, he believed, to anarchy. When he walked into the centre of Paris, passing the sideshows that now lined the half-built Champs-Elysées like a continuous circus, he heard nothing but the hot air of politics. The city was alive with political clubs and secret societies. Day and night there were 'banquets' at which orators declaimed this view or that, but almost all cried 'universal suffrage'. It was typical of the period that political mani-festations should be gastronomic and that the habit was for the guests to stroll in procession, in a kind of peaceful gourmet demo, to the appointed place. Herzen, who was in Paris from the first riots in this rainy February to the bloody outbursts of June, described with his usual scepticism in his memoirs the play-acting that went on among the self-appointed spies and secret societies. He sat among the Reds:

In the café Lamblin, where the desperate *citoyens* were sitting over their *petits verres* and big glasses, I learned that they had no plan, that the movement had no real centre of momentum and no programme. Inspiration was to descend upon them as the Holy Ghost once descended upon the apostles.

And as for the 'conspirators':

They mysteriously invite one to extraordinarily important interviews, at night if possible, or in some inconvenient place. Meeting their friends in public, they do not like saluting them with a bow, but greet them with a significant glance. Many of them keep their address a secret, never tell one what day they are going away, never say where they are going, write in cypher in invisible ink views which are plainly printed in printers' ink in the newspapers.

This was harmless and, despite the wet weather and since Parisians lived in the streets, there was almost a quickening sense of holiday and the hope of seeing some excitement. Irony had led Herzen to underrate the explosive nature of the situation: there were hungry workless men in the family crowds that came in from the working-class quarters. If the rain appeared to damp things down, it was also an exasperation. Seeing the unfamiliar sight of ministers, generals, famous orators, dashing about, the crowd felt stirrings of importance. Balzac himself felt a growing political conceit. He had also hankered after political power and had been jealous of Lamartine's office and Victor Hugo's influence.

At last the government banned a banquet. That was enough to cause an occasional scuffle and affray in far-off streets, but when the usual procession crowded down the Boulevard des Capucines to the Madeleine and found troops there and the Garde National – by luck Balzac had not been called to duty – the first shots were fired. The crowd had been peaceable and had no programme; but now, with the first dead in the street, it fled to stir up rage everywhere. That was enough. On 22 February 1848 a swarm advanced on the Tuileries. Louis-Philippe had run away; and the crowd broke into the palace. It was a mixed crowd. Some burst in merely out of curiosity and walked gaping through the corridors and royal rooms; but a wilder mob followed, made for the wine, and were soon drunkenly dressing up in court uniforms. The cry was 'To the throne room', where they sat on the throne and made satirical speeches. The corridors of the palace were soon deep in broken glass, people smashed the pictures and looting began. A large number of workers installed their families in the palace and ate up all the food – it took three weeks to get the last of them out.

At the rue Fortunée the sounds of gunfire and rioting could be distantly heard and Balzac went out that night to see what was happening at the Tuileries. The destruction he saw in the palace horrified him. Not only the monarchy was being destroyed; worse – furniture, bric-à-brac was being smashed as well. It was even worse at the Palais-Royal where the mob was tearing up the books in the magnificent library of the Orléans family. Always a collector, Balzac quietly picked up a few draperies and ornaments himself and took them home. He walked – the doctors had told him to walk more – and passed bodies being carried off on stretchers.

The news from abroad was bad. Germany and Italy were in disorder. In the next weeks the Paris banks closed, the bookshops closed, publication of books was stopped. Balzac saw his livelihood and his hopes of paying off his debts vanish in the next few months. The blow was devastating. For a while, always an opportunist, he tried to get into the public swim. He got scarcely any votes for the Republican Assembly; he was rejected by the Academy. (He had been rejected twice before.) He went back to the solitude of the rue Fortunée afraid that he would be considered an *aristo* and grew a small beard so as to look like a worker.

But there was always power of recovery in him. He was to say 'I am part of the opposition called life.' The theatres had not closed so he turned once more to writing for the theatre and wrote a play called *La Marâtre*: success for the first time in a field where he had always been defeated. He had at last discovered there is a difference between the novel and the play and he had learned to be less arrogant with theatre people. But, after a splendid first night and praise from everyone, the show closed down because people were afraid to go out. The revolutionary feeling in Paris was growing more intense. There were no letters in reply to his cries of passion to Mme Hanska for a long time and then came one of her bombshells – she told him to go and find a young wife. And her sister, Aline, the one who hated her and who was always dropping in at the rue Fortunée and lived for making trouble, offered him her own daughter, Pauline, a girl who it turned out was dying of consumption!

He packed his bags and, unable to work in the dangerous and disturbing city, went down to Saché to write four plays. He wrote to Mme Hanska a letter of desperation:

I am doing these four plays, but as a matter of conscience and if the situation in my heart and my life is what it was in December, I shall give up the struggle. I shall let myself drift with the current, like a drowning man. And you'll hear no more of Bilboquet.

And again:

Mon loup chéri, life has left me. I am wretched and alone – God might have sent me these evils one at a time; together they are enough to break any human being. I am going to Saché to make one more supreme effort.

After that, come what may, I shall have done all I can, everything that human strength is capable of. If I couldn't write and confide in you, as if I were uttering a prayer, there would be a hole in my life – for never, after sixteen years – have I lived so utterly in your heart as at the present moment. There is never a moment when in my thoughts I am alone. You are as much inside me, as my own sorrow, my work and my very blood. I told your sister that never at any time in my life had my soul known so much passion. It is the kind of passion one dies of. Only my wretchedness and work gives me the strength to fight the apathy that undermines me in everything I feel and do. I am like the surgeon who knows what his illness is, and who in the midst of his pain follows its course with a scientific eye.

At Saché he recovered for a while. He worked and even revelled with Jean de Margonne whose glum wife had long ago died. The revelling was not good for his heart. He coughed and thought he had water on the lungs. But he worked at a play called *Mercadet* – a lost cause, the theatres were closed. It turned out to be a brilliant comedy when it was cut down to three acts after his death. It is a play about a compulsive liar and speculator – for the farce was celebrating one of his many selves – and when he read it to the company of the Comédie-Française he became, like Dickens, a remarkable actor. He stripped garment by garment to his shirt-sleeves as he rushed about speaking all the parts to perfection. In the midst of his disasters, when everything had failed and when in fact he was breaking up, Balzac's reserves of mirth were always there. Gautier said 'he roared and cried and wept and raged and thundered in every conceivable tone of voice'. He evoked the swarm of Mercadet's creditors as if they 'stretched to the horizon'. We have to think of this Balzac, a true Bilboquet, when we see him playing – for was it more than that? – the whipped dog or furtive 'moujik' of Mme Hanska's imperium. A young novelist called Champfleury said he looked like a 'good-humoured wild boar, his paunch quivering with laughter and whose full-blooded lips exposed scattered teeth like fangs'. A caricature, but Balzac was, in many ways, a living caricature.

Safe at Saché, he missed the bloody rising in the sullen heat of the June days in Paris. The mob and the soldiers outdid one another in their savageries. There was an orgy of killing and cruelty. (One woman who cut off an officer's hands said afterwards 'I was in a dream.') Paris had gone mad. When Balzac returned he found the city closed down. He had only one desire: to leave France for good.

And, astonishingly, there were tender letters now from Mme Hanska. She had changed her tune. He managed to get a passport at last and in September 1848 he left. He was going for ever: in a year and a half he came back – to die.

It is difficult to know Mme Hanska. If by this time she was disillusioned and was not in love with him, why did she not break? One has to see her as the ruler of a small empire, unwilling to lose a subject. Considering how jealous she was of every woman he as much as spoke to, as though jealousy were her profession, an emotion stronger than love, it is astonishing at first that Balzac harks back so often to the 'cruelties' of the Marquise de Castries: cruelties, he rather dramatically said, that marked his life for ever. Dangerous words: but was he reminding Mme Hanska that in her evasions and angers she was a Marquise de Castries reborn? One can see why Balzac did not break: in her way Mme Hanska too was a cold mother-figure who never let a fault pass, who continually accused. One is left with the impression that Balzac was drawn by a childish terror of her as much as by her money. If he was such a deplorable liar and totally unreliable, why did she drop him and then take up with him again? The answer seems to be that she was lonely too and both felt the strong physical spell, but that the love, on both sides, had also been an affair of minds and the mind hangs on. Hence her cruelties and his deceptions.

Cholera had broken out in Paris. He set off like an emigrant with no intention of returning. Somehow, on money from his theatre contracts and some sent by Mme Hanska for her railway shares, he raised enough for the journey – not before the 'two-legged bottle of vinegar', her sister, had reported to the Ukraine that he was carrying on with an acress. This was too much: he genuinely hated actors and actresses, for they infuriated the playwright by murdering his plays. He loaded himself with enough clothes and boots for the rest of his life, quantities of perfume for the ladies, Eau de Portugal, infallible in love, and – inevitably – four dozen pairs of gloves for those beautiful hands. Also, remembering his shock at finding only one oil lamp in that rambling palace, he took five of the newly invented Carcel oil lamps with him to improve the premises! And he sneaked visits to the antique dealers in Mainz and Dresden on the way.

He had left his mother to manage his financial affairs and the care of the house in the rue Fortunée and there is now a total change in the content of his correspondence. The letters to Mme Hanska – if we except those that came after his first visit to the Ukraine onwards – are the passionate self-projection of a creative imagination and of a man in prolonged headlong love. Every ounce of him – his erotic, toiling nature, his ceaseless scheming about money, property, and his collections – goes into them; they are among the strangest love letters ever written. They are done with the whole animal.

But once in the Ukraine and writing to his mother and occasionally to Laure, Balzac's letters change. He is his mother's boy once more. The creative energy has gone, his interests have narrowed to the domestic and what to do every day at the house in the rue Fortunée. He has little to say about the Ukraine. He was of course always a man whose mind was elsewhere: in Paris, it was in the scenes of his novels and in the Ukraine; in the Ukraine his mind is on his possessions in Paris. He becomes the infinitely anxious, fussing, monotonous family meddler who worries every day about whether the floors are properly swept and the lamps spotlessly clean. Mother and son are curiously united in this. He orders and enslaves: she slaves for him, indeed the two seem closer to each other than do Balzac and Mme Hanska. One can read into this domestic surrender the decline of his health and powers. Anxiety has made him pettifogging. Mother and son are alike in their fixation on money. When he left for the Ukraine the first time she set out the story of her life in financial terms from the time she was married, the tale of exactly what losses her husband's, her son's and her own speculations had incurred. She mentions her own failures as a speculator but evading the fact – as Balzac himself did in awkward matters of his own life – that she had, as he said, 'squandered' her money on the feckless and adored Henri. The Balzacs were in their peculiar way affectionate with their 'little mother', who had once been so pretty, but they were merciless in 'bringing up the past'. Vivacity – as he called it – was strong in all of them.

In these monotonous letters from a man who knows, and refuses to know, that he is at the end of his tether, Bilboquet the man of mirth has gone. The heart attack he had had at Saché was repeated; the Polish doctor at Wierzchownia said the heart was enlarged. The patient is unable to go upstairs. If he walks in the garden Mme Hanska has to help his steps on the uneven ground. He can't even raise his arms to brush his hair and he has been told he must do no work for six months. So out pour these instructions about the payment of bills, minute orders for dealing with everything in the house from the paint to the curtains.

There are two outbursts. He has made it clear that this is the great crisis of his life and everything depends on the outcome. The family must co-operate and accept what he tells them. They must not even hint at criticism of him. The essence of the situation is that Mme Hanska – who reads all his letters – must not be put off by hard-luck stories from the family: she has had enough troubles of her own. She is a woman of fifty and will certainly not marry for a second time in order to run into more. In fact the lesser Balzacs will have to keep a polite distance. And it is in their interest. For – leaving money aside for the moment – he and Mme Hanska will be people of great social influence. Think of how that will help, he tells his sister, when it comes to the question of marrying off *her* daughters. The family must understand they are, in their turn, 'poor relations'. In other words Honoré is the only one of the family who will have 'arrived' and who can assure their happiness and security if they keep their distance.

A small mistake by the servants at the rue Fortunée started the outburst. The servants had turned away Rothschild's messenger because he had asked for Mme Sallambier: for one of Balzac's impenetrably devious reasons he had put the power of attorney in his mother's maiden name. The servants' blunder infuriated him. His mother replied coldly excusing the mistake, and addressed her son – but only in the first line of the letter – as 'vous' instead of in the intimate second person singular. The wrongs of childhood came to the surface once more:

I don't ask you to pretend to feelings that you haven't got, for God knows – and so do you – that you haven't smothered me with kisses since the day I was born. You were quite right not to do so, for if you had loved me as you loved Henri, I'd be, no doubt, in the situation he is in now – so in that sense you have been a good mother to me. What I want from you, my dear mother, is an intelligent sense of your own interests – which in fact you've never had – and not to prejudice my future, I say nothing of my happiness.

He was so annoyed by his mother's use of 'vous', that he wrote a long letter to his sister, begging her to knock sense into his mother's head. And he added the bitter words: 'If I don't achieve greatness by *La Comédie Humaine*, I shall at least achieve it in this [i.e. the marriage] if it comes off.' As for Laure's troubles – her husband, the canal-builder and engineer, was not doing well – Balzac told his sister that the right way to live is to cultivate useful people only, people like bankers or financiers and to drop friends who are failures and who drag one down.

The prospects of his marriage were poor. More crop fires had cost Mme Hanska 140,000 francs; he was treading on thin ice: 'Some marriages are like cream, the temperature can turn them in a moment and I look like remaining a bachelor.'

After these explosions Balzac settles down once more to his endless catalogue of requests. Always greedy, even at this stage of his financial troubles, he hankered after a small piece of land to round off the property at the rue Fortunée and the owner kept putting up the price and then would not sell. Balzac fusses about his new bookcases and wants to know to an exact half centimetre the depth of the shelves. He indicates where the consoles are to be placed. He wants two more consoles in gilded copper for the bedroom and a red damask bedcover – everything must be perfect for Mme Hanska – and, 'remember to see the crystal candlesticks are complete.' By October he is worrying about the curtains: to protect them in his absence they should be encased in cheap calico. And don't take up the carpets: the way to treat carpets is to brush them hard and regularly. 'Pay no attention to what the carpet dealer says': he, Balzac, knows more about keeping carpets in condition than anyone in the trade and, considering his carpet buying since the days he set up house in the rue Cassini, this is certainly true. The mother writes back that his orders about the stoves have been carried out to the letter and she has got in the coal and wood for the winter. She announces that a second coat of paint has gone on the wall. He sets out the exact duties and wages of the cook, the manservant, and the maid: she must buy her fruit and vegetables from Les Halles – not from the shops – first thing in the morning. The cook will be required to cook simple meals only when he returns: two courses for lunch and four for dinner. There is a great deal about dusting and, over and over again, he reminds his mother to see that she stands over François while he cleans the lamps. He would have been a house-proud woman.

It began to strike one that there is something odd about the silent François. Mme Balzac is strict with servants and François is her special concern. Her notion is that servants must be watched and never left idle for a moment. She obviously 'kept at' François and, lest he should go round gossiping with the Italian maid called Zanella, she teaches him to read and write and to make embroidered slippers. The poor lady, in spite of her rheumatism and a worrying heart, is in a fever of attention to her son's orders: she shares his insistence on domestic order, and she loves the luxury and the power she has. Her pension has been increased – by Mme Hanska – and at the beginning of the year she comes in from her humble lodgings at Suresnes to see all is right. Eventually she establishes herself there, accepting that when he arrives with a wife, she will leave like a servant. Her day is always the same: up at six in the morning, to bed early at night to read *The Imitation of Christ* and to leave her door open in case of burglars. This is awkward because she is sometimes alarmed that François, in one 'of his fevers' will come prowling into the room.

In the Ukraine the situation was bad. Mme Hanska had still not made up her mind and Balzac's health, which revived when he got there, had gone to pieces. Mental and emotional distress had always had a violent effect on him. The due dates of bills, the changing figures of his accountancy whirled madly round in the head of the artist who could not achieve his dream, who had ten more volumes of *La Comédie Humaine* to write and who was forbidden to work. One guesses at a life alternating between fear and deep boredom: the Promised Land was boring. He was terrified that some catastrophe would befall his house. He kept up his spirits by announcing he would be home in a month, or two months. The fact is that he could not move. In June 1849 he had another heart attack and agonizing pains in his stomach. The doctor who lived in the house with his son, also a doctor, put him on a diet of pure lemon juice to thin the blood; but this led to frightful vomiting. Balzac liked the old doctor. He played the violin to him; but his son was sceptical about Balzac's state. The climate, with its alternations of intense heat and cruel cold, Balzac said, was destroying him; it gave him headaches that did not cease day and night. He spent most of his time in bed. Neuralgia and toothache afflicted him as they used to do when he was twenty at the rue Lesdiguières. One tooth dropped out. He suffered also from trembling of the eyelids and then, suddenly, his sight almost went. Leeches were applied. The doctor took him off lemon juice and Balzac – always a believer in mysterious remedies – was put on herbal pills of a kind that were used among

Polish peasants. The pills appeared to do him good, but then the Moldavian fever attacked him. It lasted for weeks, and if he coughed he brought up blood from his lungs.

Being ill like this made him childish. He made a brief recovery when Mme Hanska and her daughter presented him with a *tessomolana*, an elaborately embroidered silk dressing-gown in Persian fashion. He was ecstatic about it and walked about in it 'like a sultan'. Everyone, he says, is so good and kind to him, but Mme Hanska is not well. Her attacks of arthritis and gout have returned. The only relief for gout, which the doctor insists on, is barbarous: plunging her swollen feet into the entrails of a newly slaughtered sucking-pig, having heard its squeals as it is killed before her eyes.

It must have been plain to her that the genius she loved and the man she mistrusted was moving towards his death. His body had wasted away: the huge belly had vanished and every attack must have seemed to her to be the last. His vitality fought back for him. If only she would make up her mind. If only the Tsar would give the sanction for the transfer of the estate to the daughter and give permission for the marriage. Balzac himself wrote to the Tsar: the permission was refused. The Russians were divided about placating the Polish nobility. In his weariness Balzac wrote to his old friend Zulma Carraud whom he loved but whose advice he had never taken. She had frankly stated that she was quite unsuited to being the queen of an aristocratic salon.

I have been taken with terrible heart trouble brought on by fifteen years of hard labour. The treatment was interrupted by one of those terrible fevers, called Moldavian fever, which starting in the Danubian marshes, spread to Odessa and ravage the steppe . . . I never cease to think of you, to love you even here . . . How different life seems after fifty . . . What a host of things, what a world of illusions have gone by the board since then. And would you believe it, except for affection, which is ever growing, I am not a whit further on where I am. How swiftly evil buds and blooms and how sorely happiness is baulked and hindered. It is enough to make one disgusted with life. I've been three years arranging a nest here, a nest which, alas, has cost a fortune, and there are no birds in it. When will they come? The years fleet by, old age is coming on and everything will wither and decay.

And, he adds, even 'the furnishings of the nest' will wither.

The winter passed. Recklessly he went with the family on a journey to Kiev to meet the Governor and to see about a passport, an expedition that cost him weeks of bronchitis. He recovered and he was now sure that he would get well if he could only get back to France. They would have to wait now for the deep snow. Then at last in March the Tsar revoked his refusal: Mme Hanska was free. It must have been plain to her that he was a dying man, but what could she do now there was no ostensible barrier? She gave in. On 14 March 1850 they drove through the snow to the church at Berdichev, a ten-hour journey, and were married and got home ill and exhausted. Mme Hanska's feet were so swollen that she could hardly walk and Balzac's heart went badly wrong. He had to rest for twelve days against the long sixteen-day journey back to Paris.

The thaw had begun in the Ukraine, the roads were flooded and there were no bridges over the swollen rivers. The risings in Galicia had led to brigandage. An enormous amount of luggage had to be got ready. While the couple waited Balzac sent dozens of detailed orders to his mother: what flowers, for example, had to be put in the various *jardinières*, and last-minute instructions on altering the pillows in the two bedrooms, the red and the blue, for everything must be perfect for the diamond of Poland, the jewel of the ancient and illustrious Rzewuski family. His own bed was to be turned round so that it did not face the door. His mother was wildly happy – and added her petty cash account at the end of her reply. At last the travellers set off. It took them a month to get as far as Dresden. Their coach sank again and again to the doors in the mud of the thaw and often sixteen men were needed to get it out. Hardly able to see or breathe, Balzac sat by the roadside in the rain, time and time again, watching it all. They stopped a month in Dresden where he kept having fainting fits. He was in bed most of the time, but he bought Mme Hanska a pearl necklace worth 25,000 francs: 'A necklace to drive a saint mad'. Some readers of her letters to her daughter think that, in desperation or indifference, she went out on a spending spree; but if she did, she also wrote that although she had known him 'for seventeen years she had not until then fully realized what an adorable creature he was. He had a quality that was entirely new to her. If only he had his health.'

They went on by train to Paris with their enormous load of luggage and once they got into France he felt better. It had been arranged that their arrival should follow a strict protocol. Mme Balzac should leave the house she had prepared and guarded for them before the arrival: the house which she said (with a dignity that would remind him that she, too, came of a distinguished family, the Sallambiers) had enabled her to enjoy once more the luxury she had been used to before she married!

Late at night their carriage arrived in the rue Fortunée. All the lights were on in festive welcome. But when the driver got down to open the gate, it was locked and barred. He hammered. No reply. Balzac himself got out and hammered and shouted. No reply. A crowd collected. A locksmith was at last found. When they got into the house they found wreckage everywhere: François the servant was standing there, wild and incoherent. He had turned out Zanella, the Italian maid, and was raving mad. He had to be seized and locked in his room.

In a day or two Balzac collapsed entirely. From then on he was a dying man. Injections, bleedings, diet, pills could do nothing. True, late in June he improved and, in a last reckless gesture of his passion for objects, he got out in a carriage and collected some of the treasures he had brought from Dresden. No doubt the toilet set his wife had bought him. After that all hope went. Blind, unable to speak, he was a ghost, unrecognizable except, some friends said, for his large, dark, arresting, and questioning eyes.

Peritonitis, kidney trouble, started. The body filled with water. Finally gangrene set in. Unable now to grasp anything, Balzac looked at his old friend Dr Nacquart, who knew the case was hopeless, and said to him suddenly 'Send for Bianchon' – the doctor he had invented in *La Comédie Humaine*. This remark has been disputed. On 18 August 1850 he died. His face had gone almost black. His wife had gone to bed. His mother was the only person with him. He himself had written:

A man who every day for fifteen years spends his nights working, who has never a spare minute during the day, who struggles against everything, has no more time for his friends or his mistresses: I've lost many mistresses and friends because of this, without regretting it, for none of them understood my situation – the longer I live the more my work piles up . . . I foresee for myself a dark destiny. I shall die the day before I achieve my desire.

Select Bibliography

Alain [Emile Auguste Chartier]. *Avec Balzac*. Paris, 1937
Arrigon, Louis Jules. *Balzac et la 'Contessa'*. Paris, 1932
Billy, André. *La Vie de Balzac*. 2 vols. Paris, 1947
Boussel, Patrice. *Les Portraits de Balzac* (catalogue). Maison de Balzac, Paris
Bouteron, Marcel, ed. *Les Cahiers Balzaciens*. 8 vols. Paris, 1923–8
Bouvier, René. *Balzac, Homme d'Affaires*. Paris, 1930
Burnand, Eugène Robert. *La Vie Quotidienne en 1830*. Paris, 1957
Curtius, Ernst Robert. *Balzac*. Berne, 1951
D'Alméras, Henri. *La Vie Parisienne sous la République de 1848*. Paris, 1921
Gautier, Théophile. *Portraits Contemporains*. Paris, 1874
Gozlan, Léon. *Balzac en Pantoufles*. Paris, 1890
Hanotaux, G. A. A., and Vicaire, G. *La Jeunesse de Balzac: Balzac Imprimeur, 1825–1828*. Paris, 1903
Hastings, Walter Scott, ed. *Balzac: Letters to his Family, 1809–1850* (text of correspondence in French). Princeton, 1934
Herzen, Alexander Ivanovich. *My Past and Thoughts*. Trans. Constance Garnett, New ed., rev. Humphrey Higgens. London, 1968
Hunt, Herbert J. *Balzac's Comédie Humaine*. London, 1959
James, Henry. *French Poets and Novelists*. London, 1878
Jameson, Fredric. '*La Cousine Bette* and Allegorical Realism', *PMLA*, Vol. 86, 1971, No. 2
Korwin-Piotrowski, Sophie de [Z. K. Piotrowska]. *Balzac et le Monde Slave: Madame Hanska et l'Oeuvre Balzacienne*. Paris, 1933
Léger, Charles, ed. *Balzac Mis à Nu*. Paris, 1928
Marceau, Félicien [Louis Carette]. *Balzac and his World*. Trans. Derek Coltman. London; New York, 1967
Maurois, André. *Prometheus: The Life of Balzac*. Trans. Norman Denny. London, 1965
May, J. Lewis, trans. *The Unpublished Correspondence of Honoré de Balzac and Madame Zulma Carraud, 1829–1850*. London, 1937

Métadier, Paul. *Balzac au Petit Matin*. Paris; Geneva, 1964
—*Balzac à Saché* (catalogue). Château de Saché
—*Balzac en Touraine*. Paris, 1968
Pierrot, Roger, ed. *Correspondance*. 5 vols. Paris, 1964
—*Lettres à Madame Hanska*. Paris, 1965
Raser, George Bernard. *Guide to Balzac's Paris*. Choisy-le-Roi, 1964
Sainte-Beuve, Charles-Augustin. *Les Causeries du Lundi*. 15 vols. Paris, 1852–62
Séché, Alphonse, and Bertaut, Jules. *Balzac: 42 Portraits et Documents*. Paris, 1910
Starkie, Enid Mary. *Petrus Borel, the Lycanthrope: His Life and Times*. London, 1954
Stoeckl, Agnes de. *King of the French: A Portrait of Louis-Philippe, 1773–1850*. London, 1957
Surville, Laure. *Balzac, sa Vie et ses Œuvres d'après sa Correspondance*. Paris, 1858
Taine, Hippolyte. *Essais de Critique et d'Histoire*. Paris, 1858
Turnell, Martin. *The Novel in France*. London, 1950
Zweig, Stefan. *Balzac*. Trans. William and Dorothy Rose. London, 1947

SOURCES OF TRANSLATIONS

Note. The following passages are quoted from the translations of Saintsbury's Temple Edition, New York, 1901: pp. 2, 9–10, 10 (2nd), 11, 16, 24, 32–3, 33–4, 34 (2nd), 64, 65, 88, 101–2, 102 (2nd), 107, 111, 112–13, 113 (2nd), 115–16, 116 (2nd), 124, 133–4, 143, 148, 159, 167–8, 169 (2nd).

Other translations quoted are: *Illusions Perdues* (Raine), pp. 14, 41, 42, 44; Maurois, *Prometheus: The Life of Balzac* (Denny), pp. 19, 20, 22 (1st), 34 (2nd), 43, 50, 54, 55 (1st), 59: 35–8, 93, 94, 95, 127, 131–2, Marccau, *Balzac and his World* (Coltman), p. 110; *Les Chouans* (Crawford), pp. 58–9; *Correspondence of Balzac and Zulma Carraud* (May), pp. 80, 81 (1st), 81–2, 82 (2nd), 83, 134 (2nd), 140, 141, 185; *Zweig, Balzac* (W. and D. Rose), pp. 155, 160 (1st); Herzen, *My Past and Thoughts* (Garnett; rev. Higgens), p. 176 (1st), 176–7.

Passages translated by the author are: *Correspondance* (ed. Pierrot), pp. 21, 22 (2nd, 3rd), 22–3, 23 (2nd), 35 (1st, 2nd), 58, (1st, 2nd), 66–7, 67: 21–3, 70, 77 (2nd), 77–8, 87, 113 (3rd). *Letters to his Family* (ed. Hastings; French text), pp. 27, 29: 12–13, 29–30, 91, 92, 98–9, 140 (2nd), 141, 175, 182, 183; Billy, *Vie de Balzac*, pp. 38–9, 39 (2nd, 3rd), 55, 56, 97; de Musset, *Confessions d'un Enfant du Siècle*, p. 38–40; Pontevice de Huessey, *Balzac en Bretagne*, 59; *Correspondance* (Editions Michel), p. 73; *Lettres à Mme. Hanska* (ed. Pierrot), pp. 106, 108 (1st), 108–9, 109 (2nd), 114, 121 (3rd), 128, 129, 130, 131 (1st), c. p. 132, 132–3, 136 (1st), 139, 142, 151, 153, 154, 157–8, 162, 170, 178, 178–9; Werdet, *Mémoires*, p. 119; Bouteron, *Une Année dans la Vie de Balzac*, pp. 120 (1st), 120–1, 121 (2nd, 3rd); Léger, *Balzac Mis à Nu*, p. 126 (1st); Gozlan, *Balzac en Pantoufles*, p. 136 (2nd); Métadier, *Balzac au Petit Martin*, p. 187.

Index

Names of characters from Balzac's works are given in single quotation marks.